HEYWOOD-WAKEFIELD
MODERN
FURNITURE

Steven Rouland and Roger W. Rouland

COLLECTOR BOOKS

A Division of Schroeder Publishing Co., Inc.

The current values in this book should be used only as a guide. They are not intended to set prices, which vary from one section of the country to another. Auction prices as well as dealer prices vary greatly and are affected by condition as well as demand. Neither the authors nor the publisher assumes responsibility for any losses that might be incurred as a result of consulting this guide.

ON THE COVER:
HEYWOOD-WAKEFIELD MODERN FURNITURE ADVERTISEMENT, 1947.
JUNIOR DINING EXTENSION TABLE - 1947–49
Table measures 34" wide by 50" long. When extended with one 14" leaf, it becomes 64" long. Height is 34".
SIDE CHAIR - 1950–55
Seat measures 18" wide by 16" deep. Height of the back is 16".
3-DRAWER BUFFET - 1948–50
Fitted with two adjustable shelves in each cabinet compartment. Top is 48" wide by 18" deep. Height is 32½".
CHINA - 1948–50
The overall height of this china is 64½". Server base is 34" wide, 17" deep, and 32½" high. Plate glass top measures 32" wide, 14½" deep, and 32" high. Both the server and the hutch have adjustable shelves.

Cover design: Beth Summers
Book design: Michelle Dowling

Searching for a Publisher?

We are always looking for knowledgeable people considered to be experts within their fields. If you feel that there is a real need for a book on your collectible subject and have a large comprehensive collection, contact us.

COLLECTOR BOOKS
P.O. Box 3009
Paducah, KY 42002-3009
www.collectorbooks.com
or
Lucky Lindy's
305 S.W. Water St.
Peoria, Illinois 61602

Dedication

*This book is dedicated with love to Ruth and John Rouland,
and Bob and Marie Stankus.*

About the Authors

Steven Rouland is a twentieth-century modern dealer and researcher from Peoria, Illinois. He and his wife Linda regularly buy and sell Heywood-Wakefield Modern and other furniture and accessories from the modern period through their store, "Lucky Lindy's." They can be contacted by writing to: Lucky Lindy's, 305 S.W. Water St., Peoria, Illinois 61602; or telephoned at: (309) 673-2637.

Roger W. Rouland is a college instructor and freelance writer and editor based in Hebron, Illinois. Specializing in company histories and business-related articles and brochures, his work has appeared in such publications as *The International Directory of Company Histories, The Chicago Tribune, Chicago Sun-Times*, and *Rockford Magazine*. His literary criticism has appeared in *The International Fiction Review* and *The Journal of Comparative Literature and Aesthetics*.

Contents

Preface

It was ten years ago that my wife Linda and I bought our first piece of Heywood-Wakefield Modern. We were drawn to Modern because of its clean style and quality construction. As we purchased more Heywood-Wakefield pieces our curiosity grew, and it became obvious that there was a frustrating lack of information about the furniture and the company which produced it. Questions regarding the names of different styles, the years pieces were produced, and even what kind of wood Modern was made from were frequently met with confusing and conflicting answers. We shared the frustrations of other Heywood-Wakefield collectors and dealers who had no source of reliable information.

Our search for this information ultimately led us around the country by phone and in person. In the process we met and talked with many wonderful people and learned more about Heywood-Wakefield and the people who were associated with it than, unfortunately, we could ever assemble in this book. We have also experienced the frustrations of having questions remain unanswered, no matter how many leads we followed. One has to marvel at how much information can be lost in only one or two generations.

In compiling our research, my brother Roger joined us in this project. The three of us collectively hope that this book will answer many of the questions about Heywood-Wakefield Modern, and thereby add to the enjoyment of this beautiful furniture.

We gratefully acknowledge those people who have given us their time and provided us with information. Although we cannot include everyone, we would like to thank the following people for their assistance: Gail Landy and the staff at the Levi Heywood Memorial Library in Gardner, Massachusetts; Mrs. Elaine Jiranek; W. Joseph Carr; Sylvia Schneidreit; Christopher Kennedy; Joanna Maitland at the American Furniture Hall of Fame in High Point, North Carolina; and the staff at the Peoria Public Library.

Steven Rouland
March, 1994

From Country Store to Modern Furniture: 100 Years of Progress

[Charting Heywood-Wakefield's history] would not be such a difficult task, if the Company . . . manufactured only the wood chairs that the five Heywood brothers began to fashion in a barn adjacent to their father's farm, in Gardner, Massachusetts, U.S.A., back in 1826. — From a 1951 speech by Richard N. Greenwood, former company president

As noted by Richard N. Greenwood, the birth of Heywood-Wakefield "Modern" furniture traces its roots back more than a century to five Heywood brothers—Walter, Levi, Seth, Benjamin and William—who in 1826 began making wooden chairs in a small barn in Gardner, Massachusetts. At a time when John Quincy Adams was president of only 24 United States and the country's first railroad tracks were only just beginning to be laid, Walter Heywood began fashioning chairs largely by hand, with his only "machine" being a foot lathe. Walter was soon joined in the chair-making enterprise by his brothers Levi and Benjamin, who began assisting in the work part-time while running a nearby country store. The brothers' chair business enjoyed quick prosperity and they soon built a new shop across the street from the store, which was disposed of around 1829.

In 1831 Levi Heywood moved to Boston where he established an outlet store to sell the Heywood chairs, while Benjamin and younger brother William remained in Gardner to manufacture the products which gradually evolved from wood-seated to cane-seated variations. In 1834 a fire destroyed the Heywood's chair shop (which was not rebuilt), prompting Levi's return to Gardner a year later. To continue chair-making operations, in 1835 a definitive partnership—B.F. Heywood & Company—was formed, initially comprised of Benjamin, Walter and William Heywood, along with Moses Wood and James W. Gates.

Upon his return to Gardner, Levi Heywood again became involved in the chair-making business. And it was Levi Heywood, the oldest of the brothers (and the one who would later achieve fame as an inventor and a patentee of chair-making machinery that revolutionized production), along with younger brother Seth and their descendants, who became the predominant figures in the development of the company in the 19th century. In 1835 Levi Heywood guided the company's move to the shores of Crystal Lake in Gardner (where a company factory would remain until the business closed its doors for good more than 140 years later). The fledgling chair-making enterprise purchased a lake-side building equipped for wood-turning and in the process gained its first "real" machinery—turning lathes and a circular saw. Initially an outlet from Crystal Lake provided the company with plenty of power, but eventually the currents of Crystal Lake proved inadequate to drive Heywood's machines and in succeeding years Levi replaced the plant's water power with steam.

Levi's insistence on the installation of new machinery dismayed his early partners, who gradually withdrew from the chair-making concern and for a period left Levi the sole Heywood owner. By 1844 a second partnership—Heywood & Wood—had been formed, with Levi and Moses Wood the apparent principal partners. By 1849 Wood's name had disappeared from the company's title—Levi Heywood & Company—and in 1851 a new name, Heywood Chair Manufacturing Company, was adopted during the formation of what amounted to a joint stock association.

The Heywood Chair Manufacturing Company, circa 1855.

LEVI HEYWOOD

WALTER HEYWOOD

SETH HEYWOOD

WILLIAM HEYWOOD

Four of the five Heywood brothers.
No known photograph of Benjamin F. Heywood exists. Family tradition had it that he
was an extremely homely man, and would never agree to have his picture taken.

In succeeding years younger brother Seth became associated with the company and in 1861 the enterprise became known as Heywood Brothers & Company. Noticeably, despite new partnership agreements, "Heywood" remained first in the company's moniker, as it would throughout the concern's history.

Levi was continually searching for improved tools and production methods which generated less waste. His inventions designed to improve production included machines to manufacture wooden chair seats and a machine for manufacturing a tilting chair. Levi's inventive genius also involved him—along with an assistant Gardner A. Watkins [1]—in the creation of several processes for wood bending. These wood-bending machines prompted Francis Thonet of Vienna (the head of what was in those days the largest chair manufacturing operation in the world) to write Levi Heywood after visiting the Gardner factory. Thonet's

8

letter included the following praise: "I must tell you candidly that you have the best machinery in the world for bending wood that I have ever seen, and I will say that I have seen and experimented a great deal in the bending of wood."

Levi was determined to not only utilize the best machinery possible, but also to improve the methods of attaining raw material and transporting his products. Initially wagons, drawn by teams of up to six horses, transported finished chairs from Gardner to the Boston market on what was then a long, 58-mile, two-day journey. By 1854 the determination of Levi had pressured builders of the Fitchburg Railroad to run their line through Gardner, rather than to the north as originally planned. As a result, the chair company gained additional outlets for its products as well as an access-route to the New Hampshire and Vermont lumber markets.

The company was not without its share of setbacks, though, including a 1862 fire which razed the Heywood operations for a second time. Levi, who watched his factory buildings burn, is said to have stopped at a neighbor's house on his way home and noted in a moment of pondering: "If the good Lord lets me live another ten years, I'll make some money yet." Levi, who would live twenty more years, and Seth, responded to the burning of their name-sake business by raising funds in town for a new factory, and soon Heywood Brothers was again making money.

Following the Civil War the company accelerated its drive for sales expansion as the United States moved into the Industrial Revolution. In 1867 Heywood Brothers opened its first warehouse, in New York City, to serve as a clearing-house for export trade. Shortly afterwards company representatives began journeying beyond domestic shores to court new business. As a result, Heywood Brothers international operations blossomed and soon cases of six and twelve chairs were being exported in the thousands to Australia, Polynesia, and the West Indies, as well as to South American and Mediterranean countries.

Through about 1870 much of the cane seating for Heywood Brothers chairs was produced outside the company's factory, with wagon-loads of

---

Unique Beginnings for Early Designs

A 19th Century Comfort Rocker

The designs of early Heywood products were both fashioned and influenced in some unique ways. Just prior to the Civil War two English brothers, Thomas and Edward Hill, joined the company and for several years the pair decorated Heywood chairs by painting them with landscapes and baskets of fruit and flowers. The brothers had an interesting method of "mass-decorating":

instead of painting one chair before beginning another, each would group a dozen chairs about him in a circle and begin dabbing a spot of one color on each chair in turn until at last twelve landscapes or twelve baskets of fruits and flowers rose from the chairs almost simultaneously. While both Hill brothers were without technical training, after leaving Heywood Brothers the Hills later became well-known regional artists, with Edward settling in New Hampshire and becoming noted for his scenes of the White Mountains, while Thomas drifted to California and became the great painter in his day of the Yosemite Valley.

Occasionally minor occurrences figured prominently in the development of a product, as in the case of one new design for a rocking chair. The design was literally found in the lay of the land after two Heywood factory workers, on their way home from the Gardner plant late one winter afternoon, began pushing each other into snowbanks. As one was picking himself up from a fall he turned and looked at his imprint and then remarked that such a form would make an excellent chair. Indeed, thought Levi Heywood, and the resulting idea gave birth to the design of the comfort rocker, a type of chair which enjoyed enormous popularity for years.

chair-seat frames and bundles of cane delivered to countryside farmhouses, where farmers' wives and children produced the cane seating by hand. But this practice began passing after Gardner A. Watkins from the Heywood plant invented a process to weave cane into a continuous web and Levi Heywood invented a machine to weave the cane webbing into chair seats. Watkins also invented a process for splicing cane, while Heywood developed machines to put Watkin's splicing method to work. Watkins went on to make other important contributions to the company and the furniture industry. Some of his more important innovations included machines for bending wood and machines for making chair springs.[2]

In 1870 Heywood Brothers began manufacturing chairs in two locations after Levi Heywood acquired a half-interest in the woodworking plant in Erving, Massachusetts, which was owned by William B. Washburn. In the mid-1870s the company expanded its furniture line to include chairs made of reed and rattan, causing the variety of Heywood Brothers products to increase rapidly. During this time the company also began manufacturing children's carriages and became one of the first firms in the country to make baby carriages of rattan and reed. To provide raw material for its rattan products, the company established an agency in Singapore where machinery for splitting and shaving rattan, in large-part designed by Levi, was installed.

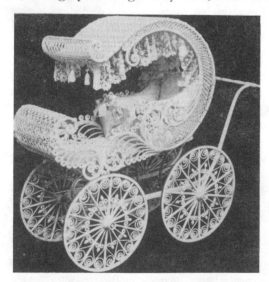

A very ornate, early baby carriage.

The efforts of Levi Heywood and his son Charles to improve the company's transportation network were instrumental in the 1874 construction of the Barre & Gardner Railroad, which further connected the Gardner factory to points north. That same year the company expanded its operations southward, and opened a second east coast warehouse, in Philadelphia. Operations were extended to the west coast in 1876, when a warehouse in San Francisco opened, followed by another warehouse in Baltimore the following year.

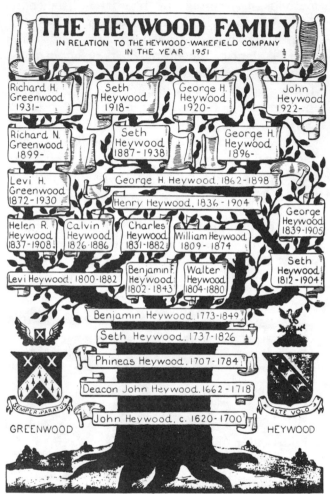

The Heywood family tree, beginning with the five Heywood brothers, as seen in "The Five Heywood Brothers (1826-1951): A Brief History of the Heywood-Wakefield Company during 125 Years."

The death of Levi Heywood and his son Charles in 1882, and the retirement of Seth Heywood that same year, placed Heywood Brothers & Company in the hands of a second generation of Heywoods. This new generation of Heywoods included Seth's sons, Henry (who succeeded Levi as president) and George; Levi's son-in-law, Alvin M. Greenwood; and Benjamin's son in law, Amos Morrill. During the late-1880s a third generation of Heywoods, in the person of George H., son of Henry Heywood, became involved in the company.

Heywood Brothers coast-to-coast expansion continued during the 1880s. Following the completion of the Northern Pacific Railway in 1883, the company opened warehouses in Portland and Los Angeles, and three years later established a warehouse in Boston. In 1884 the company began manufacturing operations in Chicago, with a decorous Chicago sales room following early the next decade.

By 1896 Heywood Brothers was operating three factories and eight warehouses and for the year recorded $1.8 million in annual sales. In a move to capitalize on the growing need for new school furniture to replace out-dated and make-shift benches and stools, in 1897 Heywood Brothers began designing and manufacturing wooden school desks and chairs.

Soon the company began making seating for trains. These early railcar seats would serve as a forerunner product to the bus and airplane seats made during the ensuing century, when a number of other companies—both competitors and affiliates of Heywood—would join the Heywood "family" and make their mark on the expanding Heywood enterprise. But the Heywood Brothers biggest pact with another company came before the close of the 19th century, with what was then Heywood's biggest competitor.

The Wakefield Rattan Company

In many ways the Wakefield Rattan Company—under the guidance of Cyrus Wakefield, the founder of the rattan and reed business in America—evolved like the Heywood enterprise. At the age of 15 Cyrus Wakefield left his home in Roxbury, New Hampshire, to seek his fortune in Boston. That was in 1826, the same year the Heywood brothers began seeking their fortunes by making chairs in nearby Gardner. Like Levi Heywood, Wakefield also teamed up with a brother to run a grocery store (in Wakefield's case, on the Boston waterfront), before turning to the industry that would capture his interest.

In 1844 Wakefield was watching a ship from his storefront when he noticed a sailor onboard preparing to throw a bundle of rattan onto the Boston wharf. Wakefield approached the sailor and asked what he intended to do with the rattan, and was told it was of little value, other than to keep cargo from shifting during long clipper ship voyages from the East. Wakefield promptly purchased the rattan for a small sum, with the transaction marking the unofficial launching of a business which would become known worldwide. (Interestingly, Wakefield's company would grow to such a magnitude that in succeeding decades the firm owned several of its own clipper ships, which hauled rattan not as dunnage, but as principal cargo.)

Wakefield sold his first bundle of rattan to basket makers, who in turn stripped off the outside covering and used only the reed or pith of the rattan in their weaving. The outer cane was later sold to chair-makers, for use in the manufacture of chair seating. Wakefield's first purchase led to others, and in 1844 he sold his interest in the grocery store to his brother, rented a Boston office and began a jobbing trade in rattan.

Having learned to strip the hard cane surface from the rattan so it could be used in basket and seat weaving, in 1855 Wakefield purchased his first plant—near Boston—marking the official beginning of the Wakefield Rattan Company. In naming his company Wakefield adopted his own spelling of "ratan," which he spelled "rattan," and his ongoing and persistent use of the latter spelling eventually forced dictionaries to follow suit.

Wakefield's new plant initially used water power furnished by mill ponds to manufacture reed baskets and skirt reeds or (hoops) for hoop-skirts. After steel became a commonplace substitute for reed in hoop-skirts, Wakefield's company entered the furniture business and began using the inside or pith of the rattan (which had previously been discarded) to make chairs and allied products. (In this case, the Heywood and the Wakefield enterprises differed; Heywood Brothers began with chairs and turned to rattan, while Wakefield began with rattan and turned to chairs.)

By the 1850s Wakefield's company was importing stripped rattan—namely the cane—from China, saving the business the labor cost of removing the reed. By the time the second Opium War (1856 to 1860) between China and trading-seeking European powers stopped Chinese shipments of rattan, Wakefield had resolved to process and manufacture his own cane, resulting in one of the company's first innovations: machines designed by Wakefield and his employees that could split cane mechanically.

Cyrus Wakefield

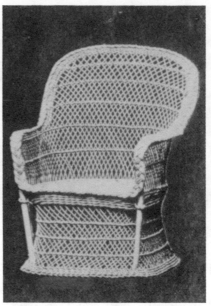

The first rattan chair made by the Wakefield Rattan Company.

The first reed chair made by the Wakefield Rattan Company.

The Wakefield Factory, circa 1865.

With the firm using both the inside of rattan for baskets and the outside of rattan for chair seating, Wakefield's invention-minded assistant, William Houston, began his quest for ways to utilize the "waste product"— the shavings and scraps from rattan—derived from stripping and cutting operations. Houston, a Scotland native born in Paisley, a town world-famous for shawls, proved invaluable in devising processes for improving production while Wakefield often invented machines to put Houston's new-founded processes to work.

During the early 1860s the pair of Wakefield and Houston devised and patented a process for spinning larger rattan shavings into usable yarn from which mats, floor coverings, and bailing cloth were made by hand. Looms were also developed to manufacture these products and in 1866 the company launched its mat and matting business after Houston utilized one of these looms to weave the first brush mat of rattan.[3] By 1870 Wakefield Rattan had introduced a loom which could weave a cane web for the seating surface of chairs. This type of loom—capable of weaving long, continuous "sheets" of cane webbing—coupled with the durability of the end product, quickly propelled the Wakefield Rattan Company into a lead position in railway and street car seating business.

With inventions and innovations improving Wakefield's production methods during the 1860s and 1870s the company's business thrived and increasingly large amounts of raw material came from the East in Wakefield's own clipper ships. Meanwhile the sale of rattan—as well as cane and reed, rattan furniture, matting, cane-seating, and a wide variety of reed baskets—was continually increasing.

Cyrus Wakefield died in 1873, but not before he—like Levi Heywood—left a mark on the community where his business developed and spurred the growth of the surrounding area's transportation network. By the time of his death Wakefield had become a director of several area railroads and the largest stockholder in two train lines. And, he had become so identified with the prosperity of South Reading—a northern suburb of Boston where his factory was located—that in 1868 the citizens of South Reading unanimously voted to change the community's name to Wakefield.

Just weeks before Wakefield's death the Wakefield Rattan Company was incorporated with Cyrus Wakefield named as president. Upon his death a nephew, Cyrus Wakefield II, was called home from Singapore where he had been serving as the company's representative in the East. Cyrus II was named president and two years later Wakefield Rattan bought out the equipment of its chief competitor, the American Rattan Company of Fitchburg, Massachusetts (located about 10 miles northeast of Gardner).

During the last quarter of the century Wakefield Rattan expanded its domestic operations and in 1876 the firm opened a warehouse in New York. Warehouses were established in San Francisco and Chicago in 1883, and four years later a factory was opened in Chicago. It was in fact the idea of a Chicago factory which first found Wakefield and Heywood interests flirting with the idea of joint operations; but before the flirting was over, such joint-venture notions resulted—for a time—in more of a competitive quarrel than a serious relationship.

The Heywood-Wakefield Fling

By the last quarter of the 19th century the Heywood and Wakefield enterprises had much in common. Both had a history of concentrating on improving manufacturing processes and machinery as well as surrounding transportation networks, both grew at about the same rate, both had worldwide reputations, both were being managed by first or second generations, and both were making related products during the final quarter of the century. It should not seem surprising then that the two companies, by the 1870s, were engaged in vigorous competition. What might seem a bit sur-

prising, given what had grown into a somewhat fierce rivalry, is that in 1883 the two companies decided to establish a joint manufacturing operation in Chicago and send representatives to that growing city where the two companies would cooperatively find and lease a suitable building. But the end result of this search was far from what was originally intended.

After a first day's quest to locate a factory proved fruitless, both parties, apparently staying in the same hotel, agreed to renew their search the following day. But upon waking Henry Heywood and his team found that the Wakefield men had taken an early breakfast and left, without leaving a message. Later in the day Cyrus Wakefield II and his party returned to the hotel and told Henry Heywood that the Wakefield Company had successfully found a suitable plant, so suitable, indeed, that the Wakefield Company had decided to purchase and operate it independently. After the ensuing stormy quarrel subsided the Wakefield representatives returned to Massachusetts, with the Heywood team staying in Chicago to locate a "suitable" factory for its operations. It is safe to say that after the attempt in Chicago with joint operations, competition between the two furniture firms was even greater than before.

A Lasting Relationship

By the mid-1890s a Wakefield was no longer running the Wakefield Rattan Company; it's operations were being guided by Charles H. Lang. In 1897 Lang and Henry Heywood agreed to put past disagreements aside and merge the former rivals. As a result, Heywood Brothers & Company and its closely-affiliated Heywood & Morrill Rattan Company were consolidated with the Wakefield Rattan Company to form Heywood Brothers & Wakefield Company. (Ironically, it was neither the Heywood Brothers Chicago factory nor the Wakefield Rattan Chicago factory that the new company used; it utilized the Chicago plant of the former Heywood & Morrill Rattan.) The newly consolidated company enjoyed the prestige of being the world's largest chair manufacturer, as well as the world's largest importer of rattan. Additionally, the company could boast of being the world's largest manufacturer of cane and reed products, mats and matting, and baby carriages.

Henry Heywood, who served as Heywood Brothers & Wakefield Company's first president, died in 1904 without a surviving son, leaving the company in the hands of a non-family member, Louis E. Carlton, for the first time. Under Carlton the company entered a new arena of seating production and in 1906 began making opera chairs in its Chicago factory. While opera chair sales opportunities were limited at the turn of the century, the venture reached a turning point in succeeding decades as the motion picture industry grew and theaters mushroomed across the country.

Lang became president in 1912, following the death of Carlton. Under Lang, in 1913 the company completed large additions to its Chicago factory, funded from the proceeds of a recently-issued one million dollars in common stock. During his nine-year tenure Lang also succeeded in guiding the company through a trio of acquisitions, which included the 50 percent interest in Washburn & Heywood Chair Company which Heywood-Wakefield did not own, the Oregon Chair Company, and Lloyd Manufacturing Company. The Lloyd Company, a manufacturer of baby carriages and woven fiber products, represented Heywood-Wakefield's most significant acquisition of the century and gave the chair manufacturer Marshall B. Lloyd's patented process for weaving fiber on the giant looms which Lloyd had designed.

The Lloyd Manufacturing Company

Marshall B. Lloyd

During the 20th century a third inventive genius—following in the footsteps of Levi Heywood and Cyrus Wakefield—found his way into the history of Heywood-Wakefield Company. Like Heywood and Wakefield, Marshall B. Lloyd was a staunch believer in the need for faster manufacturing methods and improved machinery which could produce more goods at less cost.

In 1900 Lloyd, who had already invented a combination scale and bag-holder for grocery stores as well as a scale for weighing grain, bought the manufacturing company where he had been employed and renamed the firm after himself. Adding to a line of already-in-place specialities which included wire doll carts, Lloyd's new company introduced boys' express wagons, furniture, and baby carriages made of hand-woven reed, for which Lloyd invented a wire wheel. In 1907 Lloyd reincorporated his company and moved it from Minneapolis to Menominee, Michigan, where his new factory produced boys' express wagons, collapsible go-carts, and hand-woven reed carriages.

Seeking to improve carriage production, in 1910 Lloyd and his assistant Lewis Larsen collaborated in designing a method for welding baby carriage handles. The resulting process, called the oxyacetylene tube method, involved rolling and then welding flat steel into tubing. The invention would later find numerous applications, one resulting in a contract to serve as the exclusive supplier of windshield frame tubing for Henry Ford's early Model T's.

Lloyd's greatest invention was born during a 1917 strike among his reed workers. Lloyd, who had warned his workers that their demands may defeat their purpose, worked night and day during the strike to devise new looms. When the factory reopened after a five-week shutdown, a number of workmen found their services no longer needed—they had been replaced by new power looms capable of performing the fiber-weaving work of 30 employees.

Lloyd's process for weaving fiber on giant power looms revolutionized the baby-carriage industry throughout the world, providing an alternative to the most expensive and labor-intensive process in the manufacture of carriages, namely the weaving of the wicker bodies by hand. As a result, the introduction of power looms propelled Lloyd's small company into one of the largest baby carriage factories in the world. Lloyd died in 1927, but not before patenting over 200 of his inventions.

The Washburn & Heywood Chair Company

Among the early principal partners of this company were Levi Heywood and William B. Washburn, with the latter being more notable for his political career than his business ingenuity. By the time Heywood bought a half interest in Washburn & Company in 1870, Washburn had served in both the Massachusetts Senate and the Massachusetts House of Representatives. In 1872 Washburn was elected Massachusetts governor, a post he gave up two years later after being elected a senator of the United States to fill a vacancy caused by the death of Charles Sumner. From the standpoint of Heywood-Wakefield history, the Washburn firm is noteworthy in that it provided the Heywood Brothers with a second manufacturing location, in Erving, Massachusetts, which began making chairs only after Heywood's name became part of the firm. In 1916 Heywood Brothers & Wakefield acquired complete control of Washburn & Heywood Chair Company, which was liquidated five years later when its business was consolidated into the newly-reincorporated Heywood-Wakefield Company.

The Second Reorganization

Coinciding with the acquisition of Lloyd Manufacturing, in 1921 the New Jersey corporation, Heywood Brothers & Wakefield Company, was liquidated (along with its interests in other

The Oregon Chair Company

The Oregon Chair Company was formed in 1906 after pioneer chair-maker Arthur J. Kingsley left his native Michigan to build the first Pacific Coast factory to mass produce medium and high-grade chairs. Initially Oregon Chair manufactured only oak and mahogany box-seat chairs, a product line apparently not sufficiently diversified for retail trade in a sparsely-populated area. The company later turned to cheaper grades of oak, maple, and ash to manufacture chairs, but soon recognized the need for an infusion of capital to further expand its product line. As a result, in 1915 Oregon Chair began negotiations with Heywood Brothers & Wakefield, which purchased the smaller concern in 1920 and then extended Oregon Chair's production operations and added reed furniture to its product line.

companies), and the businesses were all reincorporated in Massachusetts as a single entity, the Heywood-Wakefield Company. The new corporation's headquarters were established in a centralized Boston office which had been completed a year earlier. Late in 1921 Lang died and Levi Heywood Greenwood—great-grandson of Levi Heywood—was named president, bringing the Heywood family line back into top management. At the same time two other fourth generation Heywood descendants, Seth Heywood and Henry H. Morrill, were elected vice presidents.

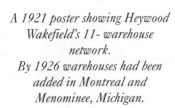

A 1921 poster showing Heywood Wakefield's 11- warehouse network.
By 1926 warehouses had been added in Montreal and Menominee, Michigan.

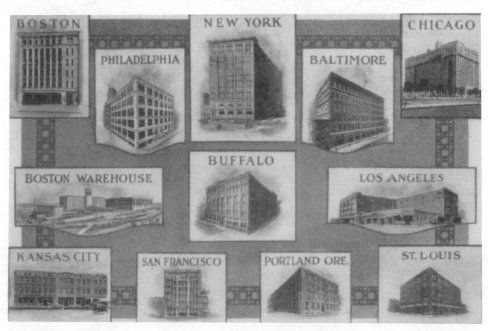

15

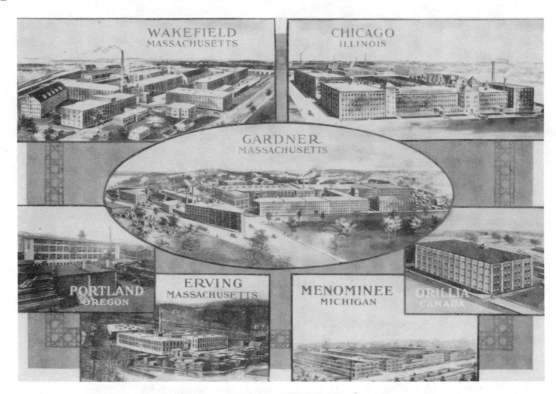

A 1921 poster illustrating Heywood-Wakefield's seven- factory network.

In 1921 the Heywood-Wakefield Company expanded its operations in the Midwest and opened warehouses in St. Louis and Kansas City. By this time Heywood-Wakefield was operating a unique warehouse system in which merchandise from factories was shipped directly to the warehouses "in the white," or unfinished, and as much as possible shipped in "knocked down" or unassembled form. This allowed warehouses to assemble and finish furniture, greatly reducing the company's freight charges and giving each warehouse an opportunity to finish and upholster goods in order to suit the desires of individual dealers.

The Roaring Twenties: The Peak of Expansion

During the 1920s Heywood-Wakefield's expansion—in terms of both personnel and operating facilities—reached its peak. By the time of its 100th anniversary in 1926, Heywood-Wakefield was producing a wide variety of cane and wood seat chairs, school furniture, baby carriages, cocoa mats and matting, railway car seats, bus seats, reed and fiber furniture, opera and theater chairs, toy vehicles, fiber webbing, and a variety of miscellaneous cane and reed items. Those numerous products were a result of a workforce which had grown to more than 5,300 employees engaged in a manufacturing and distribu-

tion network which included seven factories and 13 warehouses amounting to a combined total of 4.3 million square feet in facilities. The Gardner plant, the oldest of the company's factories, was noteworthy in that it was using a wide variety of wood in its products, including oak, beech, birch, maple, elm, chestnut, hickory, and gum, as well as spruce for crating and boxing purposes.

Entrance corridor to Heywood-Wakefield's Chicago salesrooms at the American Furniture Mart Building, circa 1926.

Throughout the 1920s the company's manufacturing operations focused on chairs and allied products – such as seating for schools, theaters, trains, buses, and stadiums – while the company enjoyed the recognition of being the largest chair manufacturer and baby carriage builder in the country. But the stock market crash in October 1929 and the ensuing Great Depression that followed served as check-valve to further expansion of the company. Ultimately the depression also contributed to the downsizing and consolidation of operations, as well as discontinuation of several product lines, including much of

Heywood-Wakefield's Chicago salesrooms, circa 1926.

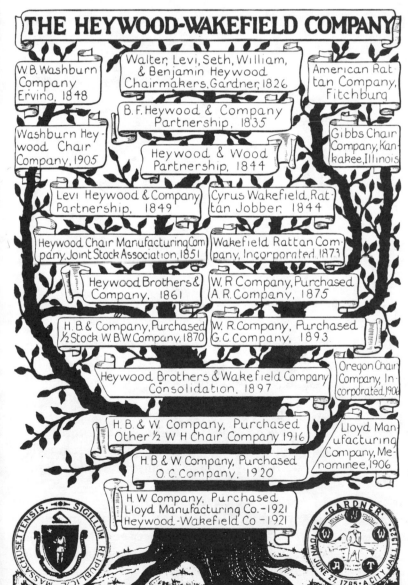

The Heywood-Wakefield company tree, as seen in "The Five Heywood Brothers (1826-1951): A Brief History of the Heywood-Wakefield Company during 125 Years."

what had been manufactured at Lloyd's factory prior to 1921.

Toward the end of the decade Heywood-Wakefield began searching for new markets which would carry the potential for long-term growth. The company aptly took note of the growing awareness of home design and decoration, caused in part by the rise in national home-oriented magazines such as *House Beautiful* and *House and Garden*. Additionally, Heywood-Wakefield recognized the public's recent discovery that with increased mass production and the resulting reduced consumer costs, a well-decorated home was no longer only for the wealthy. (It should be noted that prior to this time it had not been possible to purchase a complete, harmonious group of furniture from any one source, except as expensive custom order work.) Heywood-Wakefield concluded that there was a market for harmonious furniture groups mass produced at affordable prices and in late 1929 the company released its first complete furniture packages, in the Early American style.

Before the end of the 1920s Levi Greenwood died and his son, Richard N. Greenwood, became president of Heywood-Wakefield. By 1930 Levi Heywood's 104-year-old company had begun shrinking in size for the first time, while it began—also in a sense for the first time—to offer its customers more than a seat.

In the Modern Manner:
The Debut of Streamline Modern

A "cubist design" kitchen set from Heywood-Wakefield's 1929 catalog.
Almost all of the company's production at this time was traditional in style .

After the opening of the "L' Exposition Internationale des Arts Decoratifs et Industriels Modernes" in Paris, furniture manufacturers began producing modern styles in the United States during the late 1920s. Nonetheless, a "modern" style of furniture was not immediately embraced by the American public. From the "Modernes" Exposition a few designers such as Donald Deskey and Paul Frankl did bring a rich, understated style to the States; but many other visitors, including fashion designers and department store buyers, returned to employ only Modernes extraneous surface decorations. Ultimately cubist styles, exotic colors, and angular surface motifs contributed to a boom in modern furniture design and a commercial bust for modern at furniture stores. Reacting to the public's failure to accept this modernistic style (now sometimes referred to as "Zig-Zag Art Deco"), most furniture manufacturers abandoned modern, which was left largely in the hands of a few small, metropolitan concerns.

Heywood-Wakefield—believing there were still possibilities in a more subdued modern style, and additionally believing complete modern furniture packages could be mass produced at affordable prices—entered into an agreement with Gilbert Rohde to design a modern line, marking the first of several contracts between the furniture maker and prominent designers of the time. Rohde brought to Heywood-Wakefield a first-hand knowledge of Europe's modern styles, having traveled to Paris a few years before the Great Depression.

Upon his return home Rohde opened a design office, where he worked on "modern" interior design before being agreeing to work for Heywood-Wakefield.

In 1931 Heywood-Wakefield introduced Rohde Contemporary Furniture, the first modern furniture (as well as the first line using sectional and modular pieces) ever assembled on a production line basis. It was in fact Rohde who pioneered the development of sectional and modular furniture, which included such pieces as matching and similar-sized chests and bookcases that could be combined and rearranged in any number of different combinations.

A group of Gilbert Rohde's designs for Heywood-Wakefield in 1931.

A 1931 stick reed group designed by Gilbert Rohde.

19

Designed for flexibility and utility, Rohde's furniture was geared mainly to apartment dwellers, who seemed to be the most receptive to this new contemporary style. This line, which Heywood-Wakefield advertised as "a new mode in furniture" (while prominently displaying Rohde's name in the company's advertising), employed straight grained American walnut veneers, while a number of pieces featured the bentwood style construction that would become one of the trademarks of Rohde designs. In addition to the Contemporary line, Rohde also designed other furniture for Heywood-Wakefield, including reed and fiber furniture and an Early American line.

Part of Heywood-Wakefield's modern line in late 1932, as pictured in Furniture Record.

Part of Heywood-Wakefield's modern line in late 1932, as pictured in Furniture Record.

An advertisement which ran in Furniture Record in June 1931.

*Part of Heywood-Wakefield's modern line in late 1932, as
pictured in Furniture Record.*

*Part of Heywood-Wakefield's 1933 World's Fair Modern line,
as pictured in Furniture Record and Journal advertisements.*

*Part of Heywood-Wakefield's 1933 World's Fair Modern line,
as pictured in Furniture Record and Journal advertisements.*

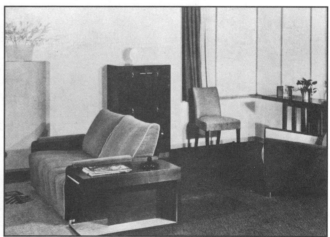

*Part of Heywood-Wakefield's 1933 World's Fair Modern line,
as pictured in Furniture Record and Journal advertisements.*

Heywood-Wakefield at the Fair

Five views of the "Design for Living" house at the Century of Progress, as pictured in Furniture Record and Journal, September, 1933.

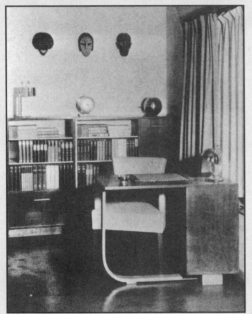

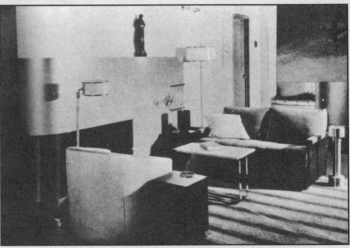

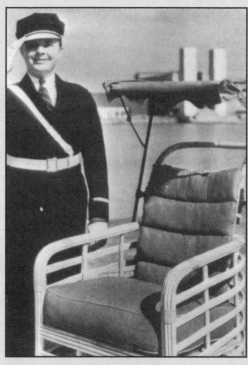

A wheeled boardwalk chair and its guide at the
Century of Progress.

A souvenir cutting board from the 1964-65
New York World's Fair.

During the time when Modern was being produced, fairs and exhibitions served as more
than entertainment for visitors; they also func-
tioned as an important advertising tool for manufacturers such as Heywood-Wakefield. Before
television brought company messages directly into
people's homes, fairs were one of the most effec-
tive ways for Heywood-Wakefield to display its
products to thousands of people a day. In addition
to this "come-and-see-it" type of advertising from
fairs and exhibitions, manufacturers often received
additional publicity through subsequent magazine
and trade journal articles featuring these international events. And like other companies, Heywood-Wakefield took advantage of opportunities
to publicize its products through fairs and exhibitions.

In 1933 Gilbert Rohde furnished the "Design
for Living" house at the Century of Progress in
Chicago with his designs for Heywood-Wakefield,
Lloyd, and Herman Miller. The Design for Living
house itself—which was featured in *House & Garden*, *Design*, and other publications—was of a contemporary style with two stories, the lower
containing a large living room with two L-wings, a
large dining room, and a library opening onto a
porch. The upper floor of this house contained two
bedrooms with a bath in between. With a flat roof

design, the entire length of the house became a
terrace for recreation or sleeping. Heywood-
Wakefield and Lloyd furnished the main floor,
while the bedrooms contained Rohde's designs
for Herman Miller. Heywood-Wakefield was
quite proud of their presence at the fair, as evi-
denced by the advertisements placed in 1933
furniture trade magazines which touted their
"World's Fair Modern" line of furniture. The
chrome tubular furniture of Lloyd so fit the
modern theme of the Century of Progress that it
was used in numerous buildings, including the
Hall of Science and the Travel and Transport
Building, as well as the displays of such companies as Kelvinator and General Electric.

Heywood-Wakefield produced boardwalk
chairs which were used at both the Century of
Progress fair and the Golden Gate Exposition.
In Chicago, around 900 of these boardwalk
chairs were pushed by college students hired by
the fair to explain the features of the Century of
Progress for $1.40 an hour. In 1939 over 1,000
Heywood-Wakefield opera chairs were on hand
at the New York World's Fair. These opera
chairs provided seating for various exhibits,
including the General Motors Futurama exhibit
which employed more than 600 chairs.

At the Golden Gate International Exposition in 1939, Heywood-Wakefield Modern was used to furnish the "Hostess House" through the efforts of Hale Brothers, a San Francisco retailer which sold Heywood-Wakefield furniture. The living room of the Hostess House featured Alfons Bach designed tables, a cane panel chair, and a sofa apparently exclusive to the company's Los Angeles factory. The Hostess House dining area was furnished with an extension table and side chairs. Salem, a finish normally used on the Old Colony line, was used on both the living and dining pieces.

Heywood-Wakefield was again present at the 1964–1965 World's Fair in New York and took part in the "American Interiors" exhibit, staged in a circular four-story building with two turret-like wings which housed over 120 exhibitors. At the exhibit, company representatives distributed a souvenir cutting board stamped with both "New York Worlds Fair" and the company's trademark.

By 1934 Rohde had contracts with a number of other furniture manufacturers including Herman Miller, Kroehler Manufacturing, and Troy Sunshade. Regardless of whether these clients kept Rohde too busy or Heywood-Wakefield desired a change, it was not Rohde who would design the company's next modern group. Heywood-Wakefield did not sever ties with Rohde completely, however, for two years later the company contracted with Rohde to redesign and redecorate its showroom at the Chicago Furniture Mart.

With Rohde's 1934 departure from active design work for Heywood-Wakefield came the arrival of Russel Wright—a newcomer at that time to the contemporary furniture field—who received a contract to design modern furniture. By mid-1934 Heywood-Wakefield was marketing its new line of modern, designed largely by Wright but still displaying a sophisticated style similar to Rohde's earlier work for the company. This largely-veneered line utilized quilted maple and plain striped walnut, though some solid beech and birch were used as well.

Wright's association with Heywood-Wakefield was short lived, and by July, 1935, Conant Ball, another Gardner-based furniture company, was showing its American Modern furniture line, which had been designed by Wright. This solid wood furniture, similar to the line Heywood-Wakefield was about to introduce, was well received and set Conant Ball sales records.

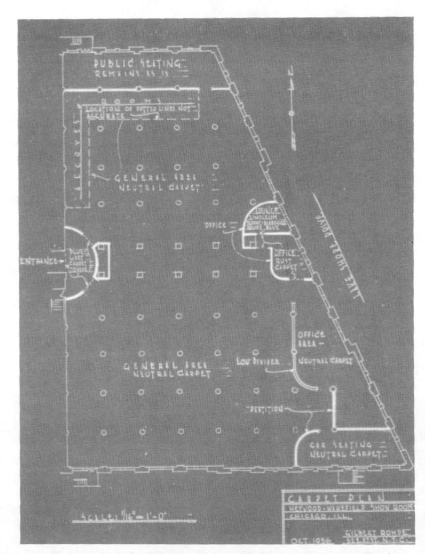

*Gilbert Rohde's floor plan for
Heywood-Wakefield's Chicago showroom,
from October, 1936.*

24

Four photos which show part of the modern group, designed largely by Russel Wright.

In late 1935 Heywood-Wakefield introduced its first Streamline Modern furniture. Initially this furniture was called Streamline Maple, because the line was made from solid close-grained Northern Maple and Birch. This line was simple and direct, with no unnecessary embellishments. Or, as noted by Heywood-Wakefield's advertisements at the time, "its clean, simple lines...are in perfect decorative harmony with quaint Colonial interiors as well as sophisticated apartment settings."

In 1935 Heywood-Wakefield built this 14 foot tall chair and placed it on the Mohawk Trail Highway in Gardner. Pictured with the chair is Seth Heywood (left) and Richard N. Greenwood (right). The chair is still in Gardner today. Photo from Furniture Record, August, 1935.

25

At first the majority of the modern pieces were shown in Amber, a maple finish, while the furniture was also available in Bleached finish or a combination of Bleached and Amber finishes (though combination finishes were available only on case pieces, and then only the drawer fronts were in the contrasting color). Reflective of Heywood-Wakefield's history of building chairs to blend with tables from other manufacturers, a dark Modern Walnut finish was also available on some chairs, allowing this line's finish to match that of other furniture makers.

Streamline Maple was designed for flexibility and utility (building on the idea pioneered by Rohde's earlier work for Heywood-Wakefield), and thus made to serve multiple uses and appeal to those living in households with limited space as well as people living on a limited budget. Streamline Maple allowed customers to buy a chest for a bedroom and when space or finances permitted, move that same chest to a dining room to be used as a server, or even the base for a china cabinet. One needn't buy a complete set all at once— matching pieces could be added later. As a matter of fact, Heywood-Wakefield made a promise in their sales literature that in later years customers would be able to purchase pieces that would match in finish and design harmony. And, for 30 years, Heywood-Wakefield kept its promise.

In 1937 Streamline Maple became Streamline Modern; Maple had been dropped from the name, if not from the construction of the modern line (between 1937 and 1939 company literature said only that Streamline Modern was made of "solid wood," while by 1940 Heywood-Wakefield-'s Modern was billed as being of "solid American Birch"). In 1937 the company also debuted its Airflow group, designed by Leo Jiranek and displaying a number of new and unique characteristics. This new Modern suite used a curved front (and was the only furniture group of the time to use the curved front design in solid wood stock). Additionally, this new line featured vertical double barred pulls, with the vertical bar motif extended to matching pieces.

The Airflow designs of Jiranek were patented and, in order to receive full legal protection, were marked with the patent numbers. The lighter Bleached finish proved to be more popular than the Amber finish and in 1937 another light finish, Wheat, was introduced and soon gained a popu-

larity that kept it in production throughout the years of Modern production.

In 1938 another well-known designer, Alfons Bach, debuted his designs in Heywood-Wakefield's Streamline Modern. Bach, who had studied his craft in Europe (and also worked for such clients as General Electric, Philco Radio, and Bigelow-Sanford Carpet Co.), designed several upholstered groups as well as occasional chairs and tables. In addition to his work on the Modern line, Bach also designed Heywood-Wakefield rattan furniture, and tubular chrome furniture for the Lloyd division. The year 1938 also brought the addition of cane to Heywood-Wakefield's Modern, with the new Swedish Modern bedroom suite employing cane wrapping on the drawer pulls and featuring cane as a decorative element on the bed and vanity bench. That same year the Airflow set received a second bed with a cane panel head and footboard, while cane panels were utilized on numerous occasional pieces and side chairs.

A tubular chrome end table designed by Alfons Bach for Lloyd Manufacturing.

Along with new designs by Alfons Bach, in 1939 Heywood-Wakefield Modern was touched by a new styling influence, in the person of Count

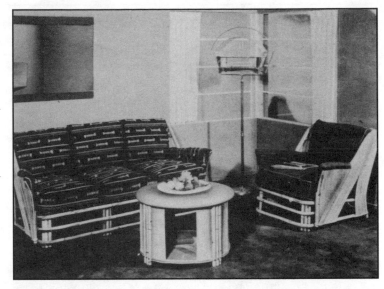

Part of the rattan "Hawaii" group designed by Alfons Bach for Heywood-Wakefield around 1938.

Alexis de Sakhnoffsky. Saknoffsky's impact on Heywood-Wakefield Modern was unmistakable, and from his drawings came the Crescendo bedroom and living room ensembles, as well as numerous other pieces.

Accompanying new 1939 styles was the introduction of a new modern finish, Champagne. Within a year Champagne—described as "a pinkish tone resembling a correctly made champagne cocktail"—became the most requested of Heywood-Wakefield's finishes. And as the popular Champagne finish was being added, Amber and Bleached (the two finishes that Streamline Modern had began with) were discontinued.

By 1940 Heywood-Wakefield had become the "fastest selling modern furniture in America." Meanwhile, the character of the furniture was coming increasingly from Heywood-Wakefield's ability to bend solid wood, with more and more pieces throughout the line displaying bow fronts and curved drawers. Using these features, Leo Jiranek designed a new bedroom suite called the Plaza.

Another new bedroom group, the Cameo, used a different new feature: plastic drawer pulls. These handles were made out of Tenite plastic that was a pastel pink color with burnished copper centers, and a Champagne finish was recommended by the company as the appropriate complement to the pinkish pulls. Such use of a non-wood material for draw pulls was a feature that was not repeated on another new Modern group until 1956.

In 1941 Heywood-Wakefield expanded its line of Modern pieces with the debut of a new Count Sakhnoffsky bedroom group, the Coronet. At the same time the company introduced Saknoffsky's Coronet living room group and his kneehole desk, the "C 3978 W," that was destined to become a Modern classic. Also new to the Heywood-Wakefield line that year was a Jiranek-designed bedroom group, the Niagara, which featured a bow-tie motif on drawer pulls and furniture bases, and the additional availability of wooden (as well as plastic) pulls for the 1940 Cameo group.

Leo Jiranek

Leo Jiranek studied engineering at Princeton University were he graduated in 1922. In 1934 he and Donald Deskey formed Amodec Inc., to allow for the manufacture and promotion of their own modern furniture designs. Marketing problems, though, soon lead to Amodec's demise. Jiranek began working with Heywood-Wakefield as a consultant sometime around 1935, with his association with the company lasting well into the 1950s. Besides designing for the Modern line, Jiranek also designed rattan summer furniture, theater seating, baby carriages, and other products for Heywood-Wakefield and its Lloyd division. With the outbreak of World War II, Jiranek assisted the company in its conversion to government work. His other clients included Kroehler Manufacturing and Basset Industries.

Count Alexis de Sakhnoffsky

As an artist-contributor to *Esquire* magazine, Count Alexis de Sakhnoffsky wrote and published drawings on streamline design. He was quoted as saying: "There is as much fashion to mechanical things as there is to clothing." Count Sakhnoffsky also worked on a line of tricycles and pedal cars for Steelcraft in 1937, along with a line of bicycles Steelcraft produced under the trade name "Mercury." The count's name was also associated with Cord, Auburn, Studebaker, and other manufacturers. He was frequently billed as "the world's premier engineering stylist," as well as "the famed exponent of streamlining." He is said to have won the Elegance Contest at the Gran Prix at Monte Carlo for his automobile designs for six consecutive years before coming to the United States around 1927. Sakhnoffsky's largest talent as a designer was his ability to "streamline" objects, and instilled in his drawings a sense of speed and movement.

A Steelcraft "Mercury" tricycle styled by Count Sakhnoffsky in 1937.

One of the last furniture groups released before the full impact of World War II on the United States had been realized was Rio, introduced at Chicago and New York furniture shows in January, 1942. Designed by Jiranek, this new set (which replaced the Cameo group) featured full length bases and cross strap pulls. The Rio group was well received and set new sales records. Rio's quick rise to popularity, though, may have been due in part to the fact that just one month before its debut war had been declared, and dealers were scrambling to stock up before the much-anticipated shortages.

"Who Serves Our Country Best": The War Years

A positively amazing change is taking place in this Massachusetts furniture factory and the story of that change is being told by a silent, mechanical conveyor, which wends its way through three miles of factory to help deliver the goods. Not so many weeks ago that conveyor was fully loaded with Streamline Modern bedroom suits; Old Colony dining pieces; smartly upholstered chairs and davenports; handsome cocktail tables. Now, it is carrying a grim, strange cargo. Here and there a lone, innocent, baby's high chair separates row upon row of dive bomber seats, gun stocks, dummy cartridges, bomb boxes, trays of bomb nose fuzes, and ack-ack projectiles . . . the hard to make tracer type!"

— From *Who Serves Our Country Best*, a Heywood-Wakefield brochure from World War II[1]

With the United States' entrance into World War II, Heywood-Wakefield was forced to make a quick shift in its production gears, drastically reducing the output of "complete and harmoniously designed furniture packages" in order to manufacture "a grim, strange cargo." As with most of the company's lines, the production of Modern was substantially pared back and less that two years after the historic bombing of Pearl Harbor the Modern line was only a third of its pre-war size.

The war, then, had several effects on Heywood-Wakefield's furniture: some temporary, some permanent. During World War II the company's Gardner plant, the oldest furniture factory in the United States, was converted to what was for the duration of the war principally an ordnance plant serving the Allied war effort. Heywood-Wakefield readily accepted the U.S. government's call to change its product line, noting: "December 7, 1941 [was] a fateful day in Heywood history, a day on which [began] an amazing story of conversion: a story of beating plowshares into swords to defend and uphold America's torch of freedom." The company suggested that Heywood-Wakefield retailers and customers at the time understood and likewise supported the war effort: "Like ourselves . . . [our customers] wish *we could serve them better*; but they prefer that Heywood-Wakefield *"serve our country best."*

The company began serving its country best in February, 1942, when an area of the Gardner factory which had been manufacturing steel baby carriage wheels was modified to produce bomb nose fuzes. In taking its first step towards an ordnance operation, Heywood-Wakefield said it was out to prove something, "that a furniture factory can make bomb nose fuzes . . . good ones, precision perfect, oodles of them, and on time."

In March, 1942, the U.S. Navy asked Heywood-Wakefield to produce Ready Room chairs for navy aircraft carriers. The Ready Room chairs—a cross between a deluxe, reclining bus seat, a school room tablet arm chair, and a personal locker—were a natural fit for Heywood-Wakefield's operations, given that the company had been producing school furniture for 45 years and had made hundreds of thousands of bus seats for customers such as Greyhound, Fifth Avenue, and Chicago Motor Coach. Once the Ready Room chairs were produced, said the company, they were placed on dozens of aircraft carriers "which roam the seven seas to deal death and destruction to all our enemies."

Heywood-Wakefield's exuberance to help the war effort was also characterized in other ways, such as: "We seem to have forgotten the trite, moss covered notion that a furniture factory is supposed to make furniture. Our executives have been flirting with the idea that we could produce anti-aircraft projectiles. Even more ridiculous; we are after a large contract for the tracer projectile which is considered by Army and Navy Ordnance Engineers more difficult to manufacture than the regular, high explosive type." As a matter of fact, in March, 1942, the company secured its first contract for ack-ack projectiles and 16 months later it was told by a Navy inspector that the Gardner factory was "one of the finest ordnance plants it has ever been my pleasure to see."

In March, 1942, the Navy also asked the company to produce dummy cartridges, or practice shells, to help train American soldiers on five-inch guns. Heywood-Wakefield's response: "We snap into action. More civilian production is necessarily thrown overboard. The race is to the swift and we have only one goal now . . . to stay right in there for the kill."

Acting swiftly for the benefit of ordnance production was not new to Heywood-Wakefield. During World War I the Gardner factory produced gun stocks, saw and pickaxe handles, and barracks chairs. The Wakefield plant had also hand-wove reed balloon baskets and produced the first stamped steel shovel in America. In addition, the company also manufactured thousands of field hospital stretchers.

In the summer of 1942 Heywood-Wakefield was again called upon to produce ambulance beds, that emblem of "the brutal, ugly, inhuman side of war." And such production apparently brought home the horror of war: "On its never ending way past the benches, machines, and work tables, the surging conveyor is a silent, moving story to every Heywood man and woman. From its stark, heartless hooks, in mute evidence of the tragedies to come, hang folding, adjustable, ambulance beds which will be used by the Army Medical Corps."

comparative ease," the company noted, "but, please God, grant that we or any other manufacturer may be called upon to produce as few as possible for our boys and those of our allies."

In August, 1942, Heywood-Wakefield's wartime product line was expanded after the company received a shipment of coir yarn from India and began producing ship fenders for Navy vessels. Eleven months later Heywood fenders sailed into Sicily. During the war the company also found its cocoa brush mats adopted by the U.S. War Department as standard equipment on road rollers which were used to prepare landing strips at vital air bases. As a result, "Heywood-Wakefield cocoa brush floor matting [was placed] on active duty at Army Posts, Naval Depots: aboard destroyer, cruiser, and battle ship decks."

War-time products displayed in front of the Heywood-Wakefield plant in Gardner, Massachusetts.

In order to conserve on critically needed steel, Heywood-Wakefield redesigned the ambulance beds and made these "products" out of the company's well-known bentwood, rather than the previously used steel tubing. "Yes, we can make wood ambulance beds in a furniture factory with

Addressing additional war-time uses for material previously used in cocoa mats, Heywood-Wakefield told its customers that cocoa matting had become "an essential part of a new type of ship fender developed in cooperation with the United States Navy. You say you have a genuine

Heywood cocoa mat on your doorstep? Well, to borrow in part from a popular slogan, you will have to 'wear it out and make it do' because every yard of coir yarn coming into the country is needed now by our Army and Navy."

A year after the bombing of Pearl Harbor—in a Gardner plant building known as "Shanghai" where workers had sorted, graded, and machined East Indian rattan until its supply of that material was cut off—Heywood-Wakefield began making one-and-a-half-ton and two-and-a-half-ton cargo bodies for Army trucks. The company anticipated the public's perception of such work for the well-known furniture maker, suggesting that people might think "that Heywood crowd must be crazy. Certainly, Heywood knows how to take a Count Sakhnoffsky sketch and turn out the swankiest Modern night table you ever saw. But, just exactly how do you jump from a gem of a night table to a massive two-and-a-half-ton truck body?" Heywood-Wakefield answered its own question. "Well, you get the right sort of patriotic, enthusiastic workmen. You back them up with sound, practical engineers. You face the future with fortitude and courage. You get a running start . . . and you jump! . . . They don't have that sleek, streamlined, Sakhnoffsky look; but they brought men and supplies which helped to save the day in Tunisia, Sicily, New Guinea, and around Orel."

By 1943 Heywood-Wakefield's line of bus, trolley, and railroad seats were being manufactured specifically for the War Production Board in order to further move "men and supplies." The production of school furniture, meanwhile, had slowed down to a trickle and was confined largely to officer candidate schools where "supplying, submerging, and shooting are taught in place of the familiar readin,' writin,' and 'rithmetic." Likewise theater chairs were being sold "on a reserve basis only, . . . reserved for Army Motion Picture Theaters, Navy Auditoriums, Coast Guard Lecture Halls, and other branches of the Armed Forces."

The one civilian product line produced in numbers closest to peace-time years was baby carriages. Heywood-Wakefield noted that "on baby carriages we have been fortunate, indeed. We were able to develop an attractive, popularly priced line of carriages which comply with conservation orders. We found a way to schedule this production without interference on any war item

in the factory."

On other production fronts the war spelled more significant changes. The company completely (and permanently) abandoned the use of rattan in favor of domestically-grown ash after the Japanese "almost bombed [Heywood-Wakefield] out of the summer furniture business when they battered Macassa into submission. Exports of rattan from this East Indian shipping port on the Island of Celebes stopped completely."

The company, though, found that the close grained ash growing right in its own New England backyard served as more than an adequate substitute and used this native hardwood to develop a complete line of summer furniture in natural finish. As a result, Heywood-Wakefield was able to maintain a sizable production volume of summer furniture during the war years without hampering its ordnance production. And, "the average consumer [could not] tell the difference between [this] smart replacement and the original rattan furniture." Believing in fact that the ash was more attractive, Heywood-Wakefield adopted steam bent ash as its standard for summer furniture, and eventually changed the name of that line to Ashcraft.

But wartime production of other furniture lines was curtailed sharply and both Old Colony and Streamline Modern Furniture were distributed on a strict quota plan as the company attempted "to make limited distribution . . . as fair and equitable as possible." By 1943 Heywood-Wakefield had released its revised and reduced basic line of Modern furniture.

And not only was the Modern line—as well as other product lines—limited in size, the company was severely limited on the number of patterns it was allowed to make. As a result, during the war years Heywood-Wakefield designs were simpler, less expensive, and easier to produce than pre-war models. And in keeping with the spirit of the war effort, furniture names also came to reflect the company's patriotism, as in the name of the Victory Group, a wartime bedroom set.

The war also found Heywood-Wakefield experimenting in other areas. To minimize the use of restricted materials such as critically-needed metals, in 1943 the company tried to replace the steel springs used in its upholstered furniture line, using bentwood in combination with plastic fiber in constructing the platform seat and back of furniture. The replacement apparently was not well received; by September, 1944, the company was once again advertising the "steel spring construction" of its upholstered line of Modern furniture.

In the end, World War II forced Heywood-Wakefield to reevaluate the importance of its products; as a result each principal line of Heywood-Wakefield domestic furniture met with production decreases. The 48-page 1941–42 Modern catalog, for instance, featured 154 designs. In stark contrast to this sizable line and its colorful portrayal were the 1943 and 1944 "catalogs," which were one-sheet posters advertising 52 and 44 Modern pieces respectively.

By September, 1944, the company had begun its post-war planning and launched a magazine ad campaign with a three-fold purpose: to keep the Heywood-Wakefield name in front of the American public, to boost sales during and after the war, and to keep the company's factories working at full capacity during the transition from war-time back to peace-time production. The advertising blitz was staged between September, 1944, and January, 1945, when quarter-page Heywood-Wakefield ads ran in leading home magazines, including *Better Homes & Gardens*, *House Beautiful* and *American Home*. These ads featured both Streamline Modern and Old Colony, the two trade or brand names Heywood-Wakefield was using during the 1940s to characterize and publicize its regular lines of furniture.

One such ad, appearing in 1944, characterized the Streamline Modern line as "charming, practical, well-styled furniture [that] adapts to your decorative schemes . . . to your ideas of gracious living." And the ad further told customers that "Heywood-Wakefield Modern is available in limited quantities just now. After the war you can buy this graceful furniture for every room in the home.

Remember, only Heywood-Wakefield makes Streamline Modern styled by America's foremost designers!"

What Heywood-Wakefield took from the war was much like what it gained from its experience weathering the Great Depression. The company became committed to a policy of line simplification and product simplification. In carrying out this move towards simplification, the company recognized what would be its most important asset in the post-war period: its reputation. Or, as Heywood-Wakefield Vice President Paul B. Posser said in a 1944 speech to employees, "this reputation for quality is our most important asset and you can do nothing better than seeing this reputation is maintained."[2]

A late 1944 advertisement designed to keep Heywood-Wakefield's name in the minds of consumers.

From Boom to Bust:
The Post-war Era

When VJ day came in September, 1945, the resumption of normal peace time production of Heywood-Wakefield furniture did not return overnight. There were still government contracts to fulfill and company factories to be retooled. In addition, the company had to contend with confusing national policies, rising labor and supply costs, and raw-material shortages. All of these post-war changes hampered operations and slowed the release of new Modern and other product lines.

In some cases the new peace made permanent war-time modifications. Soon after the war's end Heywood-Wakefield officially discontinued two staple, long-time lines of furniture: reed, and cane and fiber products. The elimination of these products ended a 100-year-era during which time (aside from years of war) Heywood and Wakefield companies had actively used these materials in furniture production.

During the first few years after the war Heywood-Wakefield drew largely on past designs which had a proven sales track record. As a matter of fact, the 1946 Heywood-Wakefield furniture lines were largely the same as those the company had been making since 1942. One thing did change: after 1946 Heywood-Wakefield no longer used the word "streamline" in its advertisement of Modern furniture. The first "new" Modern furniture came out in January, 1947, when the Riviera bedroom suite was introduced at the Chicago Furniture Mart. This Riviera suite, though, was actually the pre-war Rio bedroom group with new drawer pulls and bases.

Aside from the addition of new drawer pulls and bases, the other most distinguishing factor between Riviera and Rio was that the former used a new "M" model numbering system (for more on model numbering, see Chapter 7), as opposed to the prefix "C" used with model numbers on all wooden furniture produced before the war. As new furniture was introduced after 1946, it was marked by a new system: Modern furniture used an "M" prefix while Old Colony used a "C." (Interestingly, early in 1947 it was still possible to see company photographs with furniture using both the old and new model numbers.)

By mid-1947 a second Modern bedroom set had been added to Heywood-Wakefield's furniture lines, along with new living and dining room pieces. That same year the company also introduced a new line of Old Colony, as well as a new line of baby carriages. After moderately increasing prices in 1948, the company that year set an all time sales record of nearly $25 million, with Modern pacing furniture sales.

During the late 1940s Heywood-Wakefield introduced its tambour door cabinets (such as the M 179 illustrated in the identification guide), reflecting the influence France's Louis XVI furniture. In the construction of the new tambours, which Heywood-Wakefield had been experimenting with since before the war, the company employed a new process whereby one solid wood panel was glued to a flexible cloth material, and then the panel was grooved down to the cloth, or "duck" (as opposed to the original process in which individual wood strips—which would comprise the panel—were glued to a duck material). This new process enabled Heywood-Wakefield to create an evenness of grain in the tambour doors that would have otherwise been impossible. Tambour doors would remain a feature until the Modern line was discontinued.

The Encore line, marked by a fresh "modern" style, was introduced in 1949. Its basic design—solid wood drawer pulls extending almost the entire length of the drawer at the top edge— became one of Modern's most enduring styles of the postwar years. The Encore bedroom group and its companion pieces from the dining and living room became a staple for Heywood-Wakefield, and also lasted until Modern itself was discontinued.

In 1949 Heywood-Wakefield also introduced its new Aristocraft line, consisting of sectionals, sofas, and chairs with bentwood arms and loose cushions. Five occasional tables rounded out the line, which was designed by W. Joseph Carr, a staff designer and employee of Heywood-Wakefield since before the war. Drawing on his experience from working in the plant, Carr designed Aristocraft with a number of cost and manufacturing considerations in mind. Heywood-Wakefield's considerable experience with bending solid wood made Aristocraft's use of bentwood arms ideally suited to the company's manufacturing set up, while the loose cushion style Carr employed was less expensive to produce than fully upholstered pieces. More importantly, however, was Aristocraft's use of darker "heart" lumber (utilized in the production of Old Colony and twice as

was introduced in 1952 and lasted through the remainder of the decade. Sculptura's design was born through the collaborative work of designers Ernest Herrmann and Leo Jiranek, experimental department head Frank Parrish, and W. Joseph

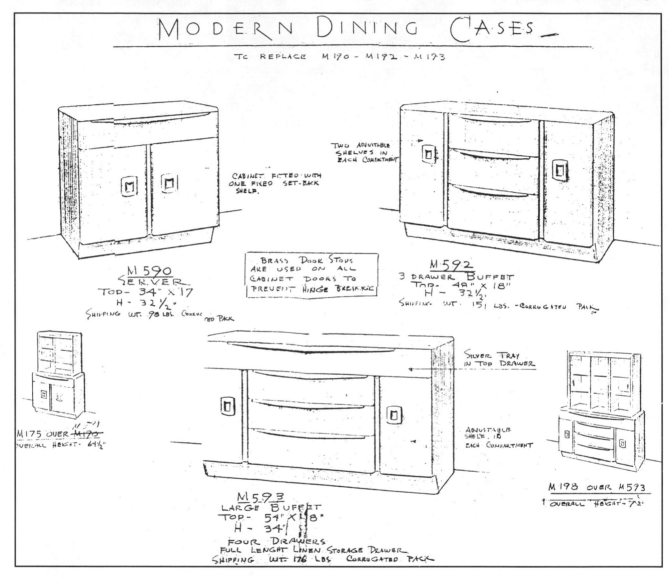

A company drawing of the M 590 series dining cases from 1950.

plentiful as the lighter "sap" lumber normally used in the production of Modern furniture), which gave the Aristocraft pieces their slightly darker tone.

Heywood-Wakefield entered the 1950s geared to meet the demands of an ever-growing market by offering an ever-changing product line. Throughout the decade numerous pieces were introduced, only to be dropped or replaced within a year or two. One exception to this rapidly evolving product base was the Sculptura bedroom group, which

Carr, who gave the Sculptura suite its name. The most dramatic styling feature of Sculptura was its drawer fronts, which curved in and out like folded ribbons.

The presence of Heywood-Wakefield's furniture not only grew domestically during the 1950s. Heywood-Wakefield, for instance, was gaining a highly-respected reputation for furniture in the modernized regions of eastern Saudi Arabia. Three towns had been built by the Arabian American Oil Company to house both Americans and Arabs

Left to right: Joseph W. Carr, Frank Parrish, and Ernest Herrmann.

The furniture specified for the sitting room was all from the standard Modern furniture line available for general sale in 1953, with the exception of the Amir's chair and telephone stand.

In 1955 Heywood-Wakefield began experimenting with new styles, materials, and finishes in the Modern line, which were similar to those being used by other contemporary furniture manufacturers. For instance, the standard finish for the newly-introduced Cadence line's living room, dining room, and bedroom furniture was Sable Grey. Another new entry to the company's product line in 1955 was the Dakar bedroom group.

working for that company in the 1940s and by the early 1950s almost one million dollars worth of Heywood-Wakefield products had been shipped to that region.

In 1953 Heywood-Wakefield Modern was requested for a unique and interesting installation. Leo Jiranek and the firm Aeon International were commissioned to decorate the new summer palace in Dammam, Saudi Arabia, for his Highness Saud ibn Jiluwi, and Jiranek specified Heywood-Wakefield Modern for the sitting rooms. Because of the high humidity in the gulf region where the palace was to be built, metal furniture was requested for the dining and bedrooms. It is not known exactly how many sitting rooms were in the palace, but following is Jiranek's specifications for one.

Dakar was made from solid mahogany and featured leaf-shaped machine carvings on the drawer fronts and headboards. That same year the Tempo bedroom group debuted, featuring a light stain with black walnut and brass pulls. All these sets were angular in appearance and—while having their own aesthetic appeal—represented a significant style change for Heywood-Wakefield. As

```
      SITTING ROOM #22 (30' X 77')
      FURNITURE: (Heywood-Wakefield Co.)
(A)   1  AMIR'S CHAIR (M-559-C)
(B)  11  SOFAS (M-597)
(C)  18  ARM CHAIRS (M-595-C)
(F)   7  LAMP TABLES (M-364-G)
(G)   2  CORNER TABLES (M-338-G)
(H)   9  TABLE LAMPS (Sandel Mfg. Co. #5845)
(I)   2  FLOOR LAMPS (Sandel Mfg. Co. #5145)
      (Note: See pages 16 & 17 for photos)
(J)   1  CARPET (James Lees & Sons Co)
      1  UNDERPAD ("Velvair")
(K)  11  pairs DRAPERIES WITH VALANCES
(T)   1  AMIR'S TELEPHONE STAND
```

Ernest Herrmann with the Kohinoor vanity he designed.

a result they never achieved the popularity of the company's more innovative Streamline Modern.

During the mid-1950s Heywood-Wakefield's Ashcraft and Old Colony continued to sell well, as did the company's school seating, which earned a mention in a 1955 *Wall Street Journal* article as one of the top two brands of school furniture. With increasingly reliance on its school and institutional furniture division, during the late-1950s the company began constructing a new manufacturing facility in Newport, Tennessee, dedicated largely to the production of movable and fixed school furniture.

While the Newport facility was being erected, the Gardner plant was becoming a source of financial and labor woes. Between 1957 and 1960 Heywood-Wakefield reported a string of annual losses, with its four-year deficit totaling in excess of $2 million. Throughout that period the Gardner plant operated in the red—losing $500,000 alone in 1960—and was the only company facility outside of Orilla, Ontario, (which opened in the early-1920s) not making money.

In January, 1961, Richard N. Greenwood announced that the one million square foot Gardner plant—then making wooden home furniture, motel and hotel furniture, as well as railroad and bus seats—would close its doors, following an unsuccessful attempt to get employees to go along for another year with a 10 percent wage reduction initiated in December, 1959. Following Greenwood's announcement the local union had a change of heart and on January 18, 1961, over 1,000 plant workers crowded into an auditorium in Gardner City Hall and agreed in a unanimous standing vote to management's terms.

The company moved back into the black in 1961, but by 1965 Heywood-Wakefield had compiled a short-term debt of over $4 million. In November, 1965, company stockholders agreed to a recapitalization plan, which among other things would more than double the company's number of outstanding shares of common stock. In early 1966 Curtis Watkins, president and sole owner of the privately held Simplex Time Recorder Company of Gardner, purchased 40 percent of Heywood-Wakefield's outstanding common stock in order to, in his words, "bring the company ownership back home." Watkins father, interestingly, had left Heywood-Wakefield in 1917 to run a clock business which grew into Simplex Time—

one of the country's largest maker of time clocks, time recorders, and timing systems.

Soon after Watkins bought into Heywood-Wakefield the proposal to increase stock shares was reversed, and Simplex Time agreed to guarantee Heywood-Wakefield's short term loans. About the same time another nearby company, Toy Town Tavern Corp., began acquiring Heywood-Wakefield stock and by mid-1966 they owned more than 10 percent of Heywood-Wakefield's outstanding common stock.

As financial problems were increasing, Heywood-Wakefield's Modern furniture line was shriveling. By 1964 the furniture that had been called Streamline Maple in 1936 had become "Classic American Furniture by Heywood-Wakefield," with only 30 pieces contained in the 1964–1965 catalog. In 1966 there was no new Modern catalog issued, only an updated price list referring to the 1965 catalog. The "M 320 W" Kneehole Desk—a direct descendant of the desk Count Sakhnoffsky had sketched in 1939—was discontinued in 1966, with the entire Modern line following suit soon after.

During Heywood-Wakefield's final years wood furniture took a back seat to institutional furniture. As the company was making this last major shift in its production focus, the reins of Heywood-Wakefield returned to the hands of a Heywood—George H., great-great-grandson of the original Seth Heywood—who became president. Heywood-Wakefield celebrated its 150th anniversary in 1976, the year of the United States' bicentennial celebration. It was about this time that the company sold its Gardner facilities, leaving Levi Heywood's company a tenant of the Massachusetts factory it had built. Then on June 13, 1979—for the first time in 153 years—no production employees reported for work at the Heywood-Wakefield factory in Gardner. The plant had been abandoned by the company and taken over by auctioneers. After the factory closed, the Gardner City Council sent a letter to the company; it was addressed simply "Gentlemen," and noted "with regret the passing of this historic Gardner industry."

By the end of 1979 the company had only two operating plants and employed less than 600. The Heywood-Wakefield name was no longer associated with wooden home furnishings and the company was comprised of two divisions: Lloyd Furniture, based in Menominee, Michigan, and consisting of metal-framed outdoor/casual and institutional furniture; and Heywood-Wakefield Public Seating, operating out of Newport, Tennessee, and producing movable and fixed school furniture as well as auditorium, church, and theater seating. (It was in fact Heywood-Wakefield's public seating division that paced the company's sales during its final years.)

In 1981 Heywood-Wakefield filed for bankruptcy, with its remaining assets placed in receivership. The following year the Lloyd plant was purchased from bankruptcy court by a group of investors led by a businessman named Don Flanders, who operated the facility under the name Bay Breeze Industries, Inc., then later—to reflect the operation's heritage—changed the company's title to Lloyd/Flanders Industries, Inc. Lloyd/Flanders introduced the first of several series of wicker furniture in 1985; and, still producing wicker in 1992, that concern celebrated its 10th anniversary.

CITY OF GARDNER
MASSACHUSETTS 01440

OFFICE OF THE
CITY COUNCIL

CHAIR CITY OF THE WORLD

PRESIDENT
JAMES E. CHARLAND

COUNCILLORS AT LARGE
JAMES E. CHARLAND
EDWARD CHITOW
PHILIP A. LaGRASSA
CHARLES P. McKEAN
ROSAIRE J. ST. JEAN
STEPHEN YABLONSKI

Ward 1
DAVID J. BESSETTE

Ward 2
ROLAND J. ALVES

Ward 3
EUGENE A. GEMBORYS

Ward 4
ROBERT F. BURKE

Ward 5
MIMI A. CANU

June 29, 1979

Heywood Wakefield Co.
206 Central Street
Gardner, MA. 01440

Gentlemen:

    The City Council of Gardner extends its sincere appreciation and thanks to the Heywood Wakefield Co. for the many years of service and support to the City of Gardner.

    The employment of our residents in this business for these many years, as also the real estate tax realized by the City, contributed to the growth and prosperity of our community.

    We note with regret the passing of this historic Gardner industry.

                    Very truly yours,
                    CITY COUNCIL OF GARDNER

                    City Clerk

It Wasn't All Modern:
Heywood-Wakefield's Other Products

Obviously Modern wasn't the only line of products Heywood-Wakefield manufactured in its 150 year history. In 1826 Heywood-Wakefield entered the furniture business by hand-crafting simple chairs and in its succeeding 15 decades of operation the company produced hundreds of different sizes and styles of chairs. But many other product and furniture lines were manufactured before, during, and after Modern. Some of the more well-known Heywood-Wakefield products included the following:

Rattan and Fiber Furniture: Heywood-Wakefield and its predecessor companies produced a wide variety of rattan and fiber furniture, which traces its roots to Cyrus Wakefield's first purchase of a small bundle of rattan in 1844. In later years Heywood and Wakefield companies certainly proved that rattan was worth more than dunnage, importing the raw material from the Far East. With the merging of Heywood and Wakefield interests in 1897, the consolidated Heywood Brothers & Wakefield Company became the largest

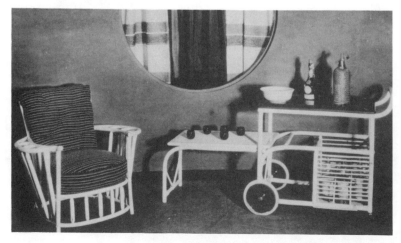

A rattan tub chair and beverage wagon from 1937.

importer of rattan in the world. During the 1920s Heywood-Wakefield began making greater use of rattan and fiber and, besides chairs, manufactured tables, serving carts, and other furniture from rattan. Heywood-Wakefield continued to manufacture and market rattan and fiber furniture until World War II brought a quick halt to rattan deliveries.

Railcar, Bus, and Airplane Seating: Seating for the mass transportation industries proved to be another use for rattan. During the 1860s looms were developed to weave sheets of cane webbing fabric out of rattan and by the 1870s rattan was recognized as the best material to cover railcar and streetcar seats. Heywood-Wakefield's streetcar seating line evolved into new materials and new uses, including bus and later airplane seats.

Mats and Mattings: Heywood-Wakefield's matting business grew out of the inventive mind of William Houston, an early employee of Cyrus Wakefield who devised a process for

A Heywood Brothers & Wakefield carriage with corduroy upholstery and a 1921 price of $74.50.

A stick reed davenport and end table from 1929.

A baby carriage produced in 1946.

Children's Furniture: Over the years Heywood-Wakefield produced a variety of children's furniture, including high chairs and bassinets.

Baby Carriages: During the 1870s Heywood Brothers & Company began making baby carriages and became one of the first companies to produce carriages out of rattan and reed. Through the acquisition of Lloyd Manufacturing Company in 1921 the newly-reorganized Heywood-Wakefield Company gained Marshall B. Lloyd's patented process for weaving fiber and creating wicker on giant looms. These looms, which revolutionized the baby carriage industry, later were used to weave fiber for the colorful Jacquard designs for furniture which made their way into a large percentage of American homes between the mid-1920s and early 1930s.

Children's Toys: The first toy vehicle Lloyd Manufacturing Company produced at Menominee, Michigan, was a boys' express wagon in 1907. By the time

spinning cane shavings into usable yarn. Houston and Wakefield then developed a loom to weave the yarn into brush mats and by 1881 over 100 of these looms were being used to weave various types of mats and mattings. By the 1930s Heywood-Wakefield was employing similar looms to weave coir yarn from the fruit of the coconut tree, using the yarn to manufacture cocoa mats and mattings.

A Heywood Brothers and Wakefield "Little Red Rider" from 1921.

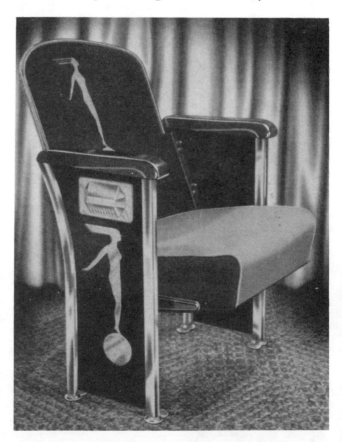

A theater seat with an art deco motif from the 1930s.

A 1950s Lloyd tubular chrome group, some of which had been in production since before WWII.

William B. Lloyd's operations were acquired by Heywood-Wakefield in 1921, Lloyd Company was also producing collapsible go-carts and hand-woven reed carriages. Production of various children's toys continued under the Heywood-Wakefield and Lloyd names into the mid-1930s, when all toy vehicles—except doll carriages—were discontinued.

Metal Furniture: Marshall B. Lloyd and his assistant Lewis Larsen patented a method of making tubing by rolling flat stock steel and then welding it. This type of tubing—utilized in the construction of baby carriages, railcar seating, and bus seating—was also used to make furniture. Metal furniture was manufactured in both Gardner and Menominee and produced under both Heywood-Wakefield and Lloyd names. Alfons Bach and Kem Weber were two of the more notable designers of this metal furniture. Weber also designed furniture for Baker Furniture, Widdicomb Furniture, and others.

A theater seat designed by Raymond Loewy.

Heywood-Wakefield school furniture at Theodore Roosevelt School in Kearny, New Jersey, in 1936.

Theater Seating: In 1906 Heywood Brothers & Wakefield Company began producing opera chairs at its Chicago factory. Along with the growth in popularity of vaudeville and motion pictures, the market for theater seating grew substantially in the 1920s. Heywood-Wakefield theater seating was designed by such figures as Leo Jiranek and Raymond Loewy (the latter whose design credits numbered in the hundreds and included such things as locomotives for Pennsylvania Railroad, refrigerators for Coldspot, and automobiles for Studebaker). Heywood-Wakefield's theater seating lines evolved to include auditorium and stadium seating.

A Trimline teachers desk from 1958.

School Furniture: The growth of the public school system fostered Heywood-Wakefield's 1897 entry into the school furniture market. The furniture, made specifically for children, was designed to replace benches and stools used at that time. Heywood-Wakefield's school furniture initially helped expand the company's wooden chair line, but later evolved into furniture made out of cast iron, steel, and in the 1950s, plastic.

Ashcraft Furniture: Ashcraft was a product born out of necessity. With shipments of rattan halted by World War II, the company turned to New England ash, which was used to develop a line of summer furniture featuring a natural finish. Convinced steam bent ash was more attractive than rattan, Heywood-Wakefield eventually adopted the Ashcraft name for its summer furniture line. The company continued making Ashcraft after the war, proving that this bent ash could be used for more than porch furniture as it designed entire lines of Ashcraft, including dining room furniture and a bedroom suite.

Old Colony Furniture and others: Old Colony was the first style Heywood-Wakefield turned to when it began designing complete furniture packages. In the Early American vein, Heywood-Wakefield's Old Colony line of furniture was made from maple and other hardwoods and recreated 17th and 18th century designs. Old Colony featured a variety of different pieces, and was thus marketed with an open stock concept, or mix and match approach, similar to Modern. Along with Early American styles, Heywood-Wakefield made wood furniture in almost every style imaginable, including Queen Anne and Chippendale.

An Ashcraft dining group.

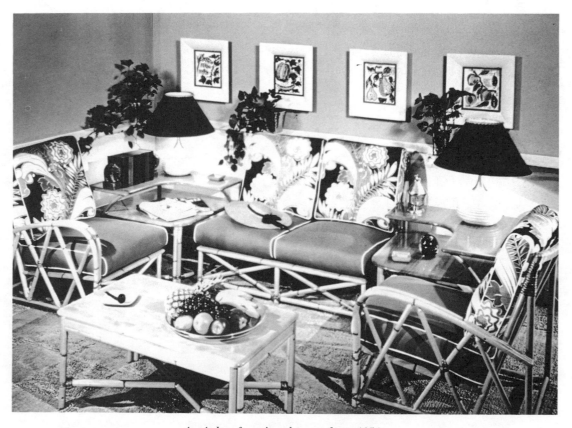

An Ashcraft sectional group from 1951.

The Crafting of Modern:
Construction & Finishes

Heywood-Wakefield was fortunate to have skilled designers, but it was the company's skilled craftsmen who turned those designs into furniture that is still appreciated today. With a battery of saws, planes, molders, lathes, and sanders, these craftsmen and women fashioned furniture out of raw lumber, much of which came from the company's own mill in Connifer, New York. In constructing Modern furniture, Heywood-Wakefield workers used solid birch exclusively, except in the case of the early Streamline Maple line which featured birch in conjunction with maple.

Modern furniture was constructed with the the outer portion of the log (called "sap" lumber), while Old Colony was made from the darker inner portion of the log (which represents about two-thirds of the tree and is called "heart lumber"). After being separated at either a plant or mill site,

the lumber was brought into the factory where it was air dried and then kiln dried. The wood was then taken to an "equalizing" room where it reabsorbed the moisture necessary to "balance" or bring the lumber to room temperature. Equalizing was an important step: it prevented warping, shrinking, or swelling during the manufacturing process.

Upon its departure from the equalizing room, the wood was cut to length, ripped, and then planed. Next the boards were matched according to color and grain to allow for design harmony when a panel was glued together. The boards then went to various parts of the plant where machining operations were done. Smaller parts such as legs or handles were machined, while matched boards were glued-up to become pieces, like table tops or chair backs (see illustration).

A line of sawyers reduce long pieces of lumber into specific lengths. Not visible is the conveyor which brought the lumber to the operators. The waste pieces dropped into a pit where they were pulverized and burnt for fuel.

44

These machines level planed the top and bottom of pieces at the same time. The machines were designed to compensate for warping, twisting, or cupping of the boards.

Much of Modern's character came from the steam-bent pieces (recall that Heywood-Wakefield had been steam-bending wood since the 19th century). Before the bending process started, air dried stock was placed into a steaming box for a period of twenty minutes to an hour. Wood that had the appropriate moisture content was then bent by hand, or pressed and heated using hydraulic presses. (Despite all of Heywood-Wakefield's skill in working with wood, 10 to 20 percent of all bentwood pieces were broken in the bending process.) After being steambent, larger parts were machined and all the parts received their first sanding.

The furniture pieces began to take shape during the assembly process. The assembly of case goods included attaching legs, and cleats on the legs; hanging doors; fitting drawers; fitting veneer back panels; and attaching hardware. Joints were glued and screwed; nails were not used at any joints. The insides of all drawers were sprayed with a drawer coater.

After the assembly process furniture was sanded in order to blend drawers, tops, and sides together. Following this sanding, Modern pieces were bleached, producing a lighter as well as more uniform wood finish. Next the pieces were spray stained, with any excess stain removed through hand wiping. After pieces were placed in a drying oven, a sanding sealer was applied, and then the pieces were further dried. Two coats of finish lacquer were applied, with the finish allowed to bake for approximately one hour. The pieces were then rubbed and waxed (mostly by air-powered machines, but also with waterproof sandpaper, Johnson-Wax, and steel wool). After the pieces had been rubbed, they were wiped dry and polished. The furniture was then given a final inspection and sent to the shipping department for distribution.

Heywood-Wakefield Finishes

Heywood-Wakefield used a variety of finishes on its Modern furniture. Aside from its first amber finish and darker finishes occasionally used on Modern pieces produced between the late 1950s and mid-1960s, Modern finishes shared one common trait: a light tone. Following are Modern finishes and the years they were used.

Amber: 1936–1939
a ruddy, maple color

Bleached: 1936–1939
a clear, sparkling blond tone

Amber and Bleached Combination: 1936
available only on case goods
(i.e., pieces with drawers)

Wheat: 1937–1966
a yellow shade resembling the color of natural, ripened grains

Champagne: 1939–1966
a pinkish tone resembling a properly-made champagne cocktail

The back of an "M 155 A" dining chair is being glued up. The stock was tongued and grooved, then lined with glue. The wood stock was then fitted in a gluing form and clamped. After the glue set, the form was removed. The excess glue was sanded away in later operations.

A hydraulic press bends the curved drawer fronts for the "M 320 W" desk.

A row of panels entered this machine with square edges and came out with rounded edges on both sides.

Platinum: 1954–1961
a natural, blond color with overtones of light gray and light beige blended to a platinum hue

Westwood: 1962–1966
an exceptionally-transparent finish with a light-honey tone

Modern Walnut: 1936–1944
a walnut-colored finish designed for use on chairs which were to be used in combination with furniture from other manufacturers

Other Finishes

Occasionally Heywood-Wakefield used darker finishes on Modern. Available in the late 1950s and 1960s (sometimes at an extra cost), these darker finishes included: Winthrop, Priscilla Maple, Sable Grey, Walnut, Topaz, Windsor, Fruitwood, Tampico, Clove, and Sherry.

The arm from an Aristocraft chair is sanded with a whip sander.

Upholstered Furniture

Heywood-Wakefield also made its own upholstered furniture. Though the company purchased fabrics from outside suppliers, it manufactured its own springs. By producing its own upholstered furniture, Heywood-Wakefield was able to design entire groupings of furniture in which tables, bookcases, and other pieces blended with the upholstered furniture.

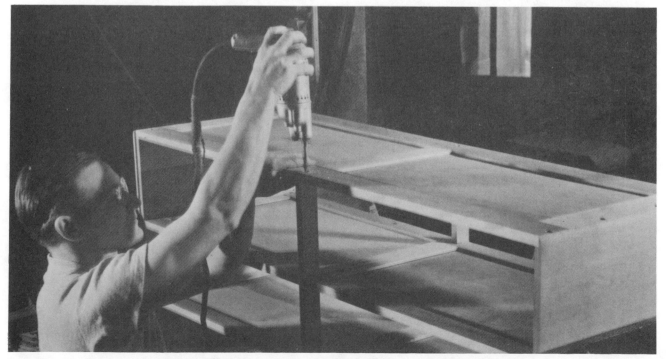

The case for a Mr. & Mrs. dresser is held in a pneumatic jig. In order to prevent the case from becoming lop-sided, the jig maintained an even pressure on the piece as it was being assembled.

A Modern desk is "cradle sanded." Sanding the assembled piece blended the individual parts together with a smooth, rounded contour.

Upholstered Furniture

Catering to tastes on the West Coast, Heywood-Wakefield offered a number of Modern design patterns which were produced exclusively from the company's Los Angeles plant. (See Identification Guide for samples of these patterns from the early 1950s). The different West Coast patterns, apparently, were generally restricted to upholstered pieces. In addition, West Coast patterns were often variations of patterns which had been discontinued at the Gardner plant, as well as variations of Heywood-Wakefield's nationally distributed line of Modern patterns.

Modern pieces were bleached with a strong solution before being stained and finished.

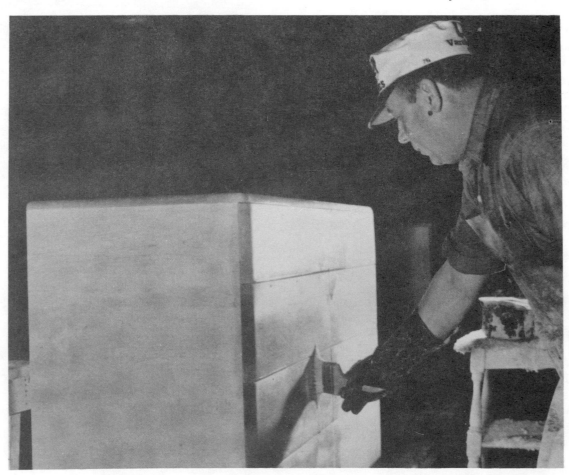

A finished "M 321" bookcase is "rubbed out" by machine.

The finished product.

A "C3363 A" side chair is "rubbed out" by hand.

Heywood-Wakefield Modern furniture was marked in numerous ways during the 30 years it was produced. Each piece of Modern was usually marked with the Heywood-Wakefield name, the style or pattern number, its respective finish color, and the inspection date.

The Heywood-Wakefield Trademark

The most distinguishing mark Heywood-Wakefield used was the Heywood-Wakefield "eagle" trademark. Adopted in 1946, the trademark was designed by Clarence Hornung, who the company labeled as "one of the foremost designers of trademarks in the country." The trademark was used on products from all Heywood-Wakefield divisions and displayed on such items as baby carriages, regular line furniture, high chairs, theater chairs, bus seats, railroad seats, and school furniture.

Hornung used the eagle because of the bird's traditional use as a decorative figure around 1826, when the company was formed. The "H" and the "W" represent the legs and the wings of the eagle as they project below the company's name plate. The trademark adopted in 1946 is the only known trademark. Prior to 1946, the company displayed no consistency in how its name was printed, and used a variety of different fonts and printing styles to portray the Heywood-Wakefield name.

The eagle trademark was branded or stamped inside the top drawer on the left side or on the bottom or back of the furniture. There were also tags that displayed the eagle trademark. These tags included the "Dupont Dulux" paper tag (with care instructions included on the back) and a cloth tag affixed under the cushions of the upholstered furniture.

The Heywood-Wakefield Label or Brand

The earliest Streamline Modern marking known is the yellow woodgrain style paper label with red print. This label is frequently found in conjunction with the blue and white style number tag made of paper. These labels were placed on the backs or bottoms of the furniture.

The woodgrain label was replaced by the red and blue paper label, which used white print. The exact date the red and blue paper label was adopted is unknown; estimates range from 1939 to no later than 1942.

There were also special emblems placed inside the top drawers on some of the furniture designed by Leo Jiranek and Count Sakhnoffsky. These emblems were made from metal or plastic and displayed the designer's name.

Style Numbers

Heywood-Wakefield Modern furniture was marked with a style or pattern number. Sometimes this number was placed on the style tag (if there was a tag); sometimes the number was stamped in block letters on the back or the bottom of the furniture. Over the years three different numbering systems were used for Modern Furniture. The first system was already in use when the Streamline Modern line was introduced in 1936, and was shared with other lines of Heywood-Wakefield wood furniture. The first numbering system used 4 digits and always included a "C" prefix. Sometimes Heywood-Wakefield used a suffix, which varied according to the type of furniture being numbered. Following are some examples of complete style numbers from the first system, known suffixes, and what those suffixes represented:

C2794 A, A	=	side chair
C2794 C, C	=	arm chair
C2932 G, G	=	table
C3539 W, W	=	desk
C3348 X, X	=	a modification or variation of a previous design

Note that a chest or a bookcase without a built-in desk would have no suffix; one that had a built-in desk had the W suffix. Additionally, a piece that was a modification or variation of a previous design had a X suffix. For example, the

The Heywood-Wakefield eagle trademark was introduced in 1946, and used through the end of Modern production.

C3348 Corner Cabinet made in 1938 and 1939 became the C3348 X when the door pulls were changed in 1940.

For sofas and sectionals, number suffixes were used to denote piece length as well as other variations, such as whether a piece was a left arm or right arm section. For example, in the C 3945 Sectional Sofa Group:

C3945 C	=	Arm Chair
C3945	=	Single Filler, Armless Section
C3945 LC	=	Left Arm Section
C3945 RC	=	Right Arm Section
C3946	=	Double Filler, Armless Section double wide
C3946-44	=	Love Seat, 44" wide seat
C3947-66	=	Davenport, 66" wide seat

In a bedroom suite, the last digit generally designated the type of furniture. Following are the style numbers used in the Crescendo bedroom suite and what the last digit of those numbers designated (note that the suite did not have a second vanity or dressing table):

C3550: bed	0 = bed
C3551: dresser	1 = dresser
C3552: 5-drawer chest	2 = chest
C3553: mirror	3 = mirror
C3554: vanity	4 = vanity
C3555: mirror	5 = mirror
none:	6 = vanity/dressing table
C3557: vanity seat	7 = vanity bench
C3558: night stand	8 = night stand
C3559: blanket chest	9 = other

In addition, if a mirror was attached to a case piece, the last 2 or 3 digits of the mirror's style

The woodgrain label was used until the late 1930s.

number became the suffix for the piece to which it was attached. For example: C3551-55 was the C3551 Crescendo dresser with the C3555 mirror attached. One note on absolutes: these guidelines will be true in most cases. However, variations did exist, especially in the case of large sets or groups that were in production for a long period of time.

After World War II there was a gradual change over to a second numbering system. As new pieces were introduced they were given a number with an "M" or a "CM" prefix. "M" designated the Modern line and "CM" designated the Contract Modern line. In the second numbering system Old Colony was the only line using the "C" prefix. The suffixes used for the first ("C") numbering system were also for the second ("M") numbering system.

In 1966 Heywood-Wakefield began using a computerized numbering system. (In most cases the first three digits of the computerized system were the last three numbers of the "M" system.) The eleven-digit computer system used the first three numbers to denote the pattern, or type of furniture. For example, these three numbers identified chairs, tables, sofas, etc. The fourth and fifth numbers designated the style and the variations of the pattern; for example, these two numbers denoted such things as bed size, number of table leaves, and other variations. The sixth and seventh numbers in the computer system designated the finish. The only three finishes used at that time and their respective numbers were: Champagne, 03; Wheat, 05; Westwood, 06. The last four numbers pertained to fabrics or other options, such as the length of bed rails.

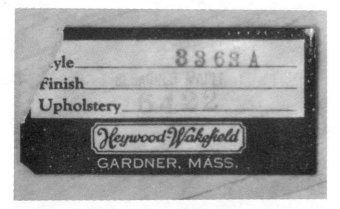

This label is usually seen with the woodgrain label.

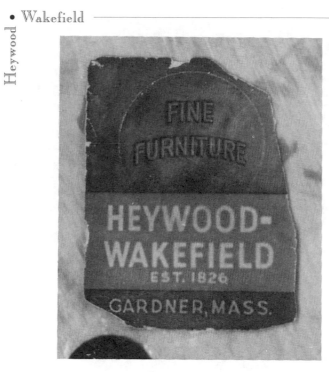

The red and blue label was used until the Heywood-Wakefield eagle trademark was phased in, beginning in 1946.

This cloth tag was used on upholstered furniture. Note the date stamp to the right of the tag.

Date Stamps

Much of the furniture produced after the war was stamped with a production or final inspection date. The date—only about one inch long—was usually stamped in red or black ink.

This paper label advertised the Dupont Dulux finish Heywood-Wakefield used for many years.

A Gardner factory worker branding drawers with the eagle mark around 1948.

Identification Guide Preface

This guide illustrates the majority of Heywood-Wakefield's Streamline Modern and Modern furniture line. The pre-1936 veneered lines of Gilbert Rhode and Russel Wright have not been included, as those lines were of a modern style unto themselves. Contemporary lines that were introduced during the mid-1950s (such as Dakar and Cadence) which were of a different style or used different materials are also not included in this guide.

Dates: Dates used in this guide are based on the documentation available from company records. The possibility exists that a piece could have been discontinued soon after a catalog was issued, or even by the time a catalog had been printed (in which case the margin of error should be no more than one or two years). The last wartime production records available were from September, 1944. However, our research indicates that pieces still in production in 1944 were likely to have been in production through at least 1946.

Designers: Design credit was taken from company records, periodicals, and trade journals contemporary to the production of pieces identified. Many designs were not documented by the company; this book leaves the attribution of those designs, even if similar to other pieces, to the reader's judgment.

Furniture Names: Names of pieces or groups of furniture identified were named by Heywood-Wakefield.

Dimensions: Dimensions have been taken largely from company records; in some cases dimensions given are a result of measurements taken from the specific piece of furniture.

Interchangeability: Modern was sold "open stock," or mix and match, and many combinations were possible. Mirrors were almost always interchangeable and were also sold as separate wall hanging units. A variety of vanity benches were sold which would match most vanities. Most china tops were also interchangeable.

West Coast Patterns: There were patterns exclusive to the West Coast during the early years of Modern, but little specific information on those patterns is available. Early 1950s styles known to be exclusive to Heywood-Wakefield's Los Angeles plant are illustrated.

DINING ROOM

C2794 A   SIDE CHAIR   *1936–41*
Designed by Gilbert Rohde. The seat is 15½" by 14½", and the height of the back is 16½". Available in Champagne, Wheat, Amber, Bleached, or Modern Walnut finishes. Yardage required 1¼ yards of 50" material.

C2794 C   ARM CHAIR   *1936–41*
Designed by Gilbert Rohde. Also available as C2794 CCB with channel back upholstery with 3 channels. Available as C2794 C 4 CB with 4 channels. The seat is 19" by 17", and the height of the back is 17". Available in Champagne, Wheat, Amber, Bleached, or Modern Walnut finishes. Yardage required 1½ yards of 50" material. 2 yards of 50" material with channels.

C2932 G   EXTENSION TABLE   *1936–39*
Size of top open is 42" by 84", with top closed 42" by 60". Height 29". Available in Champagne, Wheat, Amber, or Bleached finishes.

C2910   CENTER CABINET   *1936*
This chest was designed to be used in bedroom groupings or as the center section of the 3 piece buffet. Size of top 32" by 19". Height is 34". Available in Amber, Bleached, or a combination of both.

C2914 L OR C2915 R   LEFT OR RIGHT PIER CABINET   *1936*
The top is 16" by 19" and the height is 34". Available in Amber or Bleached finishes.

C2912   SHELF   *1936*
This piece may be used on the C2917 Server to form a dining hutch or on the C2911 W to form a secretary. Size is 31" by 11". Height is 25". Amber or Bleached finishes available.

C2917   SERVER   *1936*
Size of top is 32" by 15½". Height is 32½". Available in Amber or Bleached finishes.

DINING ROOM

C2916 A   *CHAIR*   *1936*
Seat 16" by 15½" and back 14½" high. Available in Amber or Bleached finishes. Yardage required is ¼ yard of 50" material.

C2916 G   *EXTENSION TABLE*   *1936*
Size of top open is 30" by 50". Size of top closed is 30" by 40". Height is 29". Available in Amber or Bleached finishes.

C2913   *CLOSED HUTCH CABINET*   *1936*
This piece may be used on the C2917 Server to form a closed dining hutch or on the C2910 to form a chest on chest for bedroom use. Size 31" by 14". Height 17". Available in Amber or Bleached finishes. Closed Hutch Cabinet (C2913 on C2917) has U. S. Design Patent No. 98888.

C2917   *SERVER*   *1936*
Size of top is 32" by 15½". Height is 32½". Available in Amber or Bleached finishes.

DINING ROOM

C2918 A   *SIDE CHAIR*   *1936*
Seat is 16½" by 17½". Height of back is 15½". Yardage required is ⅔ yard of 50" material. Available in Amber or Bleached finishes.

C2918 C   *ARM CHAIR*   *1936*
Seat is 16½" by 17½". Height of back is 15½". Yardage required is ⅔ yard of 50" material. Available in Amber or Bleached finishes.

C2918 G   *TABLE WITH SWING UNDER LEAVES*   *1936–38*
The two end leaves of this table swing flat under the top of this table when not in use. Size of top with leaves extended is 32" by 68", with leaves folded, 32" by 48". Height is 29". Available in Wheat, Amber, or Bleached finishes.

THREE SECTION BUFFET
This is formed by using the C2910 Center Cabinet and the C2914 and C2915 Pier Cabinets.

C2910   *CENTER CABINET*   *1936*
This chest was designed to be used in bedroom groupings or as the center section of the 3 piece buffet. Size of top 32" by 19". Height is 34". Available in Amber, Bleached, or a combination of both finishes.

C2914 L & C2915 R   *LEFT & RIGHT PIER CABINET*   *1936*
The tops are 16" by 19" and the height is 34". Available in Amber or Bleached finishes.

OPEN SHELF HUTCH CABINET.
This is formed by using the C2912 Shelf on the C2917 Server.

C2912   *SHELF*   *1936*
This piece maybe used on the C2917 Server to form a dining hutch or on the C2911–W to form a secretary. Size is 31" by 11". Height is 25". Amber or Bleached finishes available.

C2917   *SERVER*   *1936*
Size of top is 32" by 15½". Height is 32½". Available in Amber or Bleached finishes.

THE PIECES

C2910   *CENTER CABINET*   *1936–37*
This chest was designed to be used in bedroom groupings or as the center section of the 3 piece buffet. Size of top 32" by 19". Height is 34". Available in Amber, Bleached, or a combination of both.

C2912   *SHELF*   *1936–37*
This piece maybe used on the C2917 Server to form a dining hutch or on the C2911–W to form a secretary. Size is 31" by 11". Height is 25". Amber or Bleached finishes available.

C3180 G   *EXTENSION TABLE*   *1937*
Designed by Leo Jiranek.

C3180 A   *SIDE CHAIR*   *1937*
Designed by Leo Jiranek.

C3181   *SERVER*   *1937*
Designed by Leo Jiranek.

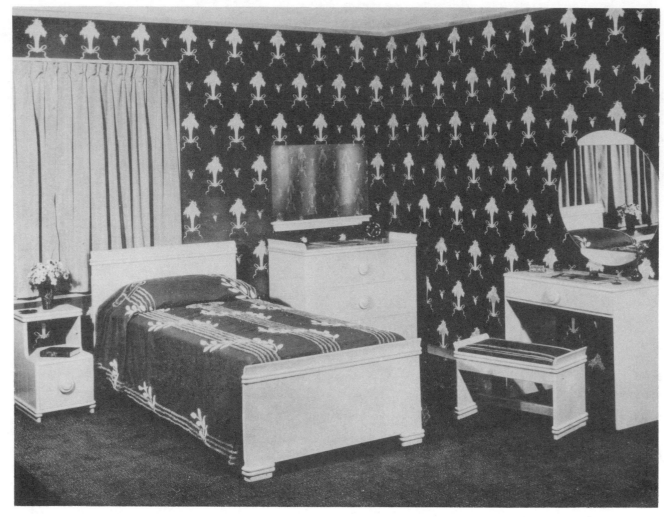

The Zephyr Bedroom Suite

C3158   *Zephyr Night Stand*   *1936–37*
Size of top is 10½" by 15". The bottom depth is 18" and the height is 23½". Available in Amber, Bleached, or combination finishes.

C3150   *Zephyr Bed*   *1936–37*
Available in 3' 3" or 4' 6" sizes. Available in Amber or Bleached finishes.

C3151   *Zephyr 3-Drawer Dresser*   *1936–37*
Size of top is 39" by 19". Height is 33½". Available in Amber, Bleached, or combination finishes.

C3153 X   *Zephyr Oblong Mirror*   *1936–37*
Mirror size 30" by 22". Available in Amber or Bleached finishes.

C3156   *Zephyr Dressing Table*   *1936*
Size of top is 34" by 17". Height is 30". Available in Amber, Bleached, or combination finishes.

C3155   *Mirror*   *1937–39*
Round mirror with wood trim on top and bottom. Available in Amber, Bleached, Wheat, or Champagne finishes.

C3157   *Zephyr Bench*   *1936–37*
Size of top is 24" by 15". Height is 17". Available in Amber or Bleached finishes. Yardage required is ½ yard of 50" material.

THE ZEPHYR BEDROOM SUITE

C3158   *ZEPHYR NIGHT STAND*   *1936–37*
Size of top is 10½" by 15". The bottom depth is 18" and the height is 23½". Available in Amber, Bleached, or combination finishes.

C3150   *ZEPHYR BED*   *1936–37*
Available in 3' 3" or 4' 6" sizes. Available in Amber or Bleached finishes.

C3152   *ZEPHYR 4- DRAWER CHEST*   *1936–37*
The height is 43" and the top is 30½" by 19". Available in Amber, Bleached, or combination finishes.

C3154   *ZEPHYR VANITY*   *1936–37*
Size of top 42" by 18". Height is 25½". Available in Amber, Bleached, or combination finishes.

C3155   *MIRROR*   *1937–39*
Round mirror with wood trim on top and bottom. Available in Amber or Bleached finishes.

THE PENTHOUSE BEDROOM GROUP

C3168   *PENTHOUSE NIGHT STAND*   *1936*
Size of top 14" by 13" and the height is 24¾". Available in Amber, Bleached, or combination finishes.

C3160   *PENTHOUSE BED*   *1936*
Available in 3' 3" or 4' 6" sizes. Available in Amber or Bleached finishes.

C3162   *PENTHOUSE 5-DRAWER CHEST*   *1936*
Size of top is 31½" by 19". The height is 41½". Available in Amber, Bleached, or combination finishes.

C3135   *ROUND MIRROR*   *1936*
Mirror is 30" in diameter. Available in Amber or Bleached finishes.

C3166   *PENTHOUSE DRESSING TABLE-DESK*   *1936*
Size of top is 34" by 17" and height is 30". Available in Amber, Bleached, or combination finishes.

C3167   *PENTHOUSE BENCH*   *1936*
Top size is 23" by 15". Height is 19". Available in Amber or Bleached finishes. Yardage required is ¾ yard of 50" material.

THE PENTHOUSE BEDROOM GROUP

C3161   PENTHOUSE 4-DRAWER CHEST   *1936*
The size of the top is 40" by 19" and the height is 34". Available in Amber, Bleached, or combination finishes.

C3163   OBLONG MIRROR   *1936*
Size is 22" by 34". Available in Amber or Bleached finishes.

C2787 C   UPHOLSTERED PULL-UP CHAIR   *1936–40*
The width of the seat is 24", depth of seat 20", and the height of the back is 15". Available in Champagne, Wheat, Amber, Bleached, or Modern Walnut. Yardage required is 2⅛" yards of 50" material.

C3167   PENTHOUSE BENCH   *1936*
Top size is 23" by 15". Height is 19". Available in Amber or Bleached finishes. Yardage required is ¾ yard of 50" material.

C3164   PENTHOUSE VANITY   *1936*
Top dimensions are 44" by 18" and the height is 30½". Available in Amber, Bleached, or combination finishes.

C3135   ROUND MIRROR   *1936*
Mirror is 30" in diameter. Available in Amber or Bleached finishes.

THE BEDROOM

C2909   *BED*   *1936*
Available in 3' 3" or 4' 6" sizes. Available in Amber or Bleached finishes.

C2902   *4-DRAWER CHEST*   *1936*
The top is 32" by 19" and the height is 43". Available in Amber, Bleached, or a combination of finishes.

C2908   *NIGHT STAND*   *1936*
Top is 14" by 13". Height is 25½". Available in Amber, Bleached, or a combination of finishes.

THE BEDROOM

C2901   *3-DRAWER CHEST*   *1936*
Top is 40" by 19" and the height is 34". Available in Amber, Bleached, or a combination.

C2903   *MIRROR*   *1936*
Mirror size is 19" by 29". Available in Amber or Bleached finishes.

C2920 C   *ARM CHAIR*   *1936*
Width of seat is 22", depth of seat is 23", and height of back is 18". Available in Amber or Bleached finishes. Yardage required is 1¾ yards of 50" material.

C2910   *CENTER CABINET*   *1936*
This chest was designed to be used in bedroom groupings or as the center section of the 3 piece buffet. Size of top 32" by 19". Height is 34". Available in Amber, Bleached, or a combination of both.

THE BEDROOM

C2907   *BENCH*   *1936*
Size of top is 14" by 13" and height is 17". Available in Amber or Bleached finishes.

C2906   *DRESSING TABLE*   *1936*
The top is 34" by 17" and the height is 30". Available in Amber or Bleached finishes, or a combination of both.

C2903   *MIRROR*   *1936*
Mirror size is 19" by 29". Available in Amber or Bleached finishes.

C2931   *5-DRAWER CHEST*   *1936*
Size of top is 40" by 19". Height is 34". Available in Amber, Bleached, or combination finishes.

THE BEDROOM

CHEST ON CHEST

This piece is formed by using the C2913 Closed Cabinet on the C2910 Chest. Chest on Chest is protected by U. S. Design Patent No. 98887.

C2913   *CLOSED HUTCH CABINET*   1936

This piece maybe used on the C2917 Server to form a closed dining hutch or on the C2910 to form a chest on chest for bedroom use. Size 31" by 14". Height 17". Available in Amber or Bleached finishes.

C2910   *CENTER CABINET*   1936

This chest was designed to be used in bedroom groupings or as the center section of the 3 piece buffet. Size of top 32" by 19". Height is 34". Available in Amber, Bleached, or a combination of both.

C2900   *BED*   1936

Available in 3' 3" or 4' 6" sizes. Available in Amber or Bleached finishes.

C2908   *NIGHT STAND*   1936

Top is 14" by 13". Height is 25½". Available in Amber or Bleached finishes or a combination.

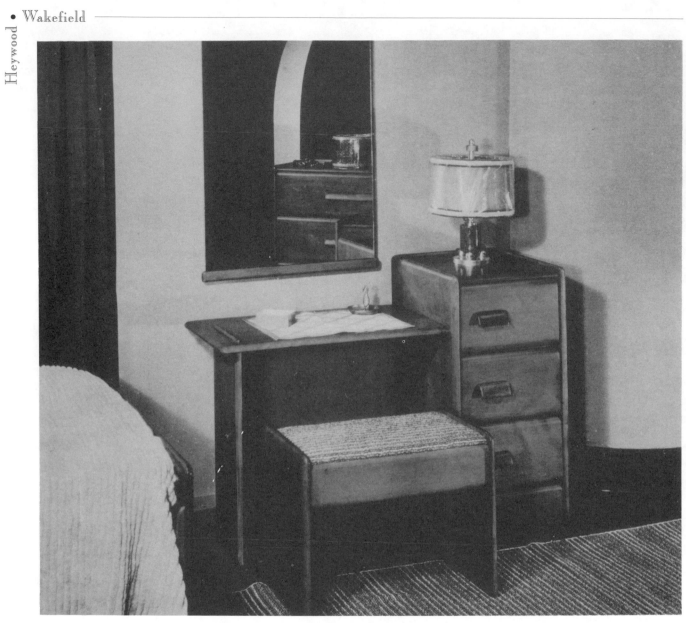

THE BEDROOM

C2907   *BENCH*   *1936*
Size of top is 14" by 13" and height is 17". Available in Amber or Bleached finishes.

C2904   *VANITY*   *1936*
Vanity has an overall length of 42", a height of 30¾", and a depth of 17". Available in Amber or Bleached finishes or a combination.

C2905   *MIRROR*   *1936*
Size 22" by 34". Available in Amber or Bleached finishes.

THE PIECES

C2787 C   *UPHOLSTERED PULL-UP CHAIR*   *1936–40*
The width of the seat is 24", depth of seat 20", and the height of the back is 15". Available in Champagne, Wheat, Amber, Bleached, or Modern Walnut. Yardage required 2⅙ yards of 50" material.

C2930 W   *KNEEHOLE DESK*   *1936*
Fully finished on rear. The top is 42" by 20". Height 30". Available in Amber, Bleached, or combination finishes.

LIVING ROOM

C2920 –60   *DAVENPORT*   *1936*

Width of seat is 60", depth of seat is 23", and the height of the back is 18". Available in Amber or Bleached finishes. Yardage required is 5 yards of 50" material.

C2923 G   *COFFEE TABLE*   *1936*

The size of top is 30" by 18" and the height is 17". Available in Amber or Bleached finishes.

C2922 G   *ROUND CORNER TABLE*   *1936–38*

The top is 28" in diameter and the height is 28". Available in Wheat, Amber, or Bleached finishes.

SECRETARY DESK

This piece is formed by using the C2912 Shelf on the C2911–W Desk Base.

C2912   *SHELF*   *1936*

Size is 31" by 11". Height is 25". Amber or Bleached finishes available.

C2911 W   *DESK CHEST*   *1936*

Size of top 32" by 19". Height is 34". Available in Amber, Bleached, or combination finishes.

THE PIECES

C2920 C   *ARM CHAIR*   *1936*
Width of seat is 22", depth of seat is 23", and height of back is 18". Available in Amber or Bleached finishes. Yardage required is 1¾ yards of 50" material.

C2929   *COMPARTMENT BOOKCASE*   *1936–38*
Fitted with a shelf inside of large closed section on left. The length is 36", the height 32½", and it is 10¾" deep. Available in Wheat, Amber, or Bleached finishes. Model number has suffix X in 1937.

C2928   *OPEN SHELF BOOKCASE*   *1936–38*
The length is 36", depth 10¾", and height 32½". Available in Wheat, Amber, or Bleached finishes.

C2794 ACB   *SIDE CHAIR WITH CHANNEL BACK*   *1936–40*
Designed by Gilbert Rohde. Same as C2794 A with channel back upholstery with 3 channels. Also available as C2794 A 4CB with 4 channels. The seat is 15½" by 14½", and the height of the back is 16½". Available in Champagne, Wheat, Amber, Bleached, or Modern Walnut finishes. Yardage required 1¼ yards of 50" material, 2 yards of 50" material with channels.

LIVING ROOM

C3170 G   *TWO-TIER END TABLE*   *1936–39*
Size of top 27" by 14". Height is 21". Available in Champagne, Wheat, Amber, or Bleached finishes.

C3172–63   *DAVENPORT*   *1936–37*
The width of the seat is 63", the depth of the seat is 22", and the height of the back is 22". Available in Amber or Bleached finishes. Yardage required is 8⅞ yards of 50" material.

C3171 G   *COFFEE TABLE*   *1936–38*
The size of the top is 34" by 16" and the height is 15". Available in Wheat, Amber, or Bleached finishes.

C2929   *COMPARTMENT BOOKCASE*   *1936–38*
Fitted with a shelf inside of large closed section on left. The length is 36", the height 32½", and it is 10¾" deep. Available in Wheat, Amber, or Bleached finishes. Model number had suffix X in 1937.

C3172 C   *ARM CHAIR*   *1936–37*
Width of seat is 22", depth of seat is 22", and the height of the back is 22". Available in Amber or Bleached finishes. Yardage required is 3⅛ yards of 50" material.

LIVING ROOM

Notice the unusual use of maple panel ends on the Davenport and Arm Chair.

C3173–66   *DAVENPORT*   *1936*
The width of the seat is 66", the depth of the seat is 24", and the height of the back is 22". Available in Amber, Bleached, or Walnut finishes. Yardage required is 9 yards of 50" material.

C2921 G   *ROUND COFFEE TABLE*   *1936–39*
The top is 28" in diameter and the height is 17". Available in Champagne, Wheat, Amber, or Bleached finishes.

C3173 C   *ARM CHAIR*   *1936*
The width of the seat is 21", the depth of the seat is 24", and the height of the back is 22". Available in Amber, Bleached, or Walnut finishes. Yardage required is 4½ yards of 50" material.

C2927 G   *END TABLE*   *1936–38*
The size of the top is 26" by 11" and it is 21" high. Available in Wheat, Amber, or Bleached finishes.

LIVING ROOM

C2926 G   *CHAIRSIDE TABLE*   *1936*
The size of the top is 26" by 12" and it is 21" high. Available in Amber or Bleached finishes.

C3174–66   *DAVENPORT*   *1936*
The width of the seat is 66", the depth of the seat is 24", and the height of the back is 21". Available in Amber, Bleached, or Walnut finishes. Yardage required is 9½ yards of 50" material.

C2924 G   *COFFEE TABLE*   *1936*
The height is 17" and the top is 24" by 19". Available in Amber or Bleached finishes.

C2925 G   *CONSOLE OR GAME TABLE*   *1936–38*
The top of this table folds and pivots. It serves as a console table, a small wall table, or with the top turned as a game table. The size of the top open is 34" square, with the top closed 32" by 16". It is 28" high. Available in Wheat, Amber, or Bleached finishes.

C3174 C   *ARM CHAIR*   *1936*
The width of the seat is 21", the depth of the seat is 24", and the height of the back is 21". Available in Amber, Bleached, or Walnut finishes. Yardage required is 5 yards of 50" material.

DINING GROUP

C2932 G   *EXTENSION TABLE*   *1936–39*
Size of top open is 42" by 84", with top closed 42" by 60". Height 29". Available in Champagne, Wheat, Amber, or Bleached finishes.

C3346 A   *SIDE CHAIR*   *1937–39*
Model number C3323 A in 1937. Seat is 16½" by 16½". Height of back is 16". Available in Wheat, Amber, Bleached, or Modern Walnut finishes. Yardage required is 1 yard of 50" material.

C3346 C   *ARM CHAIR*   *1937–39*
Model number C3323 C in 1937. Seat is 16½" by 16½". Height of back is 16". Available in Wheat, Amber, Bleached, or Modern Walnut finishes. Yardage required is 1 yard of 50" material.

C3318   *AIRFLOW BUFFET*   *1937–39*
This Airflow Buffet was designed by Leo Jiranek. Buffet has a long bottom drawer. The size of the top is 52" by 19". The height is 34". Available in Champagne, Wheat, Amber, or Bleached finishes. This piece is also marked with patent number D–105876.

CHINA
The Airflow Glass Door Hutch and Server were designed by Leo Jiranek. This is formed by using the C3316 Glass Door Cabinet on the C3317 Server.

C3316   *GLASS DOOR CABINET*   *1937–39*
It is fitted with two adjustable shelves. The size of the top is 29" by 12" and it is 34" high. Available in Champagne, Wheat, Amber, or Bleached finishes.

C3317   *AIRFLOW SERVER*   *1937–39*
May be used alone or with the C3316 China Top to form a china. The size of the top is 32" by 18" and the height is 30". Available in Champagne, Wheat, Amber, or Bleached finishes.

Dining Room

C3347 G   *EXTENSION TABLE*   *1938–39*
Fitted with two extension leaves. Size of top open is 36" by 76". Size of top closed is 36" by 54". Height is 29". Available in Champagne, Wheat, Amber, or Bleached finishes.

C3314   *SERVER*   *1937–38*
The C3314 Server maybe used with the C3312 to form an open dining hutch or the C3313 to form a closed hutch cabinet. The size of the top is 32" by 15½" and the height is 32½". Available in Wheat, Amber, or Bleached finishes.

C3324 AX   *SIDE CHAIR*   *1937–38*
Seat dimensions are 16" by 14" and the back is 16½" high. Yardage required is 1 yard of 50" material. Available in Wheat, Amber, Bleached, or Modern Walnut finishes.

C3324 AX   *ARM CHAIR*   *1937–38*
Seat dimensions are 16" by 14" and the back is 16½" high. Yardage required is 1 yard of 50" material. Available in Wheat, Amber, Bleached, or Modern Walnut finishes.

C3315   *OPEN BASE BUFFET*   *1937–38*
The size of the top is 45" by 18" and the height is 34". Available in Wheat, Amber, or Bleached finishes.

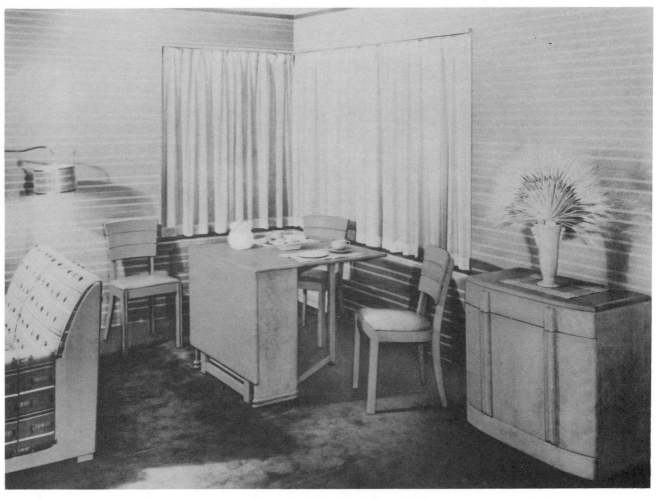

DINING ROOM

C3322 A   *SIDE CHAIR*   *1937–39*

Seat dimensions are 16½" by 15" and the back is 16" high. Yardage required is ¼ yard of 50" material. Available in Champagne, Wheat, Amber, or Bleached finishes.

C3349 G   *GATELEG TABLE*   *1938–40*

Dual purpose design as dining or console table. Top measures 36" by 60" with both leaves up, with one leaf up it is 36" square. With both leaves down table measures 36" by 13¾". Height is 29". Available in Champagne, Wheat, Amber, or Bleached finishes.

C3317   *AIRFLOW SERVER*   *1937–39*

Designed by Leo Jiranek this piece maybe used alone or with the C3316 China Top to form a china. The size of the top is 32" by 18" and the height is 30". Available in Champagne, Wheat, Amber, or Bleached finishes.

DINING ROOM

C3361 G   *EXTENSION TABLE*   *1938–39*
Fitted with one leaf. Size of top open is 30" by 50". Size of top closed is 30" by 40". Height is 29". Available in Champagne, Wheat, Amber, or Bleached finishes.

C3361 A   *SIDE CHAIR*   *1938–39*
Seat is 16" by 15" and the back is 16" high. Available in Champagne, Wheat, Amber, or Bleached finishes. Yardage required is ¼ yard of 50" material.

C3348   *CORNER CABINET*   *1938–39*
Same as C–3348 X but has horizontal pull on doors. Lower closed compartment fitted with shelf. It measures 14½" deep, 24" wide, and 65" high. Available in Champagne, Wheat, Amber, or Bleached finishes.

OPEN SHELF HUTCH
This is formed by using the C3312 Open Hutch on the C3310 Chest.

C3312   *HUTCH SHELF*   *1937–39*
This piece may also be used with the C3311–W Desk to form a secretary-desk, or with the C3314 Server to form a dining hutch. The top size is 31" by 11" and the height is 25". Available in Champagne, Wheat, Amber, or Bleached finishes.

C3310   *CHEST*   *1937–39*
This piece may also be used as an extra 4-drawer chest for the C3300 suite. The top is 32" by 19" and it is 34" high. Available in Champagne, Wheat, Amber, or Bleached finishes.

DINING ROOM

C3361 G   *EXTENSION TABLE*   *1938–39*
Fitted with one leaf. Size of top open is 30" by 50". Size of top closed is 30" by 40". Height is 29". Available in Champagne, Wheat, Amber, or Bleached finishes.

C3363 A   *SIDE CHAIR*   *1938–39*
Seat is 16½" by 15½". Height of back is 15". Available in Wheat finish. Yardage required is ⅓ yard of 50" material.

C3362   *BUFFET*   *1938–39*
Size of top 48" by 18" and it stands 35" high. Available in Champagne, Wheat, Amber, or Bleached finishes.

C2925 G   *CONSOLE OR GAME TABLE*   *1936–38*
The top of this table folds and pivots. It serves as a console table, a small wall table, or with the top turned as a game table. The size of the top open is 34" square, with the top closed 32" by 16". It is 28" high. Available in Wheat, Amber, or Bleached finishes.

Dining Room

C3319 G	*EXTENSION TABLE*	*1937–39*

Fitted with one leaf the size of the top open is 30" by 50". Size of the top closed is 30" by 40". Height is 29". Available in Champagne, Wheat, Amber, or Bleached finishes.

C3321 A	*SIDE CHAIR*	*1937–39*

Seat dimensions are 16½" by 16½" and the back is 16" high. Yardage required is ¼ yard of 50" material. Available in Champagne, Wheat, Amber, or Bleached finishes.

THE SWEDISH MODERN GROUP

The Swedish Modern pieces illustrated are from 1938 and have natural fiber drawer pulls and accents. The fiber was replaced by wood in 1939, and those pieces have an X suffix after the model number.

C3370   *SWEDISH MODERN BED*   *1938*
Available in 3' 3" or 4' 6" sizes. Available in Champagne, Wheat, Amber, or Bleached finishes.

C3371–75   *SWEDISH MODERN 3-DRAWER DRESSER*   *1938*
Size of dresser top is 42" by 20". Height is 33". Top drawer is fitted with sliding tray. Available in Champagne, Wheat, Amber, or Bleached finishes. Suffix –75 indicates attached 30" diameter mirror.

C3378   *SWEDISH MODERN NIGHT STAND*   *1938*
Fitted with drop door on lower compartment. Size of top is 14" by 13" and height is 26". Available in Champagne, Wheat, Amber, or Bleached finishes.

C3325 C   *OCCASIONAL CHAIR*   *1937–40*
Seat dimensions are 20" by 18½" and the back is 18½" high. Yardage required is 1½ yards of 50" material. Available in Champagne, Wheat, Amber, Bleached, or Modern Walnut finishes.

THE SWEDISH MODERN GROUP

C3370   SWEDISH MODERN BED   *1938*
Available in 3' 3" or 4' 6" sizes. Available in Champagne, Wheat, Amber, or Bleached finishes.

C3373   SWEDISH MODERN MIRROR   *1938*
Mirror size is 24" by 30". Available in Champagne, Wheat, Amber, or Bleached finishes.

C3374   SWEDISH MODERN VANITY   *1938*
Size of top 42" by 18" and height is 26". Available in Champagne, Wheat, Amber, or Bleached finishes.

C3377   SWEDISH MODERN BENCH   *1938*
Size of top is 22" by 13" and the height is 16". Requires ⅓ yard of 50" fabric. Available in Champagne, Wheat, Amber, or Bleached finishes.

C3378   SWEDISH MODERN NIGHT STAND   *1938*
Fitted with drop door on lower compartment. Size of top is 14" by 13" and height is 26". Available in Champagne, Wheat, Amber, or Bleached finishes.

THE SWEDISH MODERN GROUP

C3376–80   *SWEDISH MODERN VANITY WITH MIRROR*   *1938*
Size of base top is 52" by 18"and height is 22". Mirror is 40" high by 38" wide. Overall height of vanity with mirror attached is 62". Also available without mirror as C3376. Available in Champagne, Wheat, Amber, or Bleached finishes.

C3379   *SWEDISH MODERN VANITY BENCH*   *1938*
Bench top is 18" in diameter and stands 15" high. Available in Champagne, Wheat, Amber, or Bleached finishes. Yardage required is ¾ yard of 50" material.

C2787 C   *UPHOLSTERED PULL-UP CHAIR*   *1936–40*
The width of the seat is 24", depth of seat 20", and the height of the back is 15". Available in Champagne, Wheat, Amber, Bleached, or Modern Walnut. Yardage required 2⅙ yards of 50" material.

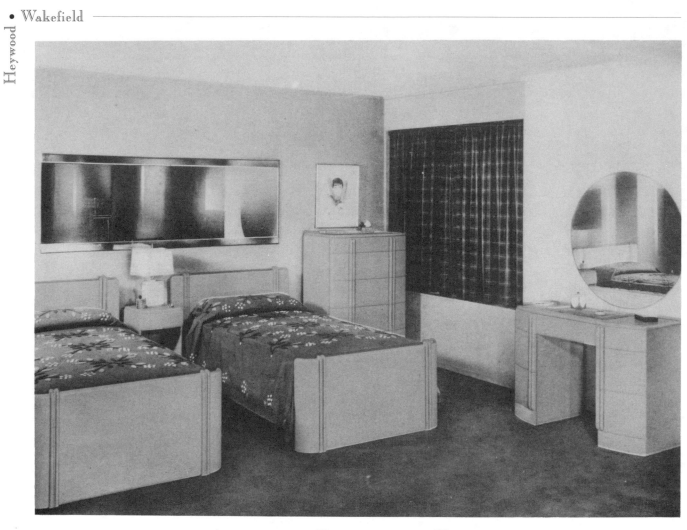

AIRFLOW BEDROOM GROUP

The Airflow Bedroom Group was designed by Leo Jiranek.

C3330   *AIRFLOW BED*   *1937–39*
Available in 3' 3" or 4' 6" sizes. Available in Champagne, Wheat, Amber, or Bleached finishes. Marked with patent number D–105663.

C3338   *AIRFLOW NIGHT STAND*   *1937–39*
Size of top is 14" by 14". Height is 25½". Available in Champagne, Wheat, Amber, or Bleached finishes. Marked with patent number D–106201.

C3332   *AIRFLOW 5-DRAWER CHEST*   *1937–39*
Size of top is 32" by 19" and chest is 46" high. Available in Champagne, Wheat, Amber, or Bleached finishes.

C3334   *AIRFLOW VANITY DESK*   *1937–39*
Top is 42" by 19". Height is 30". Available in Champagne, Wheat, Amber, or Bleached finishes.

C3335   *MIRROR*   *1937–39*
Size of mirror is 36" in diameter. Available in Champagne, Wheat, Amber, or Bleached finishes.

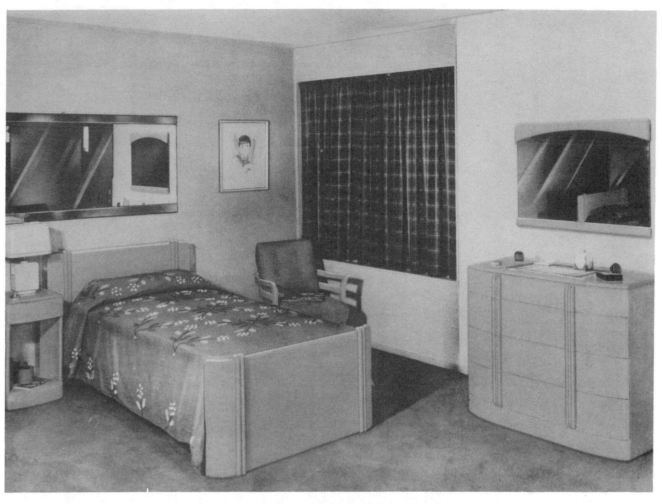

AIRFLOW BEDROOM GROUP

C3338   *AIRFLOW NIGHT STAND*   *1937–39*
Size of top is 14" by 14". Height is 25½". Available in Champagne, Wheat, Amber, or Bleached finishes. Marked with patent number D–106201.

C3330   *AIRFLOW BED*   *1937–39*
Available in 3' 3" or 4' 6" sizes. Available in Champagne, Wheat, Amber, or Bleached finishes. Marked with patent number D–105663.

C3325 C   *OCCASIONAL CHAIR*   *1937–40*
Seat dimensions are 20" by 18½" and the back is 18½" high. Yardage required is 1½ yards of 50" material. Available in Champagne, Wheat, Amber, Bleached, or Modern Walnut finishes.

C3331   *AIRFLOW 4-DRAWER DRESSER*   *1937–39*
Size of top is 42" by 20" and dresser is 34" high. Available in Champagne, Wheat, Amber, or Bleached finishes. Marked with patent number D–105874.

C3333   *AIRFLOW MIRROR*   *1937–39*
Mirror is 22" by 34". Available in Champagne, Wheat, Amber, or Bleached finishes.

AIRFLOW BEDROOM GROUP

C3340	*AIRFLOW VANITY*	*1937–39*

Top is 52" by 18" and height is 22". Overall height with mirror attached is 60½". Mirror is 48" in diameter. Available in Champagne, Wheat, Amber, or Bleached finishes. Marked with patent number D–105875.

C3337	*VANITY POUFFE*	*1937–38*

Size of top is 18" in diameter and height is 16". Available in Champagne, Wheat, Amber, or Bleached finishes. Yardage required is ⅔ yard of 50" material.

C2787 C	*UPHOLSTERED PULL-UP CHAIR*	*1936–40*

The width of the seat is 24", depth of seat 20", and the height of the back is 15". Available in Champagne, Wheat, Amber, Bleached, or Modern Walnut. Yardage required 2⅙ yards of 50" material.

Airflow Bedroom Group

C3360   *Airflow Bed with Cane Panels*   *1938*
Available in 3' 3" or 4' 6" sizes. Available in Wheat finish.

C3331   *Airflow 4-Drawer Dresser*   *1937–39*
Size of top is 42" by 20" and dresser is 34" high. Available in Champagne, Wheat, Amber, or Bleached finishes. Marked with patent number D–105874.

C3333   *Airflow Mirror*   *1937–39*
Mirror is 22" by 34". Available in Champagne, Wheat, Amber, or Bleached finishes.

C3338   *Airflow Night Stand*   *1937–39*
Size of top is 14" by 14". Height is 25½". Available in Champagne, Wheat, Amber, or Bleached finishes. Marked with patent number D–106201.

C3325 C   *Occasional Chair*   *1937–40*
Seat dimensions are 20" by 18½" and the back is 18½" high. Yardage required is 1½ yards of 50" material. Available in Champagne, Wheat, Amber, Bleached, or Modern Walnut finishes.

BEDROOM

C3309   *BED*   *1937–38*
Available in 3' 3" or 4' 6" sizes. Available in Wheat, Amber, or Bleached finishes.

C3301   *3-DRAWER DRESSER*   *1937–38*
The top measures 40" by 19" and it stands 34" high. Available in Wheat, Amber, or Bleached finishes.

C3303   *MIRROR*   *1937–38*
The glass size is 20" by 30". Available in Wheat, Amber, or Bleached finishes.

BEDROOM

| C3300 | *BED* | *1937–38* |
Available in 3' 3" or 4' 6" sizes. Available in Wheat, Amber, or Bleached finishes.

| C3302 | *4-DRAWER CHEST* | *1937–38* |
The top measures 32" by 19" and it stands 43" high. Available in Wheat, Amber, or Bleached finishes.

| C3308 | *NIGHT STAND* | *1937–38* |
Top measures 14" by 13" and the height is 25½". Available in Wheat, Amber, or Bleached finishes.

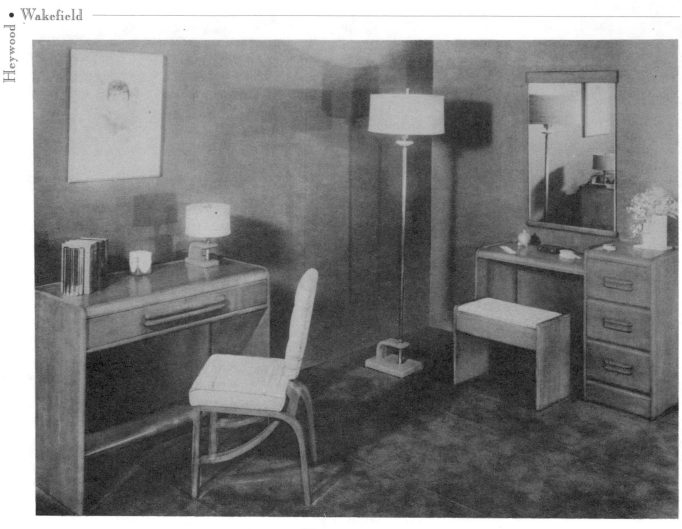

BEDROOM

C3306   *DRESSING TABLE*   *1937–38*
The top measures 38" by 17" and the height is 30". Available in Wheat, Amber, or Bleached finishes.

C3324 AX   *SIDE CHAIR*   *1937–38*
Seat dimensions are 16" by 14" and the back is 16½" high. Yardage required is 1 yard of 50" material. Available in Wheat, Amber, Bleached, or Modern Walnut finishes.

C3304   *VANITY*   *1937–38*
The overall length is 42", the depth is 17", and the height is 30¾". Available in Wheat, Amber, or Bleached finishes.

C3305   *MIRROR*   *1937–38*
Size of mirror is 22" by 34". Available in Wheat, Amber, or Bleached finishes.

C3307   *BENCH*   *1937–38*
The top measures 21" by 13" and the height is 17". Available in Wheat, Amber, or Bleached finishes. Yardage required is ⅓ yard of 50" material.

LIVING ROOM

C3342–44   *LOVE SEAT*   *1937–38*
Width of the seat is 44", depth of the seat is 23", and the back is 21" high. Available in Wheat, Amber, or Bleached finishes.
Yardage required is 6 yards of 50" material. Design patent number D–105664.

C3326 C   *BARREL CHAIR*   *1937–39*
Designed by Leo Jiranek. Seat dimensions are 23" by 22" and the back is 18½" high. Yardage required is 2½ yards of 50" material. Available in Champagne, Wheat, Amber, Bleached, or Modern Walnut finishes.

C3170 G   *TWO-TIER END TABLE*   *1936–39*
Size of top 27" by 14". Height is 21". Available in Champagne, Wheat, Amber, or Bleached finishes.

LIVING ROOM

C2927 G   *END TABLE*   *1936–38*
The size of the top is 26" by 11" and it is 21" high. Available in Wheat, Amber, or Bleached finishes.

C3341 RC OR C3341 LC   *RIGHT OR LEFT ARM CHAIR*   *1937–38*
Width of the seat is 22", depth of the seat is 23", and the back is 21" high. Available in Wheat, Amber, or Bleached finishes. Yardage required is 3¾ yards of 50" material. Design patent number number D–105664.

C3327 G   *CORNER TABLE*   *1937–38*
Designed by Count Sakhnoffsky. Table top size is 32½" square and the height is 22". Available in Wheat, Amber, or Bleached finishes.

C3341   *SINGLE FILLER OR ARMLESS CENTER SECTION*   *1937–38*
Width of the seat is 22", depth of the seat is 23", and the back is 21" high. Available in Wheat, Amber, or Bleached finishes. Yardage required is 3¼ yards of 50" material. Design patent number number D–105664.

C3342   *DOUBLE FILLER*   *1937–38*
Not illustrated but same as single filler except seat is 44" wide. Depth of the seat is 23" and the back is 21" high. Available in Wheat, Amber, or Bleached finishes. Yardage required is 5½ yards of 50" material.

LIVING ROOM

C3343–66   *DAVENPORT*   *1937–38*
Width of the seat is 66", depth of the seat is 23", and the back is 21" high. Available in Wheat, Amber, or Bleached finishes.
Yardage required is 8 yards of 50" material. Design patent number number D–105664.

C3341 C   *ARM CHAIR*   *1937–38*
Width of the seat is 22", depth of the seat is 23", and the back is 21" high. Available in Wheat, Amber, or Bleached finishes.
Yardage required is 4 yards of 50" material. Design patent number number D–105664.

C3327 G   *CORNER TABLE*   *1937–38*
Designed by Count Sakhnoffsky. Table top size is 32½" square and the height is 22". Available in Wheat, Amber, or Bleached
finishes.

C2921 G   *ROUND COFFEE TABLE*   *1936–39*
The top is 28" in diameter and the height is 17". Available in Champagne, Wheat, Amber, or Bleached finishes.

LIVING ROOM

Davenport and Chair designed by Alfons Bach.

C3367–66   *DAVENPORT*   *1938–39*
Seat is 66" wide by 21" deep. Height of back is 19". Requires 7¾ yards of 50" material. Available in Champagne, Wheat, Amber, or Bleached finishes.

C3367 C   *CHAIR*   *1938–39*
Seat is 22" wide by 20" deep. Height of back is 20". Requires 3¼ yards of 50" material. Available in Champagne, Wheat, Amber, or Bleached finishes.

C3170 G   *TWO-TIER END TABLE*   *1936–39*
Size of top 27" by 14". Height is 21". Available in Champagne, Wheat, Amber, or Bleached finishes.

C3348   *CORNER CABINET*   *1938–39*
Same as C3348 X but has horizontal pull on doors. Lower closed compartment fitted with shelf. It measures 14½" deep, 24" wide, and 65" high. Available in Champagne, Wheat, Amber, or Bleached finishes.

C3364 G   *COCKTAIL TABLE*   *1938*
Size of top is 34" in diameter and stands 16" high. Available in Wheat, Amber, or Bleached finishes.

LIVING ROOM

C3368–63   *DAVENPORT*   *1938*
Seat is 63" wide by 23" deep. Height of back is 19". Yardage required is 8 yards of 50" material. Available in Wheat, Amber, or Bleached finishes.

C3368 C   *ARM CHAIR*   *1938–39*
Seat is 22" wide by 22" deep. Height of back is 19". Yardage required is 4 yards of 50" material. Available in Wheat, Amber, or Bleached finishes.

C3345 G   *LAMP TABLE*   . *1938*
Top is 22" in diameter. Table is 26" high. Available in Wheat, Amber, and Bleached finishes.

C3312   *OPEN SHELF HUTCH CABINET*   *1937–39*
This piece may be used with the C3310 Chest to form an open shelf hutch buffet, or with the C3314 Server to form a dining hutch. The top size is 31" by 11" and the height is 25". Available in Champagne, Wheat, Amber, or Bleached finishes.

C3311 W   *DESK BASE*   *1937–39*
This desk-chest may be used alone or in combination with the C3312 shelf to form a secretary. Available in Champagne, Wheat, Amber, or Bleached finishes.

C2794 A 4CB   *SIDE CHAIR WITH CHANNEL BACK*   *1936–40*
Designed by Gilbert Rohde. Same as C2794 A but with channel back upholstery with 4 channels. The seat is 15½" by 14½", and the height of the back is 16½". Available in Champagne, Wheat, Amber, Bleached, or Modern Walnut finishes. Yardage required is 2 yards of 50" material with channels.

Living Room

C3383 C   *Cane Panel Arm Chair*   *1938*
Width of seat is 20", depth of seat is 23", and height of the back is 16". Yardage required is 1¾ yards of 50" material. Available in Wheat finish.

C2922 G   *Round Corner Table*   *1936–38*
The top is 28" in diameter and the height is 28". Available in Wheat, Amber, or Bleached finishes.

C3368 R   *Wood Frame Arm Chair*   *1938*
Seat is 22½" wide by 23" deep. Height of back is 24". Yardage required is 4¼ yards of 50" material. Available in Wheat, Amber, or Bleached finishes.

THE PIECES

C3365 A	*CANE BACK DESK CHAIR*	*1938*

Seat is 15½" by 14½" and back is 16½" high. Available in Wheat finish. Yardage required is ¼ yard of 50" material.

C3328 W	*KNEEHOLE DESK*	*1937–39*

Designed by Leo Jiranek. Fully finished including rear. Size of top is 42" by 20" and height is 30". Available in Champagne, Wheat, Amber, or Bleached finishes.

C2927 G	*END TABLE*	*1936–38*

The size of the top is 26" by 11" and it is 21" high. Available in Wheat, Amber, or Bleached finishes.

C3387 C	*ARM CHAIR*	*1938–40*

Width of seat is 24", depth of seat is 22", and height of the back is 23". Yardage required is 3¾ yards of 50" material. Available in Champagne, Wheat, Amber, Bleached, or Modern Walnut finishes.

THE PIECES

C3349 G   *GATELEG TABLE*   *1938–40*

Dual purpose design as dining or console table. Top measures 36" by 60" with both leaves up, with one leaf up it is 36" square. With both leaves down table measures 36" by 13¾". Height is 29". Available in Champagne, Wheat, Amber, or Bleached finishes.

C3386 C   *FULL UPHOLSTERED ARM CHAIR*   *1938–39*

Width of seat is 18", depth of seat is 18", and height of the back is 17". Yardage required is 1⅔ yards of 50" material. Available in Champagne, Wheat, Amber, Bleached, or Modern Walnut finishes.

C3366 W   *DESK CHEST / BOOKCASE*   *1938–39*

Length is 48", depth 12", and height 48". Available in Champagne, Wheat, Amber, or Bleached finishes.

C3385 C   *OPEN SIDE ARM CHAIR*   *1938–39*

Width of seat is 19", depth of seat is 20", and height of the back is 17". Yardage required is 1¼ yards of 50" material. Available in Champagne, Wheat, Amber, Bleached, or Modern Walnut.

THE PIECES

C3381 C   *CANE PANEL ARM CHAIR*   *1938–40*

Width of seat is 20", depth of seat is 23", and height of the back is 16". Yardage required is 1⅔ yards of 50" material. Available in Wheat finish.

C2925 G   *CONSOLE OR GAME TABLE*   *1936–38*

The top of this table folds and pivots. It serves as a console table, a small wall table, or with the top turned as a game table. The size of the top open is 34" square, with the top closed 32" by 16". It is 28" high. Available in Wheat, Amber, or Bleached finishes.

C3388 C   *UPHOLSTERED ARM CHAIR*   *1938–39*

Width of seat is 19½", depth of seat is 20½", and height of the back is 14". Yardage required is 1½ yards of 50" material. Available in Champagne, Wheat, Amber, Bleached, or Modern Walnut finishes.

THE PIECES

C3384 C   *CANE CHAIR WITH OVAL PANEL*   *1938–39*
Width of seat is 20½", depth of seat is 22", and height of the back is 18". Yardage required is 1⅔ yards of 50" material. Available in Wheat finish.

C3364 G   *COCKTAIL TABLE*   *1938*
Size of top is 34" in diameter and it stands 16" high. Available in Wheat, Amber, or Bleached finishes.

C3382 C   *CANE CHAIR WITH SQUARE PANEL*   *1938–39*
Width of seat is 20", depth of seat is 22", and height of the back is 18". Yardage required is 1¼ yards of 50" material. Available in Wheat finish.

Dining Room Group

C2932 G	*Extension Table*	*1936–39*

Size of top open is 42" by 84", with top closed 42" by 60". Height 29". Available in Champagne, Wheat, Amber, or Bleached finishes.

C3530 A	*Side Chair*	*1939–42*

Width of seat is 18", depth of seat is 17", and the back is 16" high. Yardage required is ¼ yard of 50" material. Available in Champagne, Wheat, Amber, or Bleached finishes.

C3530 C	*Arm Chair*	*1939–42*

Width of the seat is 18", depth of the seat is 17", and the back is 16" high. Yardage required is ⅓ yard of 50" material. Available in Champagne, Wheat, Amber, or Bleached finishes.

C3318	*Airflow Buffet*	*1937–39*

This piece designed by Leo Jiranek has a long bottom drawer. The size of the top is 52" by 19". The height is 34". Available in Champagne, Wheat, Amber, or Bleached finishes. This piece is also marked with patent number D105876.

China

This piece is formed by using the C3316 Glass Door Cabinet on the C3317 Server.

C3316	*Glass Door Cabinet*	*1937–39*

It is fitted with two adjustable shelves. The size of the top is 29" by 12" and it is 34" high. Available in Champagne, Wheat, Amber, or Bleached finishes.

C3317	*Airflow Server*	*1937–39*

Designed by Leo Jiranek this piece may be used alone or with the C3316 China Top. The size of the top is 32" by 18" and the height is 30". Available in Champagne, Wheat, Amber, or Bleached finishes.

THE PIECES

C3538 G   *SIDE EXTENSION TABLE*   *1939*
Designed by Count Sakhnoffsky. Fitted with one leaf. Size of top open is 30" by 50". Size of top closed is 20" by 50". Height is 29". Available in Champagne, Wheat, Amber, or Bleached finishes.

C3526 A   *SIDE CHAIR*   *1939–40*
Seat is 15½" by 14½" and the back is 16½" high. Yardage required is ¼ yard of 50" material. Available in Champagne, Wheat, Amber, or Bleached finishes.

C3387 C   *ARM CHAIR*   *1938–40*
Width of seat is 24", depth of seat is 22", and height of the back is 23". Yardage required is 3¾ yards of 50" material. Available in Champagne, Wheat, Amber, Bleached, or Modern Walnut finishes.

C3531 G   *END TABLE*   *1939*
Table top is 13½" by 26¾" and height is 20½". Available in Champagne, Wheat, Amber, or Bleached finishes.

DINETTE GROUP

C3537 G   *EXTENSION TABLE*   *1939*

Fitted with one leaf. Size of top open is 30" by 50". Size of top closed is 30" by 40". Height is 29". Available in Champagne, Wheat, Amber, or Bleached finishes.

C3536 A   *SIDE CHAIR*   *1939–40*

Seat is 16½" by 15½" and the back is 15½" high. Yardage required is ¼ yard of 50" material. Available in Champagne, Wheat, Amber, or Bleached finishes.

C3362   *BUFFET*   *1938–39*

Size of top 48" by 18" and it stands 35" high. Available in Champagne, Wheat, Amber, or Bleached finishes.

CRESCENDO GROUP

C3554   *CRESCENDO VANITY*   *1939–40*

Size of top is 54" by 18" and the height of the base is 22". Overall height is 58½". Available in Champagne, Wheat, Amber, or Bleached finishes.

C3557   *VANITY SEAT*   *1939–40*

Fitted with revolving top. Seat is 20" in diameter and 17" high. Yardage required is 1¼ yards of 54" material. Available in Champagne, Wheat, Amber, or Bleached finishes.

C2787 C   *UPHOLSTERED PULL-UP CHAIR*   *1936–40*

The width of the seat is 24", depth of seat 20", and the height of the back is 15". Available in Champagne, Wheat, Amber, Bleached, or Modern Walnut. Yardage required 2⅙ yards of 50" material.

CRESCENDO GROUP

The Crescendo Bedroom Group was designed by Count Alexis de Sakhnoffsky.

C3550   *CRESCENDO BED*   *1939–40*
Available in 3' 3" or 4' 6" sizes. Available in Champagne, Wheat, Amber, or Bleached finishes.

C3551–555   *CRESCENDO DRESSER WITH MIRROR*   *1939–40*
Dresser top is 42" by 20" and height is 33½". Size of mirror is 26" by 40". Overall height is 61". Available in Champagne, Wheat, Amber, or Bleached finishes.

C3558   *CRESCENDO NIGHT STAND*   *1939–40*
Size of top is 14" by 14" and is 25" high. Available in Champagne, Wheat, Amber, or Bleached finishes.

C3559   *BLANKET CHEST*   *1939*
Fitted with large drawer. Size of top is 44" by 14". Height is 17". Yardage required is ½ yard of 54" material. Available in Champagne, Wheat, Amber, or Bleached finishes.

CRESCENDO BEDROOM GROUP

C3539 W   *CRESCENDO VANITY / DESK*   *1939–40*
Size of top is 48" by 21". Height is 30". Available in Champagne, Wheat, Amber, or Bleached finishes.

C3553   *HANGING MIRROR*   *1939–40*
Mirror size is 26" by 40". Available in Champagne, Wheat, Amber, or Bleached finishes.

C3535 A   *SIDE CHAIR*   *1939–43*
Seat is 16" by 16½" and the back is 17" high. Yardage required is 1 yard of 50" material. Available in Champagne, Wheat, Amber, Bleached, or Modern Walnut finishes.

C3552   *CRESCENDO 5-DRAWER CHEST*   *1939–40*
Chest top is 32" by 19"and height is 48". Available in Champagne, Wheat, Amber, or Bleached finishes.

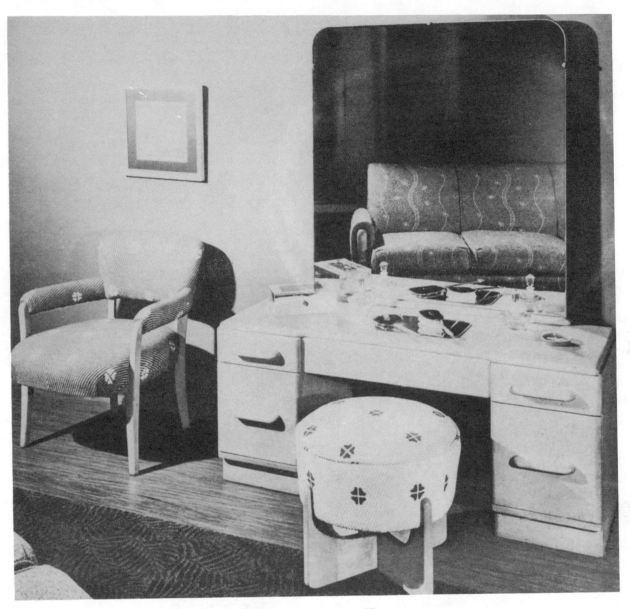

SWEDISH MODERN BEDROOM

The Swedish Modern Bedroom was changed in 1939 to wooden drawer pulls. The suffix X was added to the model number.

C3376–80 X   *SWEDISH MODERN VANITY*   *1939*
Size of base top is 52" by 18" and height is 22". Mirror is 40" high by 38" wide. Overall height of vanity with mirror attached is 62". Also available without mirror as C3376. Available in Champagne, Wheat, Amber, or Bleached finishes.

C3379 X   *SWEDISH MODERN VANITY BENCH*   *1939*
Bench top is 18" in diameter and stands 15" high. Available in Champagne, Wheat, Amber, or Bleached finishes. Yardage required is ¾ yard of 50" material.

C3388 C   *UPHOLSTERED ARM CHAIR*   *1938–39*
Width of seat is 19½", depth of seat is 20½", and height of the back is 14". Yardage required is 1½ yards of 50" material. Available in Champagne, Wheat, Amber, Bleached, or Modern Walnut finishes.

SWEDISH MODERN BEDROOM

C3370 X   *SWEDISH MODERN BED*   *1939*
Available in 3' 3" or 4' 6" sizes. Available in Champagne, Wheat, Amber, or Bleached finishes.

C3378 X   *SWEDISH MODERN NIGHT STAND*   *1939*
Fitted with drop door on lower compartment. Size of top is 14" by 13" and height is 26". Available in Champagne, Wheat, Amber, or Bleached finishes.

C3372 X   *SWEDISH MODERN 4-DRAWER CHEST*   *1939*
Two top drawers divided into sections. Top is 32" by 19" and chest is 45½" tall. Available in Champagne, Wheat, Amber, or Bleached finishes.

C3374 X   *SWEDISH MODERN VANITY*   *1939*
Size of top 42" by 18" and height is 26". Available in Champagne, Wheat, Amber, or Bleached finishes.

C3373 X   *SWEDISH MODERN MIRROR*   *1939*
Mirror size is 24" by 30". Available in Champagne, Wheat, Amber, or Bleached finishes.

C3377 X   *SWEDISH MODERN BENCH*   *1939*
Size of top is 22" by 13" and the height is 16". Requires ⅓ yard of 50" fabric. Available in Champagne, Wheat, Amber, or Bleached finishes.

Swedish Modern Bedroom

C3370 X   *Swedish Modern Bed*   *1939*
Available in 3' 3" or 4' 6" sizes. Available in Champagne, Wheat, Amber, or Bleached finishes.

C3371–75X   *Swedish Modern 3-Drawer Dresser*   *1939*
Size of dresser top is 42" by 20". Height is 33". Top drawer is fitted with sliding tray. Available in Champagne, Wheat, Amber, or Bleached finishes. Suffix –75 indicates attached 30" diameter mirror.

C3378 X   *Swedish Modern Night Stand*   *1939*
Fitted with drop door on lower compartment. Size of top is 14" by 13" and height is 26". Available in Champagne, Wheat, Amber, or Bleached finishes.

SKYLINER BEDROOM SUITE

C3560   *SKYLINER BED*   *1939–40*
Available in 3' 3" or 4' 6" sizes. Available in Champagne, Wheat, Amber, or Bleached finishes.

C3568   *SKYLINER NIGHT STAND*   *1939–40*
Top is 14" by 14" and height is 25½". Available in Champagne, Wheat, Amber, or Bleached finishes.

C3562   *SKYLINER 4-DRAWER CHEST*   *1939–40*
Top is 32" by 19" and height is 45". Available in Champagne, Wheat, Amber, or Bleached finishes.

C3564   *SKYLINER VANITY*   *1939–40*
Overall size of top is 45" by 18" and height is 25½". Available in Champagne, Wheat, Amber, or Bleached finishes.

C3567   *SKYLINER BENCH*   *1939–40*
Size of top is 21" by 13" and height is 17". Yardage required is ¼ yard of 50" material. Available in Champagne, Wheat, Amber, or Bleached finishes.

C3563   *SKYLINER MIRROR*   *1939–40*
Glass size is 35" by 42". Available in Champagne, Wheat, Amber, or Bleached finishes.

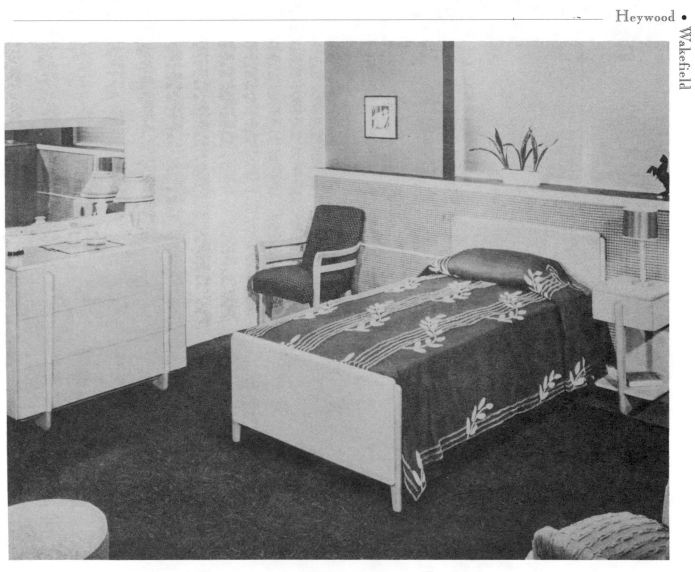

SKYLINER BEDROOM SUITE

C3560   *SKYLINER BED*   *1939–40*
Available in 3' 3" or 4' 6" sizes. Available in Champagne, Wheat, Amber, or Bleached finishes.

C3568   *SKYLINER NIGHT STAND*   *1939–40*
Top is 14" by 14" and height is 25½". Available in Champagne, Wheat, Amber, or Bleached finishes.

C3561   *SKYLINER 3-DRAWER DRESSER*   *1939–40*
Size of top is 42" by 19" and height is 33½". Available in Champagne, Wheat, Amber, or Bleached finishes.

C3563   *SKYLINER MIRROR*   *1939–40*
Glass size is 35" by 42". Available in Champagne, Wheat, Amber, or Bleached finishes.

C3325 C   *OCCASIONAL CHAIR*   *1937–40*
Seat dimensions are 20" by 18½" and the back is 18½" high. Yardage required is 1½ yards of 50" material. Available in Champagne, Wheat, Amber, Bleached, or Modern Walnut finishes.

BEDROOM SUITE

C3570   *BED*   *1939*
Available in 3' 3" or 4' 6" sizes. Available in Champagne, Wheat, Amber, or Bleached finishes.

C3578   *NIGHT STAND*   *1939*
Size of top is 13" by 14" and the height is 25½". Available in Champagne, Wheat, Amber, or Bleached finishes.

C3572   *4-DRAWER CHEST*   *1939*
The top size is 32" by 19" and the height is 43". Available in Champagne, Wheat, Amber, or Bleached finishes.

C3574   *VANITY*   *1939*
Top is 42" by 18" and height is 25". Available in Champagne, Wheat, Amber, or Bleached finishes.

C3573   *MIRROR*   *1939*
Glass size is 34" by 18". Available in Champagne, Wheat, Amber, or Bleached finishes.

C3577   *BENCH*   *1939*
Size of top is 13" by 21" and height is 17". Yardage required is ¼ yard of 50" material. Available in Champagne, Wheat, Amber, or Bleached finishes.

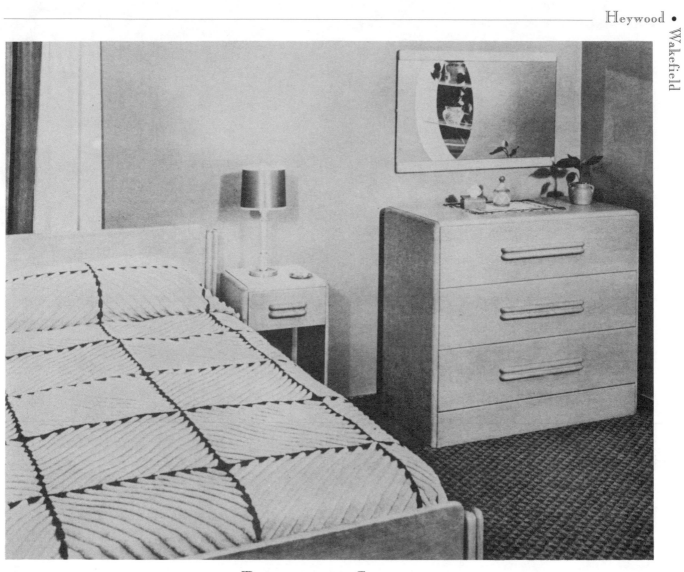

Bedroom Suite

C3570   *BED*   *1939*
Available in 3' 3" or 4' 6" sizes. Available in Champagne, Wheat, Amber, or Bleached finishes.

C3578   *NIGHT STAND*   *1939*
Size of top is 13" by 14" and the height is 25½". Available in Champagne, Wheat, Amber, or Bleached finishes.

C3571   *3-DRAWER DRESSER*   *1939*
Size of top is 19" by 40" and height is 34". Available in Champagne, Wheat, Amber, or Bleached finishes.

C3573   *MIRROR*   *1939*
Glass size is 34" by 18". Available in Champagne, Wheat, Amber, or Bleached finishes.

LIVING ROOM ENSEMBLE

Sectional sofa is from the Crescendo Group designed by Count Sakhnoffsky.

C3170 G   *TWO-TIER END TABLE*   *1936–39*
Size of top 27" by 14". Height is 21". Available in Champagne, Wheat, Amber, or Bleached finishes.

C3541 RC OR 3541 LC   *RIGHT OR LEFT ARM CHAIR*   *1939–40*
Width of the seat is 22", depth of the seat is 24", and the height of the back is 18". Yardage required is 3¾ yards of 54" material. Available in Champagne, Wheat, Amber, or Bleached finishes.

C3541   *SINGLE FILLER*   *1939–40*
Width of the seat is 22", depth of the seat is 24", and the height of the back is 18". Yardage required is 3¼ yards of 54" material. Available in Champagne, Wheat, Amber, or Bleached finishes.

C3542   *DOUBLE FILLER*   *1939–40*
Not illustrated but identical to single filler except width of the seat is 44". Depth of the seat is 24" and the height of the back is 18". Yardage required is 5⅓ yards of 54" material. Available in Champagne, Wheat, Amber, or Bleached finishes.

C3540 G   *CORNER TABLE*   *1939–40*
Top is 31½" square and height is 22". Available in Champagne, Wheat, Amber, or Bleached finishes.

C3548 G   *COCKTAIL TABLE*   *1939–40*
Fitted with revolving top which measures 32" in diameter. Height is 16". Available in Champagne, Wheat, Amber, or Bleached finishes.

CRESCENDO LIVING ROOM

All pieces in this ensemble were designed by Count Sakhnoffsky.

C3543–66   *DAVENPORT*   *1939–40*
Width of the seat is 66", depth of the seat is 24", and the height of the back is 17". Yardage required is 9½ yards of 54" material. Available in Champagne, Wheat, Amber, or Bleached finishes.

C3541 C   *ARM CHAIR*   *1939–40*
Width of the seat is 21", depth of the seat is 24", and the height of the back is 18". Yardage required is 4 yards of 54" material. Available in Champagne, Wheat, Amber, or Bleached finishes.

C3546 G   *END TABLES*   *1939–40*
Top is 28" by 15" and the height is 22". Available in Champagne, Wheat, Amber, or Bleached finishes.

C3547 G   *OVAL COCKTAIL TABLE*   *1939–40*
Top is 36" by 19" and the height is 16". Fitted with one shelf. Available in Champagne, Wheat, Amber, or Bleached finishes.

C3549 G   *LAMP TABLE*   *1939–40*
Fitted with shelf. Top is 22" in diameter and height is 26". Available in Champagne, Wheat, Amber, or Bleached finishes.

SWEDISH MODERN UPHOLSTERED SUITE

Entire ensemble designed by Alfons Bach.

C3367–66	*DAVENPORT*	*1938–39*

Seat is 66" wide by 21" deep. Height of back is 19". Requires 7¾ yards of 50" material. Available in Champagne, Wheat, Amber, or Bleached finishes.

C3367 C	*CHAIR*	*1938–39*

Seat is 22" wide by 20" deep. Height of back is 20". Requires 3¼ yards of 50" material. Available in Champagne, Wheat, Amber, or Bleached finishes.

C3532 G	*COFFEE TABLE*	*1939*

Top is 19" by 37" and height is 16½". Available in Champagne, Wheat, Amber, or Bleached finishes.

C3531 G	*END TABLE*	*1939*

Table top is 13½" by 26¾" and height is 20½". Available in Champagne, Wheat, Amber, or Bleached finishes.

C3533 G	*LAMP TABLE*	*1939*

Top dimensions are 17" by 19" and the height is 28". Available in Champagne, Wheat, Amber, or Bleached finishes.

LIVING ROOM GROUP

Davenport and arm chair are Alfons Bach designs.

C3579–63   *DAVENPORT*   *1939*
The width of the seat is 63", the depth is 23", and the height of the back is 20". Yardage required is 7 yards of 50" material. Available in Champagne, Wheat, Amber, or Bleached finishes.

C3579 C   *ARM CHAIR*   *1939*
Width of seat is 21½", depth is 23", and the back is 19" high. Yardage required is 2⅓ yards of 50" material. Available in Champagne, Wheat, Amber, or Bleached finishes.

C3532 G   *COFFEE TABLE*   *1939*
An Alfons Bach design. Top is 19" by 37" and height is 16½". Available in Champagne, Wheat, Amber, or Bleached finishes.

C3170 G   *TWO-TIER END TABLE*   *1936–39*
Size of top 27" by 14". Height is 21". Available in Champagne, Wheat, Amber, or Bleached finishes.

C3533 G   *LAMP TABLE*   *1939*
An Alfons Bach design. Top dimensions are 17" by 19" and the height is 28". Available in Champagne, Wheat, Amber, or Bleached finishes.

THE PIECES

C3521 R   *BARREL CHAIR*   *1939*
Width of seat is 27½", depth of seat is 22", and the height of the back is 19½". Yardage required is 4 yards of 54" material. Available in Champagne, Wheat, Amber, or Bleached finishes.

SECRETARY
The secretary is formed by using the C3312 Shelf on the C3311 W Desk Base.

C3312   *OPEN SHELF HUTCH CABINET*   *1937–39*
This piece may also used with the C3310 Chest to form an open shelf hutch buffet or with the C3314 Server to form a dining hutch. The top size is 31" by 11" and the height is 25". Available in Champagne, Wheat, Amber, or Bleached finishes.

C3311 W   *DESK BASE*   *1937–39*
This desk / chest may be used alone or in combination with the C3312 shelf to form a secretary. Available in Champagne, Wheat, Amber, or Bleached finishes.

C3535 A   *SIDE CHAIR*   *1939–43*
Seat is 16" by 16½" and the back is 17" high. Yardage required is 1 yard of 50" material. Available in Champagne, Wheat, Amber, Bleached, or Modern Walnut finishes.

THE PIECES

C3535 C   *ARM CHAIR*   *1939–43*
Width between arms is 17½", depth of seat is 16½", and height of the back is 17". Yardage required is 1 yard of 50" material. Available in Champagne, Wheat, Amber, Bleached, or Modern Walnut finishes.

C3539 W   *CRESCENDO VANITY / DESK*   *1939–40*
Designed by Count Sakhnoffsky. Size of top is 48" by 21". Height is 30". Available in Champagne, Wheat, Amber, or Bleached finishes.

C3326 C   *BARREL CHAIR*   *1937–39*
Seat dimensions are 23" by 22" and the back is 18½" high. Yardage required is 2½ yards of 50" material. Available in Champagne, Wheat, Amber, Bleached, or Modern Walnut finishes.

C3534   *BOOKCASE*   *1939*
Top is 12½" by 41" and height is 29¾". Available in Champagne, Wheat, Amber, or Bleached finishes.

DINING ROOM

C3706 G   *EXTENSION TABLE*   *1940–42*
Fitted with two leaves. Size of top open is 38" by 76" and closed is 38" by 54". Height is 29". Available in Champagne or Wheat finishes.

C3701 A   *SIDE CHAIR*   *1940*
Seat is 16" by 15" and back is 16" high. Yardage required is ¾ yard of 54" material. Available in Champagne or Wheat finishes.

C3701 C   *ARM CHAIR*   *1940*
Seat is 16" by 15" and back is 16" high. Yardage required is ¾ yard of 54" material. Available in Champagne or Wheat finishes.

C3708   *BUFFET*   *1940–42*
Fitted with long bottom drawer. Size of top is 52" by 19" and height is 35". Available in Champagne or Wheat finishes.

C3389 G   *CONSOLE TABLE*   *1939–42*
The top of this table folds and pivots. It serves as a small wall table, as a console table, or with the top turned as a game table. Size of top open is 32" square, folded is 32" by 16". Height is 28". Available in Champagne, Wheat, Amber, or Bleached finishes.

C 3716 G   *CONSOLE EXTENSION TABLE*   *1940*

Above & Bottom Left: Completely closed top measures 38" wide and 20" deep. Height 30". When fully extended top measures 38" by 76". Height 29". Fitted with three leaves and drop-leg attachment for center of table when fully extended. Available in Champagne or Wheat finishes.

The table and chairs in the tea set above were designed by Leo Jiranek.

C3705   *TEA TABLE*   *1940–42*
Table is 30" square and is 29" high. Available in Champagne or Wheat finishes.

C3715 A   *SIDE CHAIR*   *1940–42*
The seat on this strap-back is 16" by 15" and the back is 16½" high. Yardage required is ½ yard of 54" material. Available in Champagne or Wheat finishes.

DINING ROOM

C3594 G   EXTENSION TABLE   *1940*
Fitted with one extension leaf. Size of top open is 34" by 64". Size of top closed is 34" by 50". Available in Champagne or Wheat finishes.

C3596 A   SIDE CHAIR   *1940–44*
Seat is 16" by 16" and the back is 16" high. Yardage required is 1 yard of 54" material. Available in Champagne or Wheat finishes.

C3596 C   ARM CHAIR   *1940–44*
Width between arms is 18" and the seat is 16" deep. The back is 16" high. Yardage required is 1 yard of 54" material. Available in Champagne or Wheat finishes.

C3709   BUFFET   *1940–42*
Size of top is 48" by 18" and height is 35". Available in Champagne or Wheat finishes.

C3389 G   CONSOLE TABLE   *1939–42*
The top of this table folds and pivots. It serves as a small wall table, as a console table, or with the top turned as a game table. Size of top open is 32" square, folded is 32" by 16". Height is 28". Available in Champagne, Wheat, Amber, or Bleached finishes.

Dining Room Group

C3713 G   *EXTENSION TABLE*   *1940*
Fitted with one leaf. Size of top open is 30" by 50", closed 30" by 40". Height is 29". Available in Champagne or Wheat finishes.

C3536 A   *SIDE CHAIR*   *1939–40*
Seat is 16½" by 15½" and the back is 15½" high. Yardage required is ¼ yard of 50" material. Available in Champagne, Wheat, Amber, or Bleached finishes.

HUTCH CABINET
This is formed with the C3585 Hutch Top on the C3584 Chest Base.

C3585   *HUTCH TOP*   *1940–42*
Top is 30½" wide, 24" high, and 10¼" deep. Available in Champagne or Wheat finishes.

C3584   *CHEST BASE*   *1940*
Base has four drawers. Top is 32" wide, 17" deep, and 34" high. Available in Champagne or Wheat finishes.

C3389 G   *CONSOLE TABLE*   *1939–42*
The top of this table folds and pivots. It serves as a small wall table, as a console table, or with the top turned as a game table. Size of top open is 32" square, folded 32" by 16". Height is 28". Available in Champagne, Wheat, Amber, or Bleached finishes.

DINETTE SET

C3703 G   *EXTENSION TABLE*   *1940*
Fitted with one extension leaf. Size of top open is 30" by 50" and closed is 30" by 40". Height is 29". Available in Champagne or Wheat finishes.

C3714 A   *SIDE CHAIR*   *1940–42*
Seat is 16" by 15" and the back is 16" high. Yardage required is ½ yard of 54" material. Available in Champagne or Wheat finishes.

DINETTE SET

C3712 G   *EXTENSION TABLE*   *1940*
Fitted with one leaf. Size of top open is 30" by 50", closed 30" by 40". Height is 29". Available in Champagne or Wheat finishes.

C3588 A   *SIDE CHAIR*   *1940*
Seat is 16" by 15" and the back is 16" high. Yardage required is ½ yard of 54" material. Available in Champagne or Wheat finishes.

C3348 X   *CORNER CABINET*   *1940–43*
Designed by Leo Jiranek. Same as C3348 but has round door pulls. Lower closed compartment fitted with shelf. It measures 14½" deep, 24" wide, and 65" high. Available in Champagne or Wheat finishes.

BLANKET BENCH

C3739   *BLANKET BENCH*   *1940–42*

Size of upholstered, hinged top is 40" by 14". Height is 17½". Yardage required is 1 yard of 54" material. Available in Champagne or Wheat finishes.

PLAZA BEDROOM GROUP

The Plaza Bedroom Group was designed by Leo Jiranek.

C3730   *PLAZA BED*   *1940*
Available in 3' 3" or 4' 6" sizes. Available in Champagne or Wheat finishes.

C3731–733   *PLAZA DRESSER WITH MIRROR*   *1940*
Size of dresser top is 42" by 20" and height is 35". Mirror measures 26" by 32". Available in Champagne or Wheat finishes.

C3731   *PLAZA DRESSER*   *1940*
This is the separate dresser without mirror.

C3733   *HANGING MIRROR*   *1940*
This is the separate hanging mirror without attachment hardware. Mirror size is 26" by 32". Available in Champagne or Wheat finishes.

C3738   *PLAZA NIGHT STAND*   *1940*
Size of top is 14" square and height is 25½". Available in Champagne or Wheat finishes.

PLAZA BEDROOM GROUP

C3732   *PLAZA 5-DRAWER CHEST*   *1940*
Size of top is 33" by 20" and height is 48". Available in Champagne or Wheat finishes.

C3736   *PLAZA VANITY BASE / DESK*   *1940*
 This is a 5-drawer base. Top is 44" by 18" and height is 30". Available in Champagne or Wheat finishes.

C3735   *HANGING MIRROR*   *1940–42*
 Glass size is 36" in diameter. Available in Champagne or Wheat finishes.

C3596 C   *ARM CHAIR*   *1940–44*
Width between arms is 18" and the seat is 16" deep. The back is 16" high. Yardage required is 1 yard of 54" material. Available in Champagne or Wheat finishes.

Plaza Bedroom Group

C3734   *PLAZA VANITY*   *1940*

Size of top is 52" by 18". Height of the base is 22" and overall height is 60¼". Mirror is 48" in diameter. Available in Champagne or Wheat finishes.

C3737   *VANITY POUFFE*   *1940*

Fitted with a revolving top. Seat is 19" in diameter and height is 16". Yardage required is 1 yard of 54" material. Available in Champagne or Wheat finishes.

THE CHALLENGER BEDROOM GROUP

C3740   *CHALLENGER BED*   *1940*
Available in 3' 3" or 4' 6" sizes. Available in Champagne or Wheat finishes.

C3741   *CHALLENGER 3-DRAWER DRESSER*   *1940*
Size of top is 40" by 19" and height is 34". Available in Champagne or Wheat finishes.

C3741–725   *DRESSER WITH ATTACHED MIRROR*   *1940*
Not illustrated but same as dresser base above with 30" round mirror attached.

C3743   *HANGING MIRROR*   *1940*
Size of glass is 30" by 22". Available in Champagne or Wheat finishes.

C3748   *CHALLENGER NIGHT STAND*   *1940*
Size of top is 14" by 13" and height is 25½". Available in Champagne or Wheat finishes.

C3765 C   *ARM CHAIR*   *1940–42*
Seat is 22" by 20" and the back is 16" high. Yardage required is 2 yards of 54" material. Available in Champagne or Wheat finishes.

THE CHALLENGER BEDROOM GROUP

C3744   *CHALLENGER VANITY BASE*   *1940*
Vanity has four drawers. Size of top is 42" by 18" and the height is 25". Available in Champagne or Wheat finishes.

C3743   *HANGING MIRROR*   *1940*
Size of glass is 30" by 22". Available in Champagne or Wheat finishes.

C3747   *CHALLENGER VANITY BENCH*   *1940*
Size of seat is 22" by 16" and height is 16½". Yardage required is ½ yard of 54" material. Available in Champagne or Wheat finishes.

C3742   *CHALLENGER 4-DRAWER CHEST*   *1940*
Size of top is 32" by 19" and the height is 43". Available in Champagne or Wheat finishes.

THE LIVING ROOM

C3753 G   *2-TIER END TABLE*   *1940–44*
Top is 30" by 15" and height is 22". Available in Champagne or Wheat finishes.

C3541 RC / 3541 LC   *RIGHT OR LEFT ARM CHAIR*   *1939–40*
Width of the seat is 22", depth of the seat is 24", and the height of the back is 18". Yardage required is 3¾ yards of 54" material. Available in Champagne, Wheat, Amber, or Bleached finishes.

C3541   *SINGLE FILLER*   *1939–40*
Width of the seat is 22", depth of the seat is 24", and the height of the back is 18". Yardage required is 3¼ yards of 54" material. Available in Champagne, Wheat, Amber, or Bleached finishes.

C3542   *DOUBLE FILLER*   *1939–40*
Not illustrated. Width of the seat is 44", depth of the seat is 24", and the height of the back is 18". Yardage required is 5⅓ yards of 54" material. Available in Champagne, Wheat, Amber, or Bleached finishes.

C3540 G   *CORNER TABLE*   *1939–40*
Designed by Count Sakhnoffsky. Top is 31½" square and height is 22". Available in Champagne, Wheat, Amber, or Bleached finishes.

C3548 G   *COCKTAIL TABLE*   *1939–40*
Fitted with revolving top which measures 32" in diameter. Height is 16". Available in Champagne, Wheat, Amber, or Bleached finishes.

C3755 G   *CORNER TABLE*   *1940–44*
Shown in small view. Size of top is 29" square and height is 22½". Available in Champagne or Wheat finishes.

THE PIECES

C3542–44   *LOVE SEAT*   *1939–40*
Designed by Count Sakhnoffsky. Width of the seat is 44", depth of the seat is 24", and the height of the back is 18". Yardage required is 6⅓ yards of 54" material. Available in Champagne, Wheat, Amber, or Bleached finishes.

C3750 G   *KIDNEY-SHAPED END TABLE*   *1940*
Size of top is 36" by 19" and height is 15½". Available in Champagne or Wheat finishes.

C3719 G   *END TABLE*   *1940–42*
Fitted with drawer and two shelves. Top is 32" by 14" and height is 22". Available in Champagne or Wheat finishes.

THE PIECES

C3589–66   *DAVENPORT*   *1940*
Seat is 66" wide by 22" deep and height of back is 20". Yardage required is 7½ yards of 54" material. Available in Champagne or Wheat finishes.

C3589 C   *ARM CHAIR*   *1940*
Seat is 22" wide by 22" deep and height of back is 20". Yardage required is 4 yards of 54" material. Available in Champagne or Wheat finishes.

C3752 G   *END TABLE*   *1940*
Top is 28" by 14" and the height is 21". Available in Champagne or Wheat finishes.

C3751 G   *CLOVER LEAF COCKTAIL TABLE*   *1940*
Top is 30" in diameter and height is 15". Available in Champagne or Wheat finishes.

C3717 G   *OBLONG COCKTAIL TABLE*   *1940–42*
Shown below. Designed by Leo Jiranek. Fitted with cigarette and accessory drawer. Size of top is 37" by 17". Height is 16". Available in Champagne or Wheat finishes.

THE PIECES

C3762 C   *ARM CHAIR*   *1940*
Seat is 23" by 21" and the back is 21" high. Yardage required is 3 yards of 54" material. Available in Champagne or Wheat finishes.

C3763 LR   *LEG REST*   *1940*
Size of top is 25" by 21" and height is 15". Yardage required is 1½ yards of 54" material. Available in Champagne or Wheat finishes.

C3764 R   *WING CHAIR*   *1940*
The seat is 18½" by 20", and the height of the back is 22". Yardage required is 4 yards of 54" material. Available in Champagne, Wheat, or Modern Walnut finishes.

SECRETARY
This is formed with the C3585 Hutch Top on the C3584 W Desk/Chest.

C3585   *HUTCH TOP*   *1940–42*
Top is 30½" wide, 24" high, and 10¼" deep. Available in Champagne or Wheat finishes.

C3584 W   *DESK/CHEST*   *1940*
Top drawer has desk compartment as shown. Desk/Chest is 32" wide, 17" deep, and 34" high. Available in Champagne or Wheat finishes.

Living Room Pieces

C3761–72   *DAVENPORT*   *1940*
Seat is 72" by 21" and the back is 21" high. Yardage required is 7 yards of 54" material. Available in Champagne or Wheat finishes.

C3761 C   *ARM CHAIR*   *1940*
Seat is 23" by 21" and the back is 21" high. Yardage required is 4 yards of 54" material. Available in Champagne or Wheat finishes.

C3756 G   *OBLONG COFFEE TABLE*   *1940–42*
Top measures 42" by 20" and height is 17". Available in Champagne or Wheat finishes.

C3754 G   *LAMP TABLE*   *1940*
Fitted with lower shelf. The clover leaf top measures 24" in diameter. Height is 26½". Available in Champagne or Wheat finishes.

C3752 G   *END TABLE*   *1940*
Top is 28" by 14" and the height is 21". Available in Champagne or Wheat finishes.

LIVING ROOM PIECES

C3760–72   *DAVENPORT*   *1940*
Seat is 72" by 21" and the back is 21" high. Yardage required is 6 yards of 54" material. Available in Champagne or Wheat finishes.

C3760 C   *ARM CHAIR*   *1940*
Seat is 23" by 21" and the back is 21" high. Yardage required is 2¾ yards of 54" material. Available in Champagne or Wheat finishes.

C3348 X   *CORNER CABINET*   *1940–43*
Same as C3348 but has round door pulls. Lower closed compartment fitted with shelf. It measures 14½" deep, 24" wide, and 65" high. Available in Champagne or Wheat finishes.

C3750 G   *KIDNEY-SHAPED END TABLE*   *1940*
Size of top is 36" by 19" and height is 15½". Available in Champagne or Wheat finishes.

C3752 G   *END TABLE*   *1940*
Top is 28" by 14" and the height is 21". Available in Champagne or Wheat finishes.

The Pieces

C3387 C   ARM CHAIR   *1938–40*
Width of seat is 24", depth of seat is 22", and height of the back is
23". Yardage required is 3¾ yards of 50" material. Available in
Champagne, Wheat, Amber, Bleached, or Modern Walnut finishes.

C3544   PIER CABINET   *1939–40*
Designed by Count Sakhnoffsky. Top is 16" by 14" and height is
32½". Available in Champagne, Wheat, Amber, or Bleached finishes.

C3582   CORNER BOOKCASE   *1940*
Overall measures 28" by 28" and is 32½" high. Available in Champagne or Wheat finishes.

C3545   BOOKCASE   *1939–40*
Designed by Count Sakhnoffsky. Fitted with adjustable shelves.
Top is 36" by 11" and height is 22". Available in Champagne, Wheat,
Amber, or Bleached finishes.

C3583   CABINET BOOKCASE   *1940*
Shown in small view. Fitted with two storage compartments below. Top is 32" wide, overall depth including swelled front is
13¾", and height is 32½". Available in Champagne or Wheat finishes.

C3766   *BARREL CHAIR*   *1940*
Shown at right. Seat is 22" by 20" and the back is 20" high.
Yardage required is 2½ yards of 54" material. Available in
Champagne or Wheat finishes.

THE PIECES

C3349 G   *GATELEG TABLE*   *1938–40*
Dual purpose design as dining or console table. Top measures
36" by 60" with both leaves up, with one leaf up it is 36"
square. With both leaves down table measures 36" by 13¾".
Height is 29". Available in Champagne, Wheat, Amber, or
Bleached finishes.

C3381 C   *CANE PANEL ARM CHAIR*   *1938–40*
Width of seat is 20", depth of seat is 23", and height of the back
is 16". Yardage required is 1⅔ yards of 50" material. Available in
Wheat finish.

C3586 W   *DESK CHEST BOOKCASE*   *1940*
A compact unit suited for a small apartment. Width is 48", depth is 12", and height is 44". Available in Champagne or Wheat
finishes.

C3767 C   *READING CHAIR*   *1940–42*
Seat is 22" by 22" and the back is 24" high. Yardage required is 3¾ yards of 54" material. Available in Champagne or Wheat
finishes.

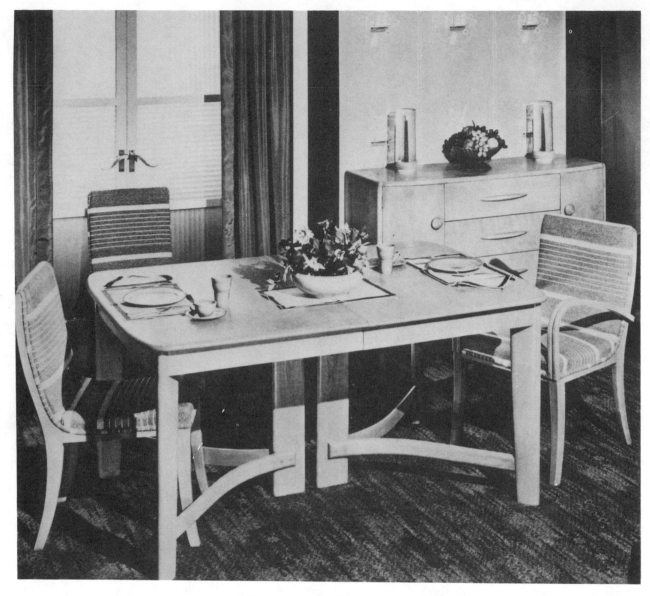

DINING GROUP

C3707 G   *EXTENSION TABLE*   *1940–42*
Fitted with two leaves. Size of top open is 42" by 84" and closed is 42" by 60". Height is 29". Available in Champagne or Wheat finishes.

C3535 A   *SIDE CHAIR*   *1939–43*
Seat is 16" by 16½" and the back is 17" high. Yardage required is 1 yard of 50" material. Available in Champagne, Wheat, Amber, Bleached, or Modern Walnut finishes.

C3535 C   *ARM CHAIR*   *1939–43*
Width between arms is 17½", depth of seat is 16½", and height of the back is 17". Yardage required is 1 yard of 50" material. Available in Champagne, Wheat, Amber, Bleached, or Modern Walnut finishes.

C3708   *BUFFET*   *1940–42*
Fitted with long bottom drawer. Size of top is 52" by 19" and height is 35". Available in Champagne or Wheat finishes.

THE PIECES

The drop-leaf table and chairs were designed by Leo Jiranek.

C3958 G   *DROP-LEAF EXTENSION TABLE*   *1941–42*
Size of top fully extended and with both extension leaves in measures 38" by 78". Size with no leaves in but both end drop leaves up is 38" by 54". Size of top with end drop leaves down is 38" by 24". Height is 29". Available in Champagne and Wheat finishes.

C3596 A   *SIDE CHAIR*   *1940–44*
Seat is 16" by 16" and the back is 16" high. Yardage required is 1 yard of 54" material. Available in Champagne or Wheat finishes.

C3596 C   *ARM CHAIR*   *1940–44*
Width between arms is 18" and the seat is 16" deep. The back is 16" high. Yardage required is 1 yard of 54" material. Available in Champagne or Wheat finishes.

HUTCH CABINET
This is formed by using the C3585 Hutch Top on the C3975 Cabinet.

C3585   *HUTCH TOP*   *1940–42*
Top shelf is adjustable. Top is 30½" wide, 24" high, and 10¼" deep. Available in Champagne or Wheat finishes.

C3975   *CABINET*   *1941–42*
This 4-drawer chest has a 32" by 17" top. Height is 34". Available in Champagne and Wheat finishes.

THE PIECES

C3957 G   GATELEG TABLE   1941–42
Dual purpose design for dining-living-foyer or console use. Top measures 36" by 60" with both drop leaves extended and 36" square with one leaf extended. Top with both leaves down measures 36" by 14". Available in Champagne and Wheat finishes.

C3951 A   SIDE CHAIR   1941–42
This chair was designed by Leo Jiranek. Seat is 15½" by 14½" and back is 16½" high. Yardage required is ½ yard of 54" material. Available in Champagne and Wheat finishes.

CHINA CABINET

This piece is formed with the C3711 X China Top on the C3710 Server.

C3711 X   CHINA TOP   1941–44
China Top has sliding glass doors and top shelf is adjustable. Size is 30" long, 13" deep, and 34½" high. Available in Champagne and Wheat finishes.

C3710   SERVER   1940–44
Top is 32" by 18" and height is 30". Available in Champagne or Wheat finishes.

DINING ROOM GROUP

C3941 G   *EXTENSION TABLE*   *1941–42*
Fitted with one 14" extension leaf. Size of top open is 34" by 64", with top closed, 34" by 50". Height is 29". Available in Champagne and Wheat finishes.

C3940 A   *SIDE CHAIR*   *1941–42*
This chair was designed by Leo Jiranek. Seat is 16" by 15" and height of back is 16". Yardage required is ¾ yard of 54" material. Available in Champagne and Wheat finishes.

C3940 C   *ARM CHAIR*   *1941–42*
This chair was designed by Leo Jiranek. Seat is 16" by 15" and height of back is 16". Yardage required is ¾ yard of 54" material. Available in Champagne and Wheat finishes.

C3954   *CREDENZA / BUFFET*   *1941–44*
Size of top is 48" by 19". Height is 34". Fitted with three center drawers and two end storage compartments. Available in Champagne and Wheat finishes.

DINING SET

C3956 G   *EXTENSION TABLE*   *1941–44*
Fitted with one 14" extension leaf. Size of top open is 34" by 64". Size of top closed is 34" by 50". Height is 29". Available in Champagne and Wheat finishes.

C3953 A   *SIDE CHAIR*   *1941–42*
Seat is 16" by 15" and back is 16" high. Yardage required is ¾ yard of 54" material. Available in Champagne and Wheat finishes.

C3953 C   *ARM CHAIR*   *1941–42*
Seat is 16" by 15" and back is 16" high. Yardage required is ¾ yard of 54" material. Available in Champagne and Wheat finishes.

C3709   *BUFFET*   *1940–42*
Size of top is 48" by 18" and height is 35". Available in Champagne or Wheat finishes.

CHINA CABINET
This is formed by using the C3711 X China Top on the C3975 Cabinet.

C3711 X   *CHINA TOP*   *1941–44*
China Top has sliding glass doors and top shelf is adjustable. Size is 30" long, 13" deep, and 34½" high. Available in Champagne and Wheat finishes.

C3975   *CABINET*   *1941–42*
This 4-drawer chest has a 32" by 17" top. Height is 34". Available in Champagne and Wheat finishes.

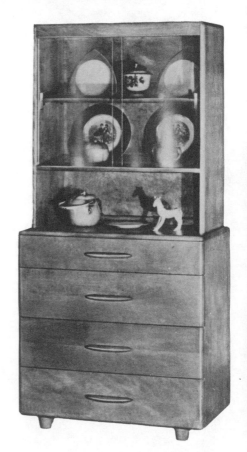

DINING ROOM GROUP

C3704 G   *OVAL EXTENSION TABLE*   *1940–41*
Fitted with one extension leaf. Size of top open is 32" by 56" and closed is 32" by 46". Height is 29". Available in Champagne or Wheat finishes.

C3702 A   *SIDE CHAIR*   *1940–42*
Seat is 16" by 15" and back is 16" high. Yardage required is ½ yard of 54" material. Available in Champagne or Wheat finishes.

C3702 C   *ARM CHAIR*   *1940–42*
Seat is 16" by 15" and back is 16" high. Yardage required is ½ yard of 54" material. Available in Champagne or Wheat finishes.

HUTCH CABINET
This is formed by using the C3585 Hutch Top on the C3972 Cabinet Base.

C3585   *HUTCH TOP*   *1940–42*
Top is 30½" wide, 24" high, and 10¼" deep. Available in Champagne or Wheat finishes.

C3972   *CABINET BASE*   *1940–42*
Fitted with two storage compartments. Base is 32" wide and 13¾" deep including bow. Height is 32½" which is the same as the bookcases. Available in Champagne and Wheat finishes.

DINING ROOM GROUP

C3704 G   *OVAL EXTENSION TABLE*   *1940–41*
Fitted with one extension leaf. Size of top open is 32" by 56" and closed is 32" by 46". Height is 29". Available in Champagne or Wheat finishes.

C3595 A   *SIDE CHAIR*   *1940–44*
Seat is 16" by 17" and the back is 16" high. Yardage required is ½ yard of 54" material. Available in Champagne or Wheat finishes.

C3595 C   *ARM CHAIR*   *1940–44*
Width between arms is 18", depth of seat is 17", and the back is 16" high. Yardage required is ½ yard of 54" material. Available in Champagne or Wheat finishes.

C3709   *BUFFET*   *1940–42*
Size of top is 48" by 18" and height is 35". Available in Champagne or Wheat finishes.

DINETTE SET

C3955 G   *EXTENSION TABLE*   *1941–42*
Fitted with one extension leaf. Size of top open is 30" by 50". Size of top closed is 30" by 40". Height is 29". Available in Champagne and Wheat finishes.

C3714 A   *SIDE CHAIR*   *1940–42*
Seat is 16" by 15" and the back is 16" high. Yardage required is ½ yard of 54" material. Available in Champagne or Wheat finishes.

C3972   *CABINET BASE*   *1940–42*
Fitted with two storage compartments. Base is 32" wide and 13¾" deep including bow. Height is 32½" which is the same as the bookcases. Available in Champagne and Wheat finishes.

DINING SET

C3940 G   *EXTENSION TABLE*   *1941–42*

Fitted with one extension leaf. Size of top open is 30" by 50", with top closed 30" by 40". Height is 29". Available in Champagne and Wheat finishes.

C3952 A   *SIDE CHAIR*   *1941–42*

Seat is 16½" by 15½" and back is 16" high. Yardage required is ½ yard of 54" material. Available in Champagne and Wheat finishes.

C3975   *CABINET*   *1941–42*

This 4-drawer chest has a 32" by 17" top. Height is 34". Available in Champagne and Wheat finishes.

C3389 G   *CONSOLE TABLE*   *1939–42*

The top of this table folds and pivots. It serves as a small wall table, as a console table, or with the top turned as a game table. Size of top open 32" square, folded 32" by 16". Height is 28". Available in Champagne, Wheat, Amber, or Bleached finishes.

DINING SET

C3955 G   *EXTENSION TABLE*   *1941–42*
Fitted with one extension leaf. Size of top open is 30" by 50". Size of top closed is 30" by 40". Height is 29". Available in Champagne and Wheat finishes.

C3700 A   *SIDE CHAIR*   *1941–44*
Seat is 16" by 15" and back is 18" high. Yardage required is ½ yard of 54" material. Available in Champagne or Wheat finishes.

C3348 X   *CORNER CABINET*   *1940–43*
Designed by Leo Jiranek. Same as C3348 but has round door pulls. Lower closed compartment fitted with shelf. It measures 14½" deep, 24" wide, and 65" high. Available in Champagne or Wheat finishes.

DINING SET

C3950 G   *EXTENSION TABLE*   *1941–43*

Fitted with one extension leaf. Size of top open is 30" by 50". Size of top closed is 30" by 40". Height is 29". Available in Champagne and Wheat finishes.

C3950 A   *SIDE CHAIR*   *1941–43*

Seat is 16" by 15" and back is 16" high. Yardage required is ½ yard of 54" material. Available in Champagne and Wheat finishes.

C3950 C   *ARM CHAIR*   *1941–43*

Seat is 16" by 15" and back is 16" high. Yardage required is ½ yard of 54" material. Available in Champagne and Wheat finishes.

C3348 X   *CORNER CABINET*   *1940–43*

Same as C3348 but has round door pulls. Lower closed compartment fitted with shelf. It measures 14½" deep, 24" wide, and 65" high. Available in Champagne or Wheat finishes.

The Coronet Bedroom Group

The Coronet Bedroom Group was designed by Count Sakhnoffsky.

C3932   *CORONET 5-DRAWER CHEST*   *1941–42*
Top measures 33" by 20" and the height is 47". Available in Champagne and Wheat finishes.

C3934   *CORONET VANITY BASE / DESK*   *1941–42*
A dual purpose piece which serves as a vanity base and also as a kneehole desk. Size of top is 44" by 18" and height is 29". Available in Champagne and Wheat finishes.

C3735   *HANGING MIRROR*   *1940–42*
Glass size is 36" in diameter. Available in Champagne or Wheat finishes.

C3535 A   *SIDE CHAIR*   *1939–43*
Seat is 16" by 16½" and the back is 17" high. Yardage required is 1 yard of 50" material. Available in Champagne, Wheat, Amber, Bleached, or Modern Walnut finishes.

THE CORONET BEDROOM GROUP

C3931–933   *CORONET DRESSER WITH MIRROR*   *1941–42*
Size of dresser top is 44" by 20". Height is 34". Glass on attached mirror measures 42" by 28". Available in Champagne and Wheat finishes.

C3535 A   *SIDE CHAIR*   *1939–43*
Seat is 16" by 16½" and the back is 17" high. Yardage required is 1 yard of 50" material. Available in Champagne, Wheat, Amber, Bleached, or Modern Walnut finishes.

C3930   *CORONET BED*   *1941–42*
Available in 3' 3" or 4' 6" sizes. Available in Champagne and Wheat finishes.

C3938   *CORONET NIGHT STAND*   *1941–42*
Size of top is 14" square and height is 25½".

C3933   *HANGING MIRROR*   *1941–42*
Same as shown but separate hanging mirror. Mirror measures 42" by 28".

THE CORONET BEDROOM GROUP

C3936   *CORONET VANITY*   *1941–42*
Size of top is 53" by 18". Height of base is 22" and total height is 65". Mirror has plate which measures 38" wide and 44" high. Lower plate in base measures 10" by 19". Vanity is fitted with glass powder shelf between the piers. Available in Champagne and Wheat finishes.

C3937   *CORONET VANITY POUFFE*   *1941–42*
Fitted with revolving top. Seat measures 20" in diameter. Yardage required is 1½ yards of 54" material. Available in Champagne and Wheat finishes.

THE NIAGARA BEDROOM GROUP

The Niagara Group was designed by Leo Jiranek.

C3926   *NIAGARA VANITY*   *1941–42*
Size of top is 53" by 18". Height of base is 23". Overall height of vanity is 61". Mirror has plate which measures 52" by 38". Lower plate in base measures 22" by 19". Vanity is fitted with glass powder shelf between piers. Available in Champagne and Wheat finishes.

C3927   *NIAGARA VANITY SEAT*   *1941–42*
Fitted with revolving top in channeled upholstery. Seat is 20" wide and height is 17". Yardage required is 1¾ yards of 54" material. Available in Champagne and Wheat finishes.

THE NIAGARA BEDROOM GROUP

C3920   *NIAGARA BED*   *1941–42*
Available in 3' 3" or 4' 6" sizes. Available in Champagne and Wheat finishes.

C3921–923   *NIAGARA DRESSER WITH MIRROR*   *1941–42*
Also available without mirror as the C3921. Size of dresser top is 42" by 20". Height of dresser base is 34". Mirror size is 40" by 28". Available in Champagne and Wheat finishes.

C3928   *NIAGARA NIGHT STAND*   *1941–42*
Size of top is 14" square. Height is 25½". Available in Champagne and Wheat finishes.

C3921–725   *NIAGARA DRESSER WITH ROUND MIRROR*   *1941–42*
Shown in single silhouette view. Size of top is 42" by 20". Height of dresser base is 34". Mirror glass is 30" in diameter. Available in Champagne and Wheat finishes.

The Niagara Bedroom Group

C3922 | *Niagara 5-Drawer Chest* | *1941–42*
Size of top is 33" by 20". Height is 47". Available in Champagne and Wheat finishes.

C3596 A *Side Chair* *1940–44*
Seat is 16" by 16" and the back is 16" high. Yardage required is 1 yard of 54" material. Available in Champagne or Wheat finishes.

C3924 *Niagara Vanity / Desk* *1941–42*
This is a 5 drawer vanity base which may also be used as a kneehole desk. Top measures 44" by 18". Height is 29". Available in Champagne and Wheat finishes.

C3923 *Hanging Mirror* *1941–42*
This is a separate mirror shown hanging over the vanity. Size of glass is 40" by 28". Available in Champagne and Wheat finishes.

C3739 *Blanket Bench* *1940–42*
Size of upholstered, hinged top is 40" by 14". Height is 17½". Yardage required is 1 yard of 54" material. Available in Champagne or Wheat finishes.

THE CAMEO BEDROOM GROUP

When introduced in 1940 this set was available only with Tenite plastic drawer pulls. The pulls are of a slight pinkish cast with burnished copper inserts. Champagne finish was recommended to harmonize with the color of the pulls. By 1941 wooden drawer pulls had been added as an option. The model number with wooden pulls has an X for a suffix.

C3720	*CAMEO BED*	*1940–42*

Available in 3' 3" or 4' 6" sizes. Available in Champagne or Wheat finishes.

C3721X–725	*CAMEO DRESSER WITH MIRROR*	*1940–42*

Size of dresser top is 42" by 20". Height is 34". Attached mirror is 30" in diameter. Available in Champagne or Wheat finishes.

C3728X	*CAMEO NIGHT STAND*	*1940–42*

Size of top is 13" by 13" and height is 26". Small top drawer and lower storage drawer. Available in Champagne or Wheat finishes.

C3992 C	*UPHOLSTERED ARM CHAIR*	*1941–42*

Seat is 20" by 18½". Height of back is 18½". Yardage required is 2½ yards of 54" material. Available in Champagne and Wheat finishes.

C3722	*CAMEO 4-DRAWER CHEST*	*1940–42*

Size of top is 32" by 19" and height is 46". Available in Champagne or Wheat finishes.

THE CAMEO BEDROOM GROUP

C3726 X   *CAMEO VANITY BASE*   *1940–42*
May be used as kneehole desk because it is finished in rear. Size of top is 44" by 18" and height is 30". Available in Champagne or Wheat finishes.

C3723   *HANGING MIRROR*   *1940–42*
Glass size is 24" by 30". Available in Champagne or Wheat finishes.

C3595 A   *SIDE CHAIR*   *1940–44*
Seat is 16" by 17" and the back is 16" high. Yardage required is ½ yard of 54" material. Available in Champagne or Wheat finishes.

C3724   *CAMEO VANITY*   *1940–42*
Shown with Tenite plastic pulls. Size of top is 29" by 18" and the base is 23" high. Mirror is 40" in diameter. Overall height is 59". Available in Champagne or Wheat finishes.

C3727   *CAMEO VANITY SEAT*   *1940–42*
Top measures 23" by 17". Height is 17". Yardage required is 1 yard of 54" material. Available in Champagne or Wheat finishes.

155

THE MIAMI BEDROOM GROUP

The Miami Bedroom Group was designed by Leo Jiranek.

C3735   HANGING MIRROR   1940–42
Glass size is 36" in diameter. Available in Champagne or Wheat finishes.

C3914   MIAMI VANITY BASE   1941–42
This is the separate vanity base with four drawers. Top of base measures 46" by 18". Height of base is 23". Available in Champagne and Wheat finishes.

SINGLE HEADBOARD FOR TWIN BEDS
C3770   1941–42
This piece designed to accommodate two twin beds will also fit today's king size mattresses. Furnished with two pivoting metal frames. Available in Champagne and Wheat Finishes.

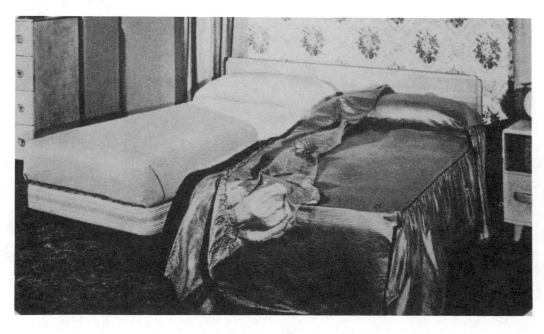

The Miami Bedroom Group

C3910   MIAMI BED   *1941–42*
Available in 3' 3" or 4' 6" sizes. Available in Champagne and Wheat finishes.

C3918   MIAMI NIGHT STAND   *1941–42*
Fitted with drawer at top and hinged storage compartment in base. Size of top is 13" by 14" and height is 25½". Available in Champagne and Wheat finishes.

C3911   MIAMI 3-DRAWER DRESSER   *1941–42*
Size of top is 42" by 19" and height is 34". Available in Champagne and Wheat finishes.

C3913   HANGING MIRROR   *1941–42*
Mirror plate size is 34" by 22". Available in Champagne and Wheat finishes.

C3915   HANGING MIRROR   *1941–42*
Not illustrated. This mirror is similar in style to the C3913 except it has a wood frame on one side of the mirror only. Glass measures 32" by 26". Available in Champagne and Wheat finishes.

C3715 A   SIDE CHAIR   *1940–42*
Seat is 16" by 15" and the back is 16½" high. Yardage required is ½ yard of 54" material. Available in Champagne or Wheat finishes.

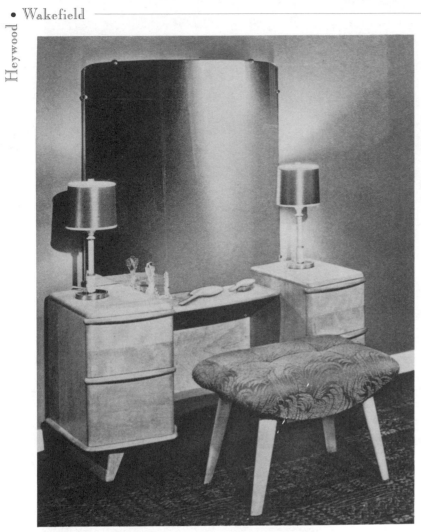

THE MIAMI BEDROOM GROUP

C3916   *MIAMI VANITY*   *1941–42*
Size of top is 46" by 18". Height of base is 23".
Mirror size is 36" by 34". Overall height is 56".
Available in Champagne and Wheat finishes.

C3917   *MIAMI VANITY BENCH*   *1941–42*
Spring filled top measures 24" by 15". Height is
17". Available in Champagne and Wheat finishes.

C3912   *MIAMI 4-DRAWER CHEST*   *1941–42*
Size of top is 32" by 19" and height is 43". Available in Champagne and Wheat finishes.

THE CATALINA BEDROOM GROUP

CATALINA DRESSER w/ROUND MIRROR
C3901–725   *1941–42*
Shown below. This dresser with attached mirror has a top 40" by 19". Height is 34". Mirror is
30" in diameter. Available in Champagne and
Wheat finishes.

THE CATALINA BEDROOM GROUP

C3902 — *CATALINA 4-DRAWER CHEST* — *1941–42*
The top is 32" by 19". Height is 43". Available in Champagne and Wheat finishes.

C3904 — *CATALINA VANITY BASE* — *1941–42*
This 4-drawer vanity base has a 42" by 18" top and is 25" high. Available in Champagne and Wheat finishes.

C3903 — *HANGING MIRROR* — *1941–42*
Size of glass is 28" by 22". Available in Champagne and Wheat finishes.

C3907 — *CATALINA VANITY BENCH* — *1941–42*
Padded top measures 22" by 16". Height is 16". Available in Champagne and Wheat finishes.

THE CATALINA
BEDROOM GROUP

C3900   *CATALINA BED*   *1941–42*
Available in 3' 3" or 4' 6" sizes. Available in Champagne and Wheat finishes.

C3901   *CATALINA DRESSER BASE*   *1941–42*
Top measures 40" by 19" and height is 34". Available in Champagne and Wheat finishes.

C3903   *HANGING MIRROR*   *1941–42*
Size of glass is 28" by 22". Available in Champagne and Wheat finishes.

C3908   *CATALINA NIGHT STAND*   *1941–42*
Size of top is 14" by 13" and height is 25". Available in Champagne and Wheat finishes.

C3765 C   *ARM CHAIR*   *1940–42*
Seat is 22" by 20" and the back is 16" high. Yardage required is 2 yards of 54" material. Available in Champagne or Wheat finishes.

CATALINA VANITY WITH ATTACHED MIRROR
C3904–923   *1941–42*
Shown at right. This complete vanity has 42" by 18" top and is 25" high. The mirror is 28" by 40". Available in Champagne and Wheat finishes.

The Living Room

C3943 G　　　　　　　　　　　ENDｰTABLE　　　　　　　　　　　*1941–44*
Size of top is 28" by 14" and height is 22". Available in Champagne and Wheat finishes.

The Coronet Sectional Sofa in this illustration was designed by Count Sakhnoffsky.

C3945 RC/3945LC　RIGHT / LEFT ARM CHAIR　*1941–42*
Seat is 22" wide by 21" deep. Height of the back is 19".
Yardage required is 4 yards of 54" material. Available in
Champagne and Wheat finishes.

C3945　　　　　SINGLE FILLER　　　　*1941–42*
This is a single size armless center section. Seat is 22"
wide by 21" deep. Back is 19" high. Yardage required is
3½ yards of 54" material. Available in Champagne and
Wheat finishes.

C3946　　　　　DOUBLE FILLER　　　　*1941–42*
Not illustrated. This is the same as single filler C3945
except seat is 44" wide. Yardage required is 6 yards of 54"
material. Available in Champagne and Wheat finishes.

C3960 G　　　　CORNER TABLE　　　　*1941–42*
Shown in large and small views. Top measures 32" square and is 22" high. Available in Champagne and Wheat finishes.

C3964 G　　　　　　　ROUND COCKTAIL TABLE　　　　　　　*1941–44*
This table was designed by Leo Jiranek. Fitted with a revolving top, 32" in diameter. Height is 17". Available in Champagne and Wheat finishes.

THE CORONET LIVING ROOM GROUP

Count Sakhnoffsky designed all pieces in this illustration.

C3947–66	*DAVENPORT*	*1941–42*

Seat is 66" wide by 21" deep. Height of back is 19". Yardage required is 9½ yards of 54" material. Available in Champagne and Wheat finishes.

C3945 C	*ARM CHAIR*	*1941–42*

Seat is 22" wide by 21" deep. Height of the back is 19". Yardage required is 4½ yards of 54" material. Available in Champagne and Wheat finishes.

C3944 G	*LAMP TABLE*	*1941–44*

Size of top is 19" by 17" and height is 26". Available in Champagne and Wheat finishes.

C3943 G	*END TABLE*	*1941–44*

Size of top is 28" by 14" and height is 22". Available in Champagne and Wheat finishes.

C3942 G	*OBLONG COFFEE TABLE*	*1941–44*

Size of top is 36" by 19" and table is 16" high. Available in Champagne and Wheat finishes.

THE LIVING ROOM

C3946–44   LOVE SEAT   *1941–42*
Designed by Count Sakhnoffsky. Seat is 44" wide by 21" deep. Height of the back is 19". Yardage required is 7 yards of 54" material. Available in Champagne and Wheat finishes.

C3948 C   CHANNEL SIDE ARM CHAIR   *1941–42*
Seat measures 28" by 20". Height of back is 16". Yardage required is 5 yards of 54" material. Available in Champagne and Wheat finishes.

C3719 G   END TABLE   *1940–42*
Fitted with drawer and two shelves. Top is 32" by 14" and height is 22". Available in Champagne or Wheat finishes.

C3963 G   ROUND COCKTAIL TABLE   *1941–42*
Diameter of top is 28" and height is 17". Available in Champagne and Wheat finishes.

THE LIVING ROOM

The upholstered pieces in this group were designed by W. Joseph Carr.

C3753 G   2-TIER END TABLE   *1940–44*
Top is 30" by 15" and height is 22". Available in Champagne or Wheat finishes.

C3985 RC OR 3985 LC   RIGHT OR LEFT ARM CHAIR   *1941–44*
Seat is 22" by 21". Back is 19" high. Yardage required is 4 yards of 54" material. Available in Champagne and Wheat finishes.

C3985   SINGLE FILLER   *1941–44*
This is single size, armless center section. Seat is 22" by 21". Back is 19" high. Yardage required is 3½ yards of 54" material. Available in Champagne and Wheat finishes.

C3755 G   CORNER TABLE   *1940–44*
Size of top is 29" square and height is 22½". Available in Champagne or Wheat finishes.

C3961 G   OVAL COCKTAIL TABLE   *1941–42*
Top measures 36" by 19". Height is 16". Available in Champagne and Wheat finishes.

THE LIVING ROOM

The upholstered pieces in this group were designed by W. Joseph Carr.

C3987–66   *DAVENPORT*   *1941–44*
Seat is 66" by 21". Back is 19" high. Yardage required is 9½ yards of 54" material. Available in Champagne and Wheat finishes.

C3986–44   *LOVE SEAT*   *1941–43*
Not illustrated. Same as Davenport C3987–66 but has two cushions and measures 44" between the arms. Seat is 22" by 21". Back is 19" high. Yardage required is 7 yards of 54" material. Available in Champagne and Wheat finishes.

C3985 C   *ARM CHAIR*   *1941–44*
Seat is 22" by 21". Back is 19" high. Yardage required is 4½ yards of 54" material. Available in Champagne and Wheat finishes.

C3549 G   *LAMP TABLE*   *1939–40*
Fitted with shelf. Top is 22" in diameter and height is 26". Available in Champagne, Wheat, Amber, or Bleached finishes.

C3717 G   *OBLONG COCKTAIL TABLE*   *1940–42*
This cocktail table was designed by Leo Jiranek. Fitted with cigarette and accessory drawer. Size of top is 37" by 17". Height is 16". Available in Champagne or Wheat finishes.

C3962 G   *END TABLE*   *1941–42*
Oval top measures 28" by 15" and height is 21". Available in Champagne and Wheat finishes.

THE PIECES

C3986   *DOUBLE FILLER*   *1941–43*
Seat is 44" by 21". Back is 19" high. Yardage required is 6 yards of 54" material. Available in Champagne and Wheat finishes.

C3978 W   *KNEEHOLE DESK*   *1941–44*
This is a 6-drawer kneehole desk finished all around. Lower left drawer is file size. Top measures 46" by 21". Height is 30". Available in Champagne and Wheat finishes.

C3535 A   *SIDE CHAIR*   *1939–43*
Seat is 16" by 16½" and the back is 17" high. Yardage required is 1 yard of 50" material. Available in Champagne, Wheat, Amber, Bleached, or Modern Walnut finishes.

C3961 G   *OVAL COCKTAIL TABLE*   *1941–42*
Top measures 36" by 19". Height is 16". Available in Champagne and Wheat finishes.

C3771 X   *STUDIO END TABLE*   *1941–42*
This table is fitted with a lower storage compartment with hinged door. It measures 32" by 19" and is 23" high. Available in Champagne and Wheat finishes.

DRAWER-TOP COCKTAIL TABLE
C3717 G   *1940–42*
Shown at right. Fitted with cigarette and accessory drawer. Size of top is 37" by 17". Height is 16". Available in Champagne or Wheat finishes.

THE PIECES

C3996 R	WING CHAIR	1941–44

Seat measures 20" by 25". Height of back is 22". Yardage required is 4 yards of 54" material. Available in Champagne and Wheat finishes.

SECRETARY
This is formed by using the C3585 Hutch Top on the C3975 W Desk/Chest.

C3585	HUTCH TOP	1940–42

Top is 30½" wide, 24" high, and 10¼" deep. Available in Champagne or Wheat finishes.

C3975 W	DESK/CHEST	1941–42

Desk/Chest is 32" wide, by 17" deep, and 34" high. Fitted with desk top in top drawer. Available in Champagne and Wheat finishes.

C3767 C	READING CHAIR	1940–42

Seat is 22" by 22" and the back is 24" high. Yardage required is 3¾ yards of 54" material. Available in Champagne or Wheat finishes.

THE LIVING ROOM

C3989–66   *DAVENPORT*   *1941–42*

Seat is 66" by 21". Height of back is 19". Yardage required is 8½ yards of 54" material. Available in Champagne and Wheat finishes.

C3989 C   *ARM CHAIR*   *1941–42*

Seat is 22" by 21". Height of back is 19". Yardage required is 4½ yards of 54" material. Available in Champagne and Wheat finishes.

C3962 G   *END TABLE*   *1941–42*

Oval top measures 28" by 15" and height is 21". Available in Champagne and Wheat finishes.

C3718 G   *HUNT COCKTAIL TABLE*   *1940–42*

Fitted with semi-circular drawer. Overall measurement of top is 41" by 19". Height is 16". Available in Champagne or Wheat finishes.

THE LIVING ROOM

C3981–68	*DAVENPORT*	*1941–42*

Seat is 68" by 21". Height of back is 21". Yardage required is 7½ yards of 54" material. Available in Champagne and Wheat finishes.

C3981 C	*ARM CHAIR*	*1941–42*

Seat is 23" by 21". Height of back is 21". Yardage required is 4½ yards of 54" material. Available in Champagne and Wheat finishes.

C3753 G	*2-TIER END TABLE*	*1940–44*

Top is 30" by 15" and height is 22". Available in Champagne or Wheat finishes.

C3756 G	*OBLONG COFFEE TABLE*	*1940–42*

Top measures 42" by 20" and height is 17". Available in Champagne or Wheat finishes.

C3549 G	*LAMP TABLE*	*1939–40*

Designed by Count Sakhnoffsky. Fitted with shelf. Top is 22" in diameter and height is 26". Available in Champagne, Wheat, Amber, or Bleached finishes.

THE PIECES

All pieces in the large illustration were designed by
Leo Jiranek.

C3997 C   UPHOLSTERED ARM CHAIR   *1941–42*
Seat measures 22" by 22". Height of back is 24". Yardage
required is 4¼ yards of 54" material. Available in Champagne and Wheat finishes.

C3977 W   DESK / CHEST BOOKCASE   *1941–42*
Larger than the C3976 this piece measures 60" wide, 12"
deep, and 44" high. Available in Champagne and Wheat
finishes.

C3995 C   OPEN FRAME ARM CHAIR   *1941–42*
Seat is 23" by 21". Height of back is 21". Yardage
required is 3¾ yards of 54" material. Available in Champagne and Wheat finishes.

C3990 LR   LEG REST   *1941–42*
Size of top is 25" by 21". Height is 5". Yardage required is
1¾ yards of 54" material. Available in Champagne and
Wheat finishes.

C3976 W   DESK / CHEST BOOKCASE   *1941–42*
This is a smaller bookcase shown to the right. Overall
measures 48" wide, 12" deep, and 44" high. Available in
Champagne and Wheat finishes.

THE LIVING ROOM

C3980–68   *DAVENPORT*   *1941–44*
Seat is 68" by 21". Height of back is 21". Yardage required is 7 yards of 54" material. Available in Champagne and Wheat finishes.

C3980 C   *ARM CHAIR*   *1941–44*
Seat is 23" by 21". Height of back is 21". Yardage required is 3½ yards of 54" material. Available in Champagne and Wheat finishes.

C3962 G   *END TABLE*   *1941–42*
Oval top measures 28" by 15" and height is 21". Available in Champagne and Wheat finishes.

C3942 G   *OBLONG COFFEE TABLE*   *1941–44*
Designed by Count Sakhnoffsky. Size of top is 36" by 19" and table is 16" high. Available in Champagne and Wheat finishes.

C3348 X   *CORNER CABINET*   *1940–43*
Designed by Leo Jiranek. Same as C3348 but has round door pulls. Lower closed compartment fitted with shelf. It measures 14½" deep, 24" wide, and 65" high. Available in Champagne or Wheat finishes.

C3973   *3-DRAWER BOOKCASE-CHEST*   *1941–42*
This piece can be used with sectional bookcase. Top measures 28" by 14". Height is 32½". Available in Champagne and Wheat finishes.

THE PIECES

C3974   *PIER CABINET*   *1941–42*
Shown at right. Fitted with four drawers. Size of top is 16" by 14". Height is 32½". Available in Champagne and Wheat finishes.

C3970   *STRAIGHT FRONT BOOKCASE*   *1941–44*
Shown at right. Bookcase is fitted with adjustable shelves. Top measures 36" by 11" and height is 32½". Available in Champagne and Wheat finishes.

C3957 G   *GATELEG TABLE*   *1941–42*
Dual purpose design for dining-living-foyer or console use. Top measures 36" by 60" with both drop leaves extended and 36" square with one leaf extended. Top with both leaves down measures 36" by 14". Available in Champagne and Wheat finishes.

C3777 WX   *BOOKCASE-END DESK*   *1941–42*
This desk was designed by Leo Jiranek. It is fitted with only three drawers as the bookcase end takes up right drawer space. Top measures 42" by 20" and height is 29". Available in Champagne and Wheat finishes.

C3530 A   *SIDE CHAIR*   *1939–42*
Width of seat is 18", depth of seat is 17", and the back is 16" high. Yardage required is ¼ yard of 50" material. Available in Champagne, Wheat, Amber, or Bleached finishes.

C3997 C   *UPHOLSTERED ARM CHAIR*   *1941–42*
Seat measures 22" by 22". Height of back is 24". Yardage required is 4¼ yards of 54" material. Available in Champagne and Wheat finishes.

THE PIECES

C3992 C   *UPHOLSTERED ARM CHAIR*   *1941–42*
Seat is 20" by 18½". Height of back is 18½". Yardage required is 2½ yards of 54" material. Available in Champagne and Wheat finishes.

C3908   *RADIO TABLE*   *1941–42*
This is also the Catalina night stand. Size of top is 14" by 13" and height is 25". Available in Champagne and Wheat finishes.

C3757   *TABLE DESK*   *1940–42*
Fitted with drawer. Top measures 36" by 18" and height is 29". Available in Champagne or Wheat finishes.

C3991 C   *WOOD FRAME ARM CHAIR*   *1941–47*
Seat is 20" by 18½". Height of back is 18½". Yardage required is 1¾ yards of 54" material. Available in Champagne and Wheat finishes.

THE RIO GROUP

C3790   *RIO BED*   *1943–44*
The Rio Bedroom Group was designed by Leo Jiranek. Available in 3' 3" or 4' 6" sizes. Available in Champagne and Wheat finishes.

RIO 3-DRAWER DRESSER WITH MIRROR
C3791–795   *1943–44*
Top measures 42" by 20". Height of dresser is 33". Mirror measures 32" by 34". Available in Champagne and Wheat finishes.

C3791   *RIO 3-DRAWER DRESSER*   *1943–44*
Top is 20" by 42". Height is 33". Available in Champagne and Wheat finishes.

C3792   *RIO 4-DRAWER CHEST*   *1943–44*
Top measures 19" by 32". Height is 45". Available in Champagne and Wheat finishes.

THE RIO GROUP

C3798   *RIO NIGHT STAND*   *1943–44*
Top is 13" by 13" and height is 25½". Available in Champagne and Wheat finishes.

C3797   *VANITY POUFFE*   *1943–44*
Revolving top pouffe fitted with cotton filled cushion. Top is 20" in diameter and height is 17". Available in Champagne and Wheat finishes.

C3796   *RIO VANITY WITH MIRROR*   *1943–44*
Deluxe vanity with attached mirror. Top measures 18" by 49" and base height is 21½". Overall height is 61½". Available in Champagne and Wheat finishes.

Heywood

The Victory Group

C4140   VICTORY BED   1943–44
Available in 3' 3" or 4' 6" sizes. Available in Champagne or Wheat finishes.

C4141   VICTORY DRESSER BASE   1943–44
Dresser top measures 40" by 19". Height is 33½". Available in Champagne or Wheat finishes.

C4143   HANGING MIRROR   1943–44
Hanging mirror plate measures 28" by 22". Available in Champagne or Wheat finishes.

C4141–795   VICTORY DRESSER WITH MIRROR   1943–44
Dresser top measures 40" by 19". Height is 33½". Mirror plate measures 32" by 34". Available in Champagne or Wheat finishes.

THE VICTORY GROUP

C4144   *VICTORY VANITY BASE*   *1943–44*
Top measures 44" by 18" and height is 25". Available in Champagne or Wheat finishes.

VICTORY NIGHT STAND
C4148   *1943–44*
Compartment has hinged door. Top is 13" by 14". Height is 24". Available in Champagne or Wheat finishes.

C4142   *VICTORY 4-DRAWER DRESSER*   *1943–44*
Top measures 32" by 19" and height is 42½". Available in Champagne or Wheat finishes.

VICTORY VANITY BENCH
C4147   *1943–44*
Slip seat upholstered top measures 22" by 16". Height is 16". Available in Champagne or Wheat finishes.

C4146   *VICTORY VANITY WITH MIRROR*   *1943–44*
Top of vanity base measures 44" by 18". Height is 24½". Mirror plate measures 28" by 34". Available in Champagne or Wheat finishes.

C3965   EXTENSION TABLE   *1943–44*

Fitted with one extension leaf. Top measures 30" by 50" with leaf in and 30" by 40" without leaf. Available in Champagne and Wheat finishes.

C4154 G   EXTENSION TABLE   *1943–44*

Table fitted with two leaves. With leaves installed top is 42" by 84", without leaves, 42" by 60". Available in Champagne or Wheat finishes.

C3970   *STRAIGHT FRONT BOOKCASE*   *1941–44*
Bookcase is fitted with adjustable shelves. Top measures 36" by 11"
and height is 32½". Available in Champagne and Wheat finishes.

C3971   *CORNER BOOKCASE*   *1941–44*
Overall measurements are 28" by 28". Height is 32½". Available in
Champagne and Wheat finishes.

C3994 C   *CHANNEL BACK ARM CHAIR*   *1941–44*
Seat measures 20" by 22". Height of back is 19". Yardage required is 3
yards of 54" material. Available in Champagne and Wheat finishes.

THE KOHINOOR SUITE

The Kohinoor Suite was named for the famous British diamond. Designed by Ernest Herrmann, it featured concave and convex drawer fronts, which was something new for the Modern furniture line when first introduced.

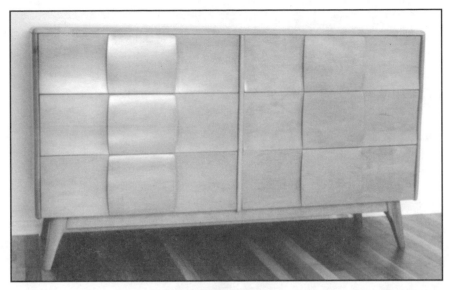

M 144   *Kohinoor Mr. & Mrs. Dresser*   *1949–51*
Size of top 56" by 19". Height 32½".

M 148   *Kohinoor Night Stand*   *1949–51*
Size of top 20" by 16". Height 24".

M 146   *Kohinoor Vanity*   *1949–51*
Base has tambour door and measures 50" by 18". Height of base
23". Overall height 58". Plate glass size 44" by 36".

KOHINOOR DRESSER WITH DECK TOP
M 149 ON M 141   *1949–51*
Dresser measures 44" wide, 19" deep, 32½" high. Deck top is a separate piece which adds two more drawers. It measures 42" wide, 17½" deep, 10½" high. Overall height is 43".

KOHINOOR DRESSER WITH ATTACHED MIRROR
M 141– M145   *1949–51*
Size of top 44" by 19". Height is 32½". Glass size 36" by 28".

KOHINOOR VANITY BENCH

M 147   *1949–51*

Revolving top measures 20" in diameter. Height 17". Yardage required: 1 yard of 54" material.

M 546   *KOHINOOR DESK / VANITY*   *1949*

This Modern design styled to the Kohinoor bedroom grouping serves as both a vanity and desk. The base measures 50" by 22" and base height is 28". Fitted with Tambour doors. Plate glass is 38" wide by 26" high. Overall height is 54".

M 142   *KOHINOOR CHEST*   *1949–51*

Size of top 34" by 19". Height 45".

M 140   *KOHINOOR BED*   *1949–51*
Available in 3' 3" and 4' 6" sizes. Also available as a footless bed M 140 X.

THE RIVIERA BEDROOM SUITE

Heywood-Wakefield introduced the Riviera Bedroom Suite at the Chicago Furniture Mart in January, 1947. While the Riviera was heralded as the company's first new post-war modern bedroom suite, it was not really new at all, but a restyled version of the World War II era Rio Bedroom Suite.

M 186   *RIVIERA VANITY*   *1947–48*
Top measures 18" by 49". Height is 21½".

M 187   *REVOLVING POUFFE*   *1947–48*
Diameter 20". Height 17".

M 182   RIVIERA 4-DRAWER CHEST   *1947–48*
Chest stands 45" high with a top that measures 32" by 19".

Not Shown:
M 181   RIVIERA 3-DRAWER DRESSER   *1947–48*
The top measures 20" by 42". It stands 33" high.

M 188   RIVIERA NIGHT STAND   *1947–48*
Top measures 13" by 13". It stands 28½" high.

M 180   RIVIERA BED   *1947–48*
Available in 3' 3" and 4' 6" sizes.

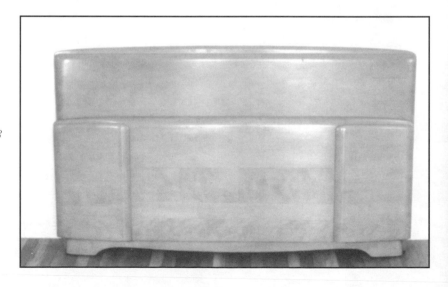

modern

. . . with a "nice-to-live-with" look

Heywood-Wakefield's distinctly pleasant flow of line warms your heart to Modern as Modern should be. "Home Planned" designs and light finishes assure harmony of feeling as you add pieces to living room, dining room, bedroom. Ask for this livable new Modern by Heywood-Wakefield at better furniture and department stores.

HEYWOOD-WAKEFIELD
EST. 1826
GARDNER, MASS.

| M 116 | *DELUXE VANITY* | *1947–48* |

Mirror has 38" high glass plate.

| M 117 | *VANITY BENCH* | *1947–48* |

Vanity Bench has coil spring seat.

Shown Below:

| M 110 | *BED* | *1947–48* |

Available in 3' 3" or 4' 6" sizes.

| M 118 | *NIGHT STAND* | *1947–48* |

Fitted with two small drawers and a compartment for a small radio or telephone.

| M 114 | *MR. & MRS. DRESSER* | *1947–48* |

Heywood-Wakefield's first Mr. and Mrs. Dresser.

| M 135 | *HANGING MIRROR* | *1947* |

Mirror has plate glass that is 40" long by 28" high.

Heywood

M 112   5-DRAWER CHEST   *1947–48*
Two small drawers on top instead of one large drawer.

M 111   3-DRAWER DRESSER   *1947–48*
Designed to line up perfectly with bottom three drawers of
M 112 Chest when placed side by side.

M 115   HANGING MIRROR   *1947–48*
Wood trim at bottom of mirror.

ENC**O**RE BEDROOM

The Encore bedroom group was introduced in 1949, and featured drawer pulls, which extended almost the full length of each drawer at the top edge. The style was quite popular and Heywood-Wakefield added new pieces and discontinued older ones until 1956, when an all new Encore suite was introduced.

M 510	*BED*	1948–53

Bed was available in 3' 3" and 4' 6" sizes. Also available without footboard as M 510 X.

M 518	*ENCORE NIGHT STAND*	1948–55

Fitted with adjustable shelf. Top measures 15" by 14". Height is 26".

ENCORE MR. & MRS. DRESSER

M 524		1948–55

Top measures 54" wide by 19" deep. Height is 34".

M 525	*LARGE MIRROR*	1948–59

The M 525 mirror was available with looped clips for hanging, or could be attached to a dresser. Plate glass size is 40" wide by 28" high. It was also available in the Contract Package.

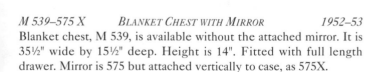

M 539–575 X   BLANKET CHEST WITH MIRROR   1952–53
Blanket chest, M 539, is available without the attached mirror. It is 35½" wide by 15½" deep. Height is 14". Fitted with full length drawer. Mirror is 575 but attached vertically to case, as 575X.

M 536   *ENCORE VANITY*   *1950–53*

Fitted with full length mirror, plate glass shelf, and pin tray in top drawer. Overall height is 65". Wood pier measures 26" by 18". Overall width 54". Height of base 24".

M 537   *VANITY BENCH*   *1950–53*

Spring filled top measures 26" wide by 17" deep. Height is 15". Yardage required: 1½ yards of 54" material, or 2 yards of 36" material.

M 577   *VANITY BENCH*   *1951–52*

Revolving top measures 20" in diameter. Height is 17". Yardage required: 1 yard of 54" material.

M 587   *VANITY BENCH*   *1953*
Spring filled top measures 31" long by 25" wide. Height 15". Yardage
required: 1¾ yards of 54" material.

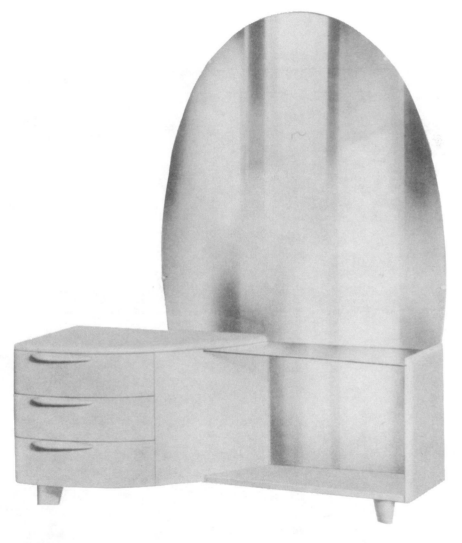

ENCORE DELUXE VANITY
M 586   *1953–54*
Fitted with full length mirror and plate
glass shelf. Overall height 62½". Overall width 50". Depth of base 18",
height of base 20".

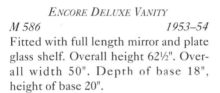

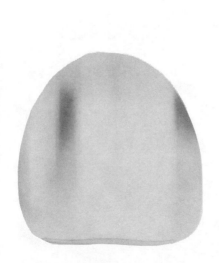

M 583   *HANGING MIRROR*   *1953*
Plate glass size 32" wide by 34" high.

191

M 516   *VANITY*   *1948–49*
The 4-drawer base is 49" by 18". The overall vanity height is 60". The mirror is shield shaped plate glass that measures 38" by 42".

M 517   *VANITY BENCH*   *1948–49*
Bench has a spring filled top that measures 22" by 15". It stands 16" high. Yardage required is 1 yard of 54" material.

M 538   *ENCORE NIGHT STAND*   *1950–55*
Fitted with drawer. Open back for telephone or radio wires. Tier top measures 19" by 13". Overall width 20", depth 16", height 26".

ENCORE DOUBLE CHEST
M 532   *1954–55*
This double chest has seven drawers.
Top measures 44" by 19". Height is 46".

M 523   *ENCORE UTILITY CASE*   *1948–54*
Top measures 30" by 19" deep. Height is 34". A pair of
these cases forms an extra wide Mr. and Mrs. dresser
arrangement.

M 529–575   *ENCORE TRIPLE DRESSER WITH MIRROR*   *1952–55*
Fitted with nine drawers. Top measures 60" by 19". Height is 34". Mirror M 575 has plate glass 50" by 34".

M 780 4/6   *CABINET UTILITY HEADBOARD*   *1952–55*
This 4' 6" headboard is 82" wide, including the built-in night stands. It is 11" deep and 32½" high. Night stands have drop-door that level into shelves. Also Shown: M 567 C Ladies' Pull-Up Chair.

M 534   *ENCORE UTILITY CABINET*   *1950–53*
Useful as a server, china base, dresser, or living room
piece. Grain runs horizontal on sides to eliminate
sticky or loose drawers with temperature changes.
Center drawer glides. Top measures 34" by 15½".
Height is 32½".

ENCORE 4-DRAWER DRESSER WITH MIRROR
M 521–525   *1948–55*
Fitted with pin tray in top drawer. Top measures 42"
wide by 19" deep. Height is 34". Mirror has plate glass
40" wide by 28" high.

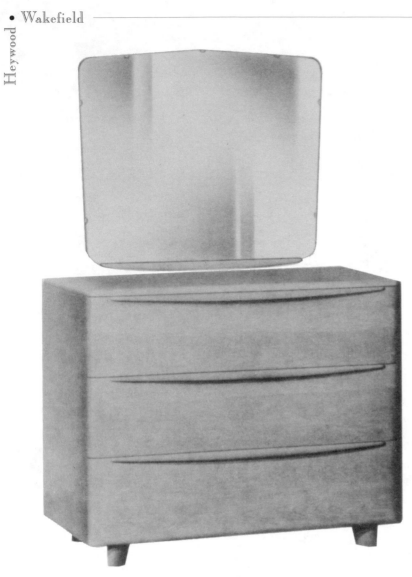

ENCORE 3-DRAWER DRESSER WITH MIRROR
M 511–515   *1948–50*
Top measures 42" by 19" and the height is 34".
Over the dresser is the shield-shaped mirror M 515.
It has a wood trimmed base and measures 34" wide
and 28" high.

M 512   *ENCORE 4-DRAWER CHEST*   *1948–50*
Top measures 32" by 19" . Height is 42".

M 923   *CHEST MIRROR*   *1954–55*
This chest mirror is designed to fit on any chest in the
Heywood-Wakefield line. Mirror has a plate-glass size
24" wide by 12" high. It cannot be attached and is
readily movable.

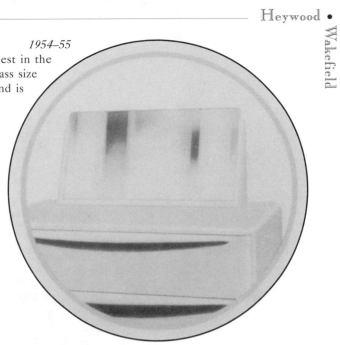

M 522   *ENCORE 5-DRAWER CHEST*   *1948–55*
Top measures 34" by 19". Height is 46".

M 520   *SHELF HEADBOARD BED*   *1952–53*
Available in 3' 3" and 4' 6" sizes. Overall length of single headboard 40½"; of double headboard 55½". Overall height 34½". Shelf
height 32½" . Fitted with Seng frame equipped with pin hinges so
that metal frame can be swung in either direction or removed
completely.

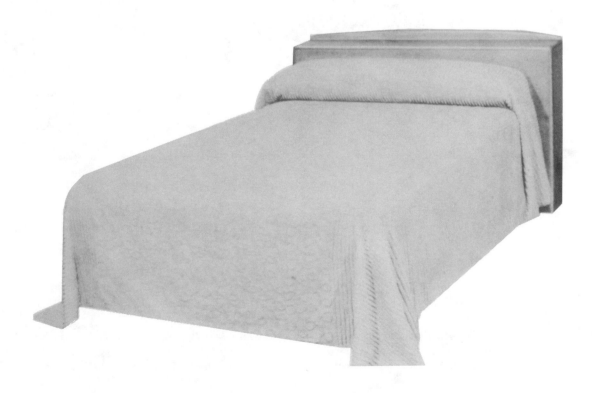

UTILITY HEADBOARD
M 540   *1950–53*
Available in 3' 3" and 4' 6" sizes. Double headboard is 55½" wide; single size is 27¼" wide. Depth 9", height 40". Headboard has three compartments fitted with two ribbed sliding door panels.

M 540 6/6   *DOUBLE UTILITY HEADBOARD WITH SWING-APART TWIN BED FRAMES*   *1953–54*
Each twin headboard has three compartments fitted with two solid wood, ribbed sliding door panels. Double (6' 6") headboard consists of two single headboards clamped together; can be used as twin beds. Headboard is 81" wide, 9" deep, and 40" high.

M 530   *BED*   *1950–53*
Bed was available in 3' 3" and 4' 6" sizes.
Also available as a footless bed M 530 X.

M 790 6/6   *DOUBLE UTILITY HEADBOARD*   *1953–54*
One-piece headboard is 81" wide, 37" high, and 11" deep. Closed center section has sliding doors and open end sections to accommodate books, a small radio, and other bedside accessories. With two single bed frames.

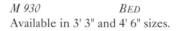

UTILITY HEADBOARD

M 790   1953–55

Available in 3' 3" and 4' 6" sizes. Shelf headboard has three compartments and two sliding, solid wood door panels. Twin headboard is 40½" wide, 37" high, and 10" deep; the double size is 55½" wide. The metal frame that supports the mattress is fitted with pin hinges which permits the frame to be swung either left or right, or removed completely from the headboard.

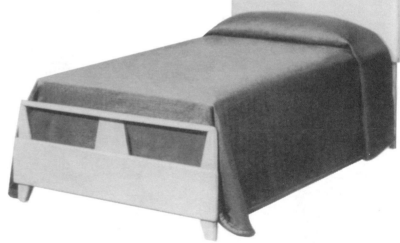

M 930   *BED*   *1954–55*

Available in 3' 3" and 4' 6" sizes.

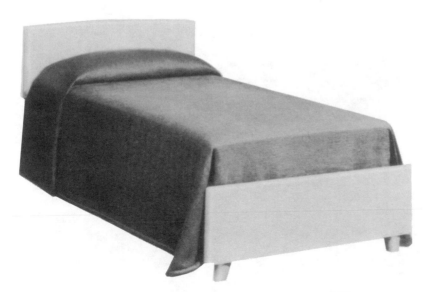

M 920   *BED*   *1954–55*

Available in 3' 3" and 4' 6" sizes.

M 578   TROPHY SUITE NIGHT STAND   1951–52
Size of top 20" by 16". Height is 24".

TROPHY SUITE DELUXE VANITY
M 576   1951–52
Base measures 50" by 18". Height
of base 23". Plate glass size 44" by
36". Overall height is 58".

TROPHY SUITE MR. AND MRS. DRESSER WITH MIRROR
M 574–575   1951–52
Top measures 56" by 19". Height is 32". Mirror
plate glass size is 50" by 34".

M 572   *TROPHY SUITE CHEST*   1951–52
Size of top 34" by 19". Height is 44".

TROPHY SUITE DRESSER WITH MIRROR
M 571–573   1951–52
Size of top is 44" by 19". Height is 32". Mirror
available only as attached mirror. Plate glass size
34" wide by 32" high.

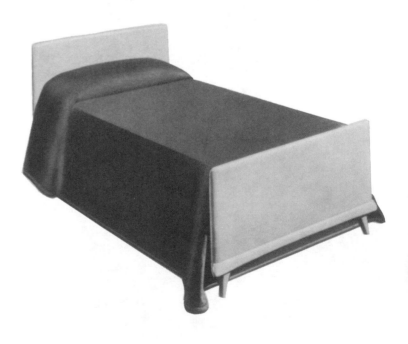

M 570   *TROPHY SUITE BED*   1951–52
Available in 3' 3" and 4' 6" sizes. Also available as a footless bed M 570 X.

202

THE SCULPTURA SUITE

The Sculptura Suite featured drawer fronts with built-in pulls that curved in and out like folded ribbons. Along with Encore, the Sculptura line was the other truly successful Modern bedroom group, lasting for seven years. This suite was a result of the collaborative work of designers Ernest Herrmann, Leo Jiranek, Frank Parrish, and W. Joseph Carr.

M 770	*BED*	*1952–59*

Bed was available in 3' 3" and 4' 6" sizes. Also available as a footless bed, M 770 X, and as a king size footless bed, M 770 6' 6" in 1956.

M 772	*SCULPTURA CHEST*	*1952–59*

Fitted with four drawers; top drawer has removable shirt partition. Top measures 38" by 19". Height is 39".

M 778	*SCULPTURA NIGHT STAND*	*1952–59*

Fitted with drawer. Overall width 20". Overall depth 16". Height 24".

M 779–575	*SCULPTURA TRIPLE DRESSER WITH MIRROR*	*1952–59*

Fitted with nine drawers. Top measures 62" by 19". Height is 31". Mirror has 50" by 34" plate glass. Mirror attaches flush to dresser with two-bracket stationary standard.

SCULPTURA SINGLE DRESSER WITH MIRROR
M 771–525   1952–56
Top measures 46" by 19". Height is 31". Attached mirror has 40" by 28" plate glass.

M 776   *SCULPTURA VANITY*   1952–59
Plate glass mirror which extends to bottom shelf, measures 42" high by 38" wide. Plate glass shelf. Vanity base is 50" wide by 18" deep. Base height is 20".

M 777   *VANITY BENCH*   1952–59
Revolving spring filled top measures 20" in diameter. Height is 16". Yardage required: 1 yard of 54" material.

M 778   *SCULPTURA NIGHT STAND*   1952–59
Fitted with drawer. Overall width is 20", overall depth is 16", and the height is 24".

11221

200.00

8/7/2004

Sonia E. Ayerdi
Maid

CITIBANK   8/3 & 8/7

PAYMENT
RECORD

11221

200.00

8/7/2004

Sonia E. Ayerdi
Maid

CITIBANK   8/3 & 8/7

wheat 1774 Dessau

wheat 792

SCULPTURA DECK TOP ON SCULPTURA SINGLE DRESSER
M 781 ON M 771   *1952–53*
Dresser top is 46" by 19". Height is 31". Deck-top is designed to fit on top of Sculptura 3-drawer chest. Top measures 42" by 16". Height is 19".

SCULPTURA MR. & MRS. DRESSER WITH MIRROR
M 774–525   *1952–59*
Fitted with six drawers. Top measures 56" by 19". Height is 31". Plate glass size is 40" wide by 28" high. Mirror is attached with two-bracket, adjustable, tilting standard.

M 792   *SCULPTURA 5-DRAWER CHEST*   *1953–59*
Fitted with five drawers; second drawer has removable shirt partition. Size of top is 38" by 19". Height is 48".

CONTRACT FURNITURE

Heywood-Wakefield was a large producer of furniture for commercial and institutional use. The Contract Furniture line was designed for use by various businesses, hotels, hospitals, government facilities, and institutions. The model numbers for this type of furniture has the prefix "CM." This furniture was not usually available for sale to the general public.

CM 1911   *BACHELOR'S CHEST WITH PLASTIC TOP*   1958
Two are shown: Fitted with matching laminated plastic top and three drawers. The top measures 30" by 19". It is 30" high. Available only in the Contract Package.

CM 1915   *TABLE DESK WITH PLASTIC TOP*   1958
Shown between the two chests: Fitted with matching laminated plastic top. Desk measures 36" by 19". It is 30" high. Available only in the Contract Package.

M 1560   *BED WITH OR WITHOUT FOOTBOARD*   1958–65
Available in 3' 3" or 4' 6" sizes and with or without footboard. The suffix H is used to denote without footboard.

M 549 C   *CAPTAINS CHAIR*   1953–66
Seat measures 20" wide by 17" deep. Height of back is 14". Overall height is 30".

M 1533   *HANGING MIRROR*   1958–66
This hanging mirror has plate glass 36" by 28", the overall size of the mirror is 38" by 30". The mirror may be hung vertically or horizontally.

CM 1908   *NIGHT TABLE WITH PLASTIC TOP*   1958
Fitted with matching laminated plastic top. The top measures 18" by 16". It is 24" high. Available only in the Contract Package.

CM 1927   *ARM CHAIR*   1958
Fitted with "Wall-Saver" legs. Overall dimensions: 27" wide; 32½" deep; 30" high. 2 yards of 54" material required.

CM 1914–1535   *DOUBLE DRESSER WITH PLASTIC TOP AND ATTACHED MIRROR*   1958
Dresser has matching plastic top. Fitted with six drawers it measures 54" wide by 19" deep. It is 30" high. Overall size of mirror is 42" by 28". The dresser is available only in the Contract Package.

CM 1912   *4-DRAWER CHEST WITH PLASTIC TOP*   1958
Chest has matching laminated plastic top and is fitted with four drawers. Top measures 36" by 19". It is 37½" high. Available only in the Contract Package.

M 1560   *BED WITH OR WITHOUT FOOTBOARD*   1958–65
Available in 3' 3" or 4' 6" sizes and with or without footboard. The suffix H is used to denote without footboard.

CM 1917   *LUGGAGE BENCH*   1958
Upholstered top measures 26" by 17". Height is 18". Available only in the Contract Package. Yardage required: ¾ yard of 54" material.

CM 1916   *DESK/DRESSER*   1958
The desk has matching plastic top and is fitted with four drawers. Top measures 54" by 19" and the height is 30". This desk was available only in the Contract Package.

M 1551 A   *SIDE CHAIR*   1956–66
The seat measures 18" by 16" and the overall height is 31½". Yardage required: ½ yard of 54" material.

CM 716   *DRESSER / DESK*   *1956–57*
The plastic top of this dresser desk measures 48" wide by 19"
deep. It stands 30" high. It was only available in the Contract
Package. Also Shown: M 552 A Side Chair, M 525 Hanging Mirror.

CM 708   *NIGHT STAND*   *1956–57*
The plastic top of this night stand mea-
sures 18" wide by 16" deep. It is 25" high.
It was only available in the Contract
Package.

CM 712   *4-DRAWER CHEST*   *1956–57*
The plastic top measures 36" wide by 19" deep. The
height of the chest is 37½". It was only available in the
Contract Package.

CM 714   Double Dresser   1956–57
This six drawer Mr. and Mrs. Dresser
has a plastic top that measures 48" wide
by 19" deep. It is 30" high. It was only
available in the Contract Package.

CM 715   Table / Desk   1956–57
The plastic top of this table measures 36" wide by 19"
deep. It stands 30" high and is fitted with a desk drawer. It was only available in the Contract Package.

CM 717   Luggage Bench   1956–57
The upholstered top of this bench measures 26" wide by 17"
deep. It is 18" high and ¾ of a yard of 54" material is required. It
was only available in the Contract Package.

THE HARMONIC BEDROOM

The Harmonic bedroom group was introduced in 1954 along with a Harmonic dining group. According to Heywood-Wakefield sales literature, Harmonic featured "a rhythmic flow of lines...a contrast of light and shadows...a harmonious combination of good styling, sound construction, and solid value."

M 910   *HARMONIC BED*   *1954*
Available in 3' 3" and 4' 6" sizes. Headboard height is 35", footboard height is 18".

M 911–573   *HARMONIC DRESSER WITH MIRROR*   *1954*
Two-bracket arrangement mounts mirror to dresser top flush and stationary. Mirror M 573 has plate glass 34" by 42". Dresser top measures 46" by 19". Height is 31".

M 912   *HARMONIC 5-DRAWER CHEST*   *1954*
Top measures 38" by 19". Height is 45½".

M 916   HARMONIC DESK / VANITY   *1954*
This desk/vanity is fully finished at the back and
will not, therefore, accommodate an attached mirror. Size of top is 44" by 22". Height is 30".

M 777   VANITY BENCH   *1952–59*
Revolving spring filled top measures 20" in diameter. Height is 16". Yardage required: 1 yard of 54"
material.

M 914   HARMONIC MR. & MRS. DRESSER   *1954*
This 6-drawer double dresser has a top that measures 60" by 19". Height is 31".

HARMONIC NIGHT STAND / LAMP TABLE
M 918   *1954*
Fitted with drawer and shelf. Top measures
20" by 18". Height is 25½".

THE ENCORE BEDROOM

An all new Encore bedroom group was introduced in 1956. This group had two features which had not been seen in the Modern line since the late 1930s. The group re-employed the use of cane panels and drawer pulls that were made out of something other than wood. With the introduction of the new group, Encore case goods could be ordered with either legs or bases that went to the floor. All cases that went to the floor were furnished with ball-bearing swivel caster dollies.

M 1509   *ENCORE CANE DOOR CHEST*   *1956–59*
Fitted with two cane door compartments. The left compartment has two trays and the right is equipped with an adjustable shelf. Chest measures 40" wide, 19" deep, 50" high.

M 1514–1525   *DOUBLE DRESSER WITH MIRROR*   *1956–61*
Fitted with six drawers. Top measures 56" by 19". Height is 32". Mirror has plate glass 34" by 52". Mirror is attached to case top flush and stationary with two-bracket standard. Overall height of dresser and mirror is 68".

M 1530 4/6 WITH M 1518   *UTILITY HEADBOARD BED WITH NIGHT STANDS*   *1956*
Headboard is fitted with two open front end compartments. Sliding doors have cane panels. Bed has Seng or Harvard metal frame. Headboard is 101½" wide, 37" high, 10¼" deep. This bed was also available with footboard as M 1530 4/6X . Available with wood sliding doors as M 1530 4/6 WD. Pier cabinets not included.

ENCORE LAMP TABLE / NIGHT STAND
M 1538   *1958–59*
Fitted with one drawer. Has closed back. Overall
size is 19" wide, 15" deep, 25" high.

ENCORE 3-DRAWER DECK ON SINGLE DRESSER
M 1531 ON M 1521   *1956*
M 1531 deck is fitted with three full length drawers with center partition
in each drawer. Deck is 39½" wide, 17" deep, 19" high. Single dresser has
four drawers. Dresser top measures 42" by 19". Height is 32". Overall
height of deck and dresser is 51".

M 1511   *BACHELOR'S CHEST*   *1958–59*
Fitted with four drawers. Top measures 30"
by 18". Height is 31".

M 1521   *SINGLE DRESSER*   *1956*
Fitted with four drawers. Top measures 42" by 19". Height is 32".

213

M 1500   *ENCORE BED*   *1956–66*
Above: Available in 3' 3" and 4' 6" sizes with or without a footboard. The suffix H in the model number denotes no footboard. Metal frame was furnished with footless bed. Also available in the Contract Package.

M 1528   *ENCORE NIGHT STAND*   *1956–66*
Above: Fitted with drawer. Night Stand measures 20" wide, 15" deep, 25" high.

M 1508   *ENCORE NIGHT STAND*   *1956*
Right: Drop front conceals storage space fitted with tray/drawer. Back wall is white Plastone. Top measures 22" by 17½". Height is 26".

M 1510   *PANEL BED*   *1956*
Below: Available in 3' 3" and 4' 6" sizes. This bed was also available without footboard as M 1510 3/3H or 4/6H.

M 1512   ENCORE 5-DRAWER CHEST   1956–61
Fitted with five drawers. Top measures 36" by 19".
Height is 44".

ENCORE TRIPLE DRESSER WITH MIRROR
M 1529–1525   1956–66
Fitted with twelve drawers. Top measures 62" by
19". Height of dresser is 32". Mirror has plate glass
34" by 52". Mirror is attached to case top flush and
stationary with two-bracket standard. Overall
height of dresser and mirror is 68".

ENCORE CABINET UTILITY HEADBOARD BED
M 1540   1956–57
Available as 4' 6" only. Headboard has built-in
night stands. Night stands have drop doors. Fitted
with Seng or Harvard metal frame.

ENCORE DOUBLE DRESSER WITH MIRROR
M 1514–1515   *1956–57*
Fitted with six drawers. Top measures 56" by 19". Height is 32". Mirror has plate glass 32" by 44". Mirror is attached to case top flush and stationary with two-bracket standard. Overall height of dresser and mirror is 68".

ENCORE NIGHT STAND / PIER CABINET
M 1518   *1956*
Equipped with three drawers. Top measures 22" by 17". Height is 26".

ENCORE TRIPLE DRESSER WITH ATTACHED MIRROR
M 1519–1525   *1956*
Fitted with nine drawers. Top measures 62" by 19". Height of dresser is 32". Mirror has plate glass 34" by 52". Mirror is attached to case top flush and stationary with two-bracket standard. Overall height of dresser and mirror 68".

M 1520   *UTILITY HEADBOARD BED*   *1956–66*
Available in 3' 3" and 4' 6" and 6' 6" sizes. The 3/3 and 4/6 beds are available with foot
boards as M 1520 X. Available with cane doors as M 1520 CD.

M 1522   *ENCORE 5-DRAWER CHEST*   *1956–66*
Fitted with five drawers. Top drawer has a removable
shirt partition. Chest has four swivel caster wheels. Top
measures 38" by 19". Height is 44".

ENCORE DOUBLE DRESSER WITH MIRROR
M 1524–1515   *1956–66*
Fitted with eight drawers. Top measures 56" by 19". Height of
dresser is 32". Mirror has plate glass 32" by 44". Mirror attached with
two-bracket, adjustable, tilting standard. Overall height of mirror
and dresser is 67".

217

ENCORE DOUBLE DRESSER WITH MIRROR
M 1534–1533   1958–59
Fitted with six drawers. Top measures 52" by
18". Height 31". Mirror has plate glass 36" by
28". Mirror is attached with two bracket,
adjustable, tilting standard. Overall height of
dresser and mirror is 62".

ENCORE TAMBOUR DECK UTILITY CABINET ON
SINGLE DRESSER
M 1536 ON M 1521   1956
M 1536 Deck Cabinet is fitted with two Tambour sliding doors and contour-front
adjustable shelf. Deck is 39½" wide, 17" deep,
and 19" high. Dresser has four drawers. Top
measures 42" by 19", height 32". Overall
height of deck and dresser is 51".

ENCORE TRIPLE DRESSER WITH MIRROR
M 1539–1535   1958–59
Fitted with nine drawers. Top measures 58"
by 18". Height 31". Mirror has plate glass 40"
by 28". Mirror is attached to dresser with a
two-bracket, adjustable, tilting standard.
Overall height of mirror and dresser is 62".

M 1582   *ENCORE 5-DRAWER CHEST*   *1958–59*
Fitted with five drawers. The third drawer has a removable shirt partition. Top measures 34" by 18". Height is 43".

M 1920   *KING-SIZE HEADBOARD*   *1962–65*
One-piece paneled headboard has full-length cap. Headboard is fitted with two "Swing-Away" metal bed frames which can be locked together. Available in 6' 6" size only. No footboard. Width: 82½", height: 37½".

M 1930   *ENCORE BOOKCASE HEADBOARD BED*   *1958–59*
Available in 3' 3" and 4' 6" sizes. Headboard is 33" high and 8½" deep.

ENCORE UTILITY HEADBOARD
M 1940   *1958–61*
Headboard has open cabinet at each end fitted with drawer. Available only in 4' 6" size. Headboard is 91" wide, 32" high, and 12" deep.

THE SYMPHONIC BEDROOM

M 1932   SYMPHONIC 4-DRAWER CHEST   1958–59
Fitted with four drawers. Second drawer is extra deep for shirts; removable partition. Chest top measures 34" by 18". Height is 43".

SYMPHONIC DOUBLE DRESSER WITH HANGING MIRROR
M 1934 WITH M 1533   *1958–59*
Fitted with six drawers. Top measures 52" by 18". Height is 31". Hanging Mirror has plate glass 36" by 28". Mirror may be hung vertically or horizontally. It is fitted with hanging clips for use with wire.

M 1938   SYMPHONIC NIGHT STAND   1958–59
Fitted with one drawer. Has closed back. Overall
size of night table is 19" wide, 15" deep, 25" high.

BED WITH OR WITHOUT FOOTBOARD
M 1560   1958–65
Available in 3' 3" or 4' 6" sizes and with or without
footboard. The suffix H is used to denote with-
out footboard. Available also in the Contract
Package.

SYMPHONIC TRIPLE DRESSER
WITH ATTACHED MIRROR
M 1939–1535   1958–59
Fitted with nine drawers. Top measures 58" by
18". Height is 31". Mirror has plate glass 40" by
28". Mirror is attached to dresser with a two-
bracket, adjustable, tilting standard. Overall
height of dresser and mirror is 62".

CABINETS, UTILITY CASES, DESKS, AND BOOKCASES

M 926   *VANITY DESK*   *1954–56*
Steam-bent drawer fronts. Top measures 50" by 22". Height is 30". Also Shown: M554 A Side Chair.

M 327 W   TABLE DESK   *1950–54*
This table desk can be used as a server, dressing table, foyer piece, or as a desk. Top measures 40" by 20". Height 30".

M 328 W   DESK BOOKCASE   *1951–54*
This large utility wall piece is especially useful as a storage unit. Fitted with three drawers and adjustable bookcase shelves. Front panel door forms desk writing surface 29" high. "Pigeon-hole" desk section is adjustable for height and is removable for added storage space. Size of top is 60" wide by 13" deep. Overall height is 42".

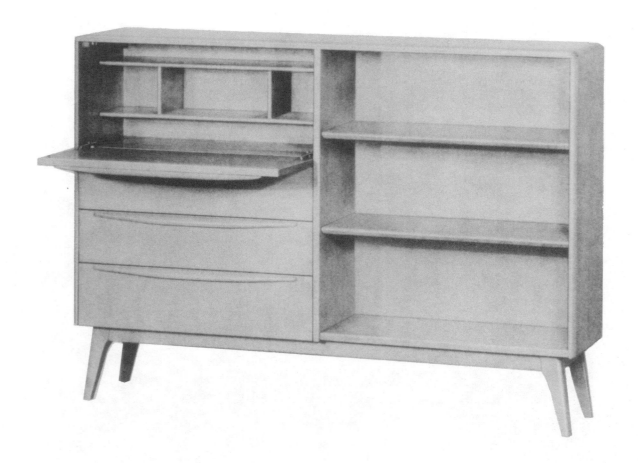

M 389 W   *DESK CHEST*   *1952–54*
Left: Top measures 30" by 13". Height is 42".
Desk top looks like drawer front when closed.

M 315 W   *KNEEHOLE DESK*   *1947–49*
Below: Finished in back with solid wood. Steam
bent drawer fronts. Deep file drawer on left. Top
measures 50" x 24". Height is 30". Note difference in feet from M320 W. Also Shown: M157 C
Arm Chair, M 321 Bookcase.

M 320 W   *KNEEHOLE DESK*   *1950–65*
Above: Finished in back with solid wood, not
veneer. Steam bent drawer fronts. Deep file drawer
on left. Top measures 50" by 24". Height is 30".
Note difference in feet from M 315 W.

M 783 W   *STUDENT'S DESK*   *1952–61*
Right: Finished in back with solid wood, not veneer.
Full length top drawer and file drawer at left. Top
measures 44" by 22". Height 30".

M 314 W   *STUDENT'S DESK*   *1950–51*
Below: Finished in back with solid wood, not
veneer. Adjustable shelf at right. Full length top
drawer and deep file drawer at left. Top measures
44" by 22". Height is 30".

One of the keys to Heywood-Wakefield's success was its flexibility, as displayed in the production of its bookcase and cabinet pieces. Many of these cases were built to a uniform 32½" height, allowing the pieces to be used in a variety of sectional arrangements. Among these cases are the M 326 cabinet bookcase, the M 528 pier cabinet, and the M 534 utility cabinet.

M 526   *UTILITY CABINET*   1952–53
Hinge construction permits full door swing in butted sectional arrangements. Fitted with two adjustable shelves. Top 34" by 15½". Height is 32½".

M 528   *PIER CABINET*   1952–54
Ideal for sectional wall arrangements or as a night table and bedroom piece where wall space is limited. Top measures 18" by 15½". Height is 32½".

M 322   *CORNER BOOKCASE*   1947–61
Above: Top measures 28" by 11". Height is 32½". Fitted with
two adjustable shelves.

M 326   *CABINET BOOKCASE*   1952–61
Right: Fitted with an adjustable shelf inside cabinet doors. This
piece lines up perfectly with M 321 and M 322 bookcases. Top
measures 36" by 11". Height is 32½".

M 321   *STRAIGHT BOOKCASE*   1947–65
Below: Fitted with two adjustable shelves. Top measures 36" by
11". Height 32½".

M 934 W   STARTER CHEST WITH DESK DRAWER   1954
Above: Fitted with desk drawer at top. Top measures 32" by 18". Height is 32½".

M 934   STARTER CHEST   1954
Below: Top measures 32" wide by 18" deep. Height is 32½" which is the same as bookcases and many utility cabinets.

TAMBOUR DOORS

The tambour door (or shutter), according to Heywood-Wakefield, "[came] from the French influence in the period of Louis XVI." Following the end of World War II Heywood-Wakefield revived tambour door use and improved the tambour construction process. Instead of gluing individual strips of wood to the flexible duck material, with the new process solid wood panels were glued to the fabric. Then the wood panels were grooved to the duck, allowing for an evenness of wood grain not possible when gluing individual strips.

M 179   *TAMBOUR UTILITY CASE*   *1950–54*
Above: This tambour front case is 32½" high to fit in with sectional bookcase units. Fitted with an adjustable shelf inside. Roomy enough for small radio, record player, and records. Top measures 24" wide by 17" deep.

M 178   *TAMBOUR FRONT 4-DRAWER CHEST*   *1947–48*
Right and Below: Tambour front hides four drawers in metal frame. Top is 44½" by 20". Height is 34".

229

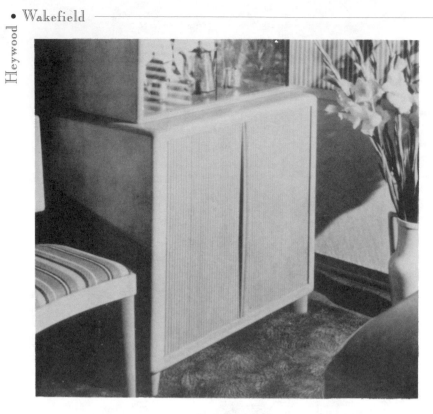

M 177   *TAMBOUR FRONT CHEST*   *1947–48*
Top Left: Tambour hides 4 drawers on a steel frame. Height 32½".
Width approximately 34", depth unknown.

M 1925   *CORNER CABINET*   *1958–59*
Top Right: Fitted with door and adjustable shelf. Top measures 24" by
24". Height is 30".

M 1924   *WALL CABINET*   *1958–59*
Left: Fitted with two doors and one adjustable shelf. Top measures 24"
by 24". Height is 30".

M 1923   *CORNER DESK*   *1958–59*
Bottom Left: Fitted with one drawer. Mounted on three legs. Top measures 31" by 31". Height is 30".

M 1922   *CORNER BOOKCASE*   *1958–59*
Fitted with adjustable shelf. Top measures 24" by 24".
Height is 30".

M 1921   *STRAIGHT BOOKCASE*   *1958–59*
Fitted with adjustable shelf. Top measures 36" by
12". Height is 30".

M 504 UNDER M 505   *ROOM DIVIDER*   *1953–56*
The base has two distinctive sides for added usefulness and flexibility. Both sides are completely finished. The base can be
used as a room divider, or it can serve as a wall piece. The sliding tray under the base top has stops that prevent it from pulling
out all the way. Adjustable shelves on both sides and cabinets on the dining room end add to its usefulness. Base is 60" wide,
11" deep, and 30" high. The overall height is 60".

DINING ROOMS

M 163 G   *JUNIOR DINING EXTENSION TABLE*   *1947–49*
Top Left: Table is 34" wide and 50" long. Extended with one 14" leaf it becomes 64" long. It stands 34" high.

M 154 A   *SIDE CHAIR*   *1950–55*
Top Right: Seat measures 18" wide by 16" deep. Height of back is 16½". Yardage required: ½ yard of 54" material.

M 192   *3-DRAWER BUFFET*   *1948–50*
Below: Fitted with two adjustable shelves in each cabinet compartment. Top measures 48" wide by 18" deep. Height is 32½".

M175 ON M 190   *CHINA*   *1948–50*
The overall height of this china is 64½". Server base is 34" wide, 17" deep, and 32½" high. Plate glass top measures 32" wide, 14½" deep, and 32" high. Both the server and the hutch have adjustable shelves.

DINETTE EXTENSION TABLE
M 160 G   *1950*
Right: Fitted with a 10" leaf. Size of top closed 32" by 42"; open 32" by 52". Height 29".

LARGE DINING EXTENSION TABLE
M 165 G   *1947–52*
Middle Right: Fitted with center leg and two 15" leaves. Top measures 60" by 42" closed. Extends to 75" and 90". Height 29".

DROP-LEAF DINING TABLE
M 166 G   *1947–55*
Bottom Left: Fitted with modern gate legs. Top size, with both leaves down, 36" by 14"; with one leaf up, 36" by 37"; with both leaves up, 36" by 60". Height 29".

DROP-LEAF EXTENSION TABLE
M 167 G   *1949*
Bottom Right: With leaves down 26" wide. Expands to 94" by 40". Additional length by adding two 18" leaves. Stands 29" high.

233

M 168 G   OVAL DINING TABLE   1950
Fitted with 10" leaf. Top measures 32" by 48"
closed; open 32" by 58". Height is 29".

JUNIOR DINING EXTENSION TABLE
M 169 G   1950–55
Fitted with 14" leaf. Top measures
34" by 50" closed; 34" by 64" open.
Height 29".

JUNIOR DINING EXTENSION TABLE
M 189 G   1951–55
Fitted with 18" leaf with aprons to
match boxing. Top measures 36" by 54"
closed; 36" by 72" open. Height is 29".

M 197 G   PEDESTAL DROP-LEAF EXTENSION TABLE   1948–55
Above: Butterfly supports for drop-leaves keep table top level
when extended. Fitted with two 18" extension leaves. Top
measures 40" by 26" closed; 40" by 58" with drop leaves up;
40" by 94" with leaves up and extension leaves in place.
Height is 29".

M 199 G   CONSOLE EXTENSION TABLE   1950–52
Right and Below: Size of top closed is 38" by 20". Extends to
76" with three 12" leaves inserted and top extended. Fitted
with two folding legs under top for added support when
extended. Steam-bent front boxing. Height is 29".

M 313 G   *PIVOT TOP CONSOLE TABLE*   1951–52
Left: Useful as a tea or game table when fully opened up to
32" by 32" size. Space under top in boxing is useful for
storing ashtrays, cards, table games, etc. Size of top folded
is 32" by 16". Height is 29".

M 394 G   *SERVICE WAGON*   1951–52
Middle & Bottom Right: Fitted with ball-bearing caster wheels.
Roomy lower shelf. Size of top with leaves up is 48" by 38".
The size with the leaves down is 38" by 20". Height is 28½".

236

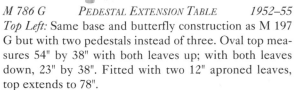

M 786 G   PEDESTAL EXTENSION TABLE   1952–55
Top Left: Same base and butterfly construction as M 197 G but with two pedestals instead of three. Oval top measures 54" by 38" with both leaves up; with both leaves down, 23" by 38". Fitted with two 12" aproned leaves, top extends to 78".

GAME DINING TABLE
M 787 G   1952–53
Top Right & Middle Left: Size of top with both leaves down, 22" by 36"; with both drop leaves raised 40" by 36". Top extends to 88" with four 12" leaves inserted.

EXTENSION GAME DINING TABLE
M 788 G   1953–54
Middle Right & Bottom Right: Fitted with two 15" leaves. Top measures 34" by 34" closed; with one leaf in 34" by 49"; with both leaves 34" by 64". Height is 29".

LARGE DINING EXTENSION TABLE
M 789 G   *1953–55*
Above: Fitted with center leg and two 15" leaves that can be stored under top when not in use. Top measures 60" by 42" closed; extends to 75" and 90". Height is 29".

M 950 G   ROUND EXTENSION TABLE   *1954–55*
Left: Size of top closed is 48" in diameter. With one 14" extension leaf top measures 62" long by 48" wide. Height is 29".

PLASTIC TOP DINING EXTENSION TABLE
M 952 G   *1955*
Below: This table is available only with Wheat, Champagne, or Platinum plastic top. Fitted with one 14" leaf with aprons to match boxing. Leaf can be stored under top when not in use. Top measures 34" by 48" closed; 34" by 62" when extended with leaf inserted.

HARMONIC DROP-LEAF EXTENSION TABLE
M 989 G   1954–55
Above: Table has a 42" by 26½" top with both leaves
down and no extension leaves inserted. With one
drop-leaf up, the top measures 45" by 42". With
both leaves up and no extension leaves inserted,
the top measures 63" by 42". With two 10" leaves
inserted and both drop leaves up, the top extends
to 83". Butterfly supports and center legs offer
added rigidity at every table size.

M 1549 G   DROP-LEAF EXTENSION TABLE   1956–66
Right: Size of top: with both leaves down, 42" by
26½"; with both leaves up, 42" by 63"; with both
leaves up and top extended with two 10" leaves
inserted, 42" by 83". Height 29".

M 1550 G   ROUND EXTENSION TABLE   1956
Below: Size of top: closed, 48" in diameter. Extended with 14" leaf inserted, 48" by 62". Height 29".

*Two-Pedestal Drop-Leaf
Extension Table*
M 1556 G   *1956–61*
Size of top: with both leaves down,
38" by 23"; with both leaves up, 38"
by 54"; with both leaves up and two
12" leaves inserted, 38" by 78".
Height 29".

*Three-Pedestal Drop-Leaf
Extension Table*
M 1557 G   *1956–66*
Size of top: with both leaves
down, 40" by 26"; with both
leaves up, 40" by 58"; with
both leaves up and two 18"
leaves inserted, 40" by 94".
Height 29".

*Encore Junior Dining
Extension Table*
M 1558 G   *1956–66*
Size of top: closed, 38" by 54";
top extended with 18" leaf insert-
ed is 38" by 72". Height 29".

LARGE DINING EXTENSION TABLE
M 1559 G   1956–61
Top: Size of top: closed, 42" by 60"; top extended with two 15" leaves inserted is 42" by 90". Height 29".

M 1566 G   DROP-LEAF DINING TABLE   1956
Middle: Size of top: with both leaves down, 36" by 14", with both leaves up 36" by 60". Height is 29".

M 1567 G   DINING EXTENSION TABLE   1958–59
Left: Size of top: closed, 36" by 48"; top extended with one 12", self-storing leaf, inserted, 60". Height is 29". Available with plastic top as M 1567 GP.

M 1568 G   Round Dining Extension Table   1958–59
Left: Size of top: 48" in diameter; top extends to 48" by 72" with two 12" leaves inserted. Height is 29". Available with plastic top as M 1568 GP.

M 1569 G   Junior Dinning Extension Table   1956
Middle: Size of top: 34" by 50". Top extended with 14" leaf inserted, 34" by 64". Height 29".

M 1589 G   Large Dining Extension Table   1962–66
Below: Table is fitted with two 15" extension leaves that have matched boxing. Without leaves top is 42" by 60", extends to 42" by 90" with both leaves. Height is 29".

M 151 A   *SIDE CHAIR*   *1950*
Seat measures 17" wide by 15" deep. Height of back is 16". Yardage required is ½ yard of 54" material.

M 152 A   *SIDE CHAIR*   *1947–1950*
Seat measures 17" wide by 15" deep. Height of back is 16". Yardage required is ½ yard of 54" material.

M 153 A   *SIDE CHAIR*   *1950*
Seat measures 17" wide by 15" deep. Height of back is 16". Yardage required is ½ yard of 54" material.

M 154 A   *SIDE CHAIR*   *1950–55*
Seat measures 18" wide by 16" deep. Height of back is 16½". Yardage required: ½ yard of 54" material.

M 154 C   *ARMCHAIR*   *1950–55*
Seat measures 18" wide by 16" deep. Height of back is 16½". Yardage required: ½ yard of 54" material.

M 155 A   SIDE CHAIR   *1947–50*
Seat measures 18" wide by 16" deep.
Height of back is 15". Yardage
required: ½ yard of 54" material.

M 155 C   ARM CHAIR   *1947–50*
Seat measures 18" wide by 16" deep.
Height of back is 15". Yardage required:
½ yard of 54" material.

M 157 A   SIDE CHAIR   *1947–50*
Seat measures 18" wide by 16" deep.
Height of back is 17". Yardage required:
1¼ yard of 54" material.

M 157 C   ARM CHAIR   *1947–50*
Seat measures 18" wide by 16" deep.
Height of back is 17". Yardage required:
1¼ yard of 54" material.

M 158 A   SIDE CHAIR   *1950*
Seat measures 18" wide by 17" deep.
Height of back is 17". Yardage required:
1¾ yards of 54" material.

M 158 C   ARM CHAIR   *1950*
Seat measures 22" wide by 17" deep.
Height of back is 17". Yardage required:
2 yards of 54" material.

M 549 C   CAPTAINS CHAIR   *1953–66*
Seat measures 20" wide by 17" deep. Height of
back is 14". Overall height is 30". Also available in
the Contract Package.

M 551 A   SIDE CHAIR   *1952–55*
Seat measures 17" wide by 16" deep.
Height of back is 16".

M 552 A   SIDE CHAIR   *1953–55*
Seat measures 18" wide by 15½" deep.
Height of back is 15". Overall height is 31½".

M 552 C   ARM CHAIR   *1953–55*
Seat measures 18" wide by 15½" deep. Height
of back is 15". Overall height is 31½".

Heywood

M 553 A   SIDE CHAIR   1950–53
Seat measures 17" wide by 15" deep.
Height of back is 15". Overall height
is 32". Yardage required is ½ yard of
54" material.

M 553 C   ARM CHAIR   1950–53
Seat measures 18" wide by 16" deep. Height
of back is 15". Overall height is 32". Yardage
required is ½ yard of 54" material.

M 554 C   ARM CHAIR   1953–55
Seat measures 18" wide by 16½" deep.
Height of back is 16". Overall height is
33½".

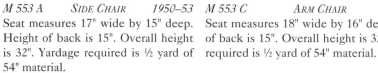

M 554 A   SIDE CHAIR   1953–55
Seat measures 18" wide by 16½" deep.
Height of back is 16". Overall height is 32".

M 555 C   ARM CHAIR   1950–55
Seat measures 21" wide by 17" deep.
Height of back is 17". Overall height is 34".
Yardage required: ½ yard of 54" material.

M 555 A   SIDE CHAIR   1950–55
Seat measures 18" wide by 16" deep.
Height of back is 16". Overall height is 32".
Yardage required: ½ yard of 54" material.

M 556 A   SIDE CHAIR   *1952–54*
Seat measures 18" wide by 16" deep.
Height of back is 15". Overall height is 31".

M 556 C   ARM CHAIR   *1952–54*
Seat measures 18" wide by 16" deep.
Height of back is 15". Overall height
is 31".

M 557 C   ARM CHAIR   *1952*
Width of seat 20½". Depth of seat 16½".
Overall height is 35".

M 557 A   SIDE CHAIR   *1952*
Width of seat 18½". Depth of seat 16".
Overall height is 34".

M 6107 A   SIDE CHAIR   *1952*
This chair was available only from
the Los Angeles plant. The width of
the seat is 17", the depth is 24", and
the height is 35". The yardage
required: 1¼ yards of 50" material.

M 6107 C   ARM CHAIR   *1952*
The width of the seat on this California
only chair is 23", the depth is 24", and the
height is 35". The yardage required: 1½
yards of 50" material.

M 953 A   Side Chair   *1954–55*
Seat measures 17" wide by 15" deep.
Height of back 15". Overall height 32".

M 953 C   Arm Chair   *1954–55*
Seat measures 18" wide by 16" deep.
Height of back is 15", overall height 32".

M 1551 A   Side Chair   *1956–66*
The seat measures 18" by 16" and the
overall height is 31½". Also available in
the Contract Package. Yardage
required: ½ yard of 54" material.

M 1551 C   Arm Chair   *1956–66*
The seat measures 18" by 16" and the
overall height is 31½". Yardage
required: ½ yard of 54" material.

M 1552 C   Arm Chair   *1956*
Seat: 19" wide by 17" deep. Back height
15", overall height is 32".

M 1552 A   Side Chair   *1956*
The seat measures 19" by 17" and the
height is 32". This chair was also available
in the Contract Package. Yardage
required: ½ yard of 54" material.

M 1553 A   SIDE CHAIR   *1956–66*
Overall: Height 32½"; width 19"; depth 19½".

M 1553 C   ARM CHAIR   *1956–66*
Overall: Height 32½"; width 23½"; depth 19½".

M 1554 C   ARM CHAIR   *1957–58*
Seat is 18" wide by 16" deep. Back height is 16" and overall height is 32½".

M 1554 A   SIDE CHAIR   *1956–66*
Seat is 18" wide by 16" deep. Back height is 16" and overall height is 32½".

M 1555 A   SIDE CHAIR   *1956–59*
Seat is 18" wide by 16" deep. Back height is 15" and overall height is 32¼".

M 1555 C   ARM CHAIR   *1956–59*
Seat is 18" wide by 16" deep. Back height is 15" and overall height is 32¼".

M 1561 C   *ARM CHAIR*   1958–59
Overall: Height is 31½"; width is 21½";
depth is 19½".

M 1561 A   *SIDE CHAIR*   1958–59
Overall: Height is 31½"; width is
18½"; depth is 19½".

M 1562 C   *CANE ARM CHAIR*   1956
Seat: 20½" wide by 19" deep. Back
height is 15", overall height 31½". Also
available with a foam rubber seat cushion
as M 1562 C RU.

M 1562 A   *CANE SIDE CHAIR*   1956
Seat: 20½" wide by 19" deep. Back
height is 15", overall height is 31½". Also
available with a foam rubber seat cushion
as M 1562 A RU.

M 1563 A   *SIDE CHAIR*   1956
Seat: 20½" wide by 19" deep. Back
height is 14". Overall height is 31½".

M 1563 C   *ARM CHAIR*   1956
Seat: 20½" wide by 19" deep. Back height is
14". Overall height is 31½".

M 1564 A　　SIDE CHAIR　　*1956–61*
Seat is 19" wide by 17" deep. Back height is
16" and overall height is 32".

M 1564 C　　ARM CHAIR　　*1956–61*
Seat is 19" wide by 17" deep. Back height is 16"
and overall height is 32".

M 1593　　SIDE CHAIR　　*1958–59*
Overall: Height 34"; width 19½"; depth 20".

M 1594 A　　SIDE CHAIR　　*1958–59*
Overall: Height 34"; width 20"; depth 20".

M 1594 C　　ARM CHAIR　　*1958–59*
Overall: Height 35"; width 24½"; depth 21".

M 173   *CREDENZA*   1947
Top Left: Credenza has full length bottom drawer. Top is 54" by 19" and height is 34".

M 176   *CORNER CABINET*   1948–55
Top Right: This full size corner cabinet is 68" high, 28" wide, and 16" deep. Lower compartment is fitted with an adjustable shelf.

CHINA TOP ON SERVER BASE
M 175 ON M 170   1947
Left: Plate glass top measures 32" wide, 14½" deep, and 32" high. Shelves are adjustable.

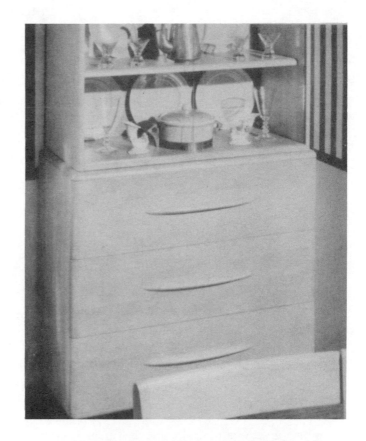

GLASS TOP HUTCH ON UTILITY CASE
M 175 ON M 334   *1949*
Top Left: Hutch top measures 34" by 18". It stands 32½"
high. The Utility Case top is 34" wide and 15½" deep. It
stands 32½" high, the same height as bookcases so it can
be used in a sectional bookcase arrangement. The three
drawers are extra deep.

M 324   *UTILITY CHEST*   *1947–48*
Top Right: Height of chest is 32½" giving the flexibility
of being grouped with bookcases.

M 175 ON M 190   *CHINA*   *1948–50*
Right: The overall height of this china is 64½". Server
base is 34" wide, 17" deep, and 32½" high. Plate glass top
measures 32" wide, 14½" deep, and 32" high. Both the
server and the hutch have adjustable shelves.

Heywood

M 590   SERVER   *1950–55*
Top Left: Fitted with shelf inside of cabinet doors. Top measures 34" wide and 17" deep. Height is 32½". Shelves are adjustable.

M 527 ON M 526   CHINA WITH OPEN HUTCH   *1952–53*
Top Right: The M 526 server base is 34" wide, 15½" deep, and 32½" high. It is fitted with two adjustable shelves inside of the cabinet doors. The M 527 open hutch is 32" wide, 12" deep, and 25" high. Overall height is 57½".

M 196 W   CREDENZA WITH DESK DRAWER   *1950*
Below: Designed by W. Joseph Carr. Fitted with desk drawer at top center. Size of top is 54" wide, 18" deep, and 34" high. Two regular drawers at the top and a full length drawer at the bottom. Two base cabinets are fitted with adjustable shelves. Also available with out a desk drawer as M 196.

M 175 on M 194   CHINA TOP ON SERVER   1950
Top Left: The base of this china was designed by W. Joseph Carr. It is fitted with swivel wheels. The server top measures 34" by 18" and is 32½" high. The overall height of the server and china top is 64½". The plate glass top is fitted with two adjustable shelves. The base has a full length drawer and an adjustable shelf inside.

CREDENZA WITH GLASS-TOP HUTCH
M 198 on M196   1950
Top Right: This modern utility case is 72" overall and is equipped with ball-bearing swivel wheels. The credenza base is 54" wide, 34" high, and 18" deep. The plate glass top is 52" wide, 38" high, and 14" deep. The base is fitted with three drawers at the top and a full length bottom drawer. The two base cabinets are fitted with adjustable shelves. The china hutch has six adjustable shelves.

M 195   JUNIOR BUFFET   1950
Left: Designed by W. Joseph Carr. Fitted with ball-bearing, swivel wheels. Full length top drawer. Two adjustable shelves in larger left compartment and one in right-hand section. Top measures 48" wide by 18" deep. Height is 32½".

M 593   *CREDENZA*   *1950–55*
Top: Fitted with full length top drawer and adjustable shelves inside of cabinets. Top measures 54" by 18". Height 34". Silver tray in top drawer.

M 192   *3-DRAWER BUFFET*   *1948–50*
Middle Right: Fitted with two adjustable shelves in each cabinet compartment. Top measures 48" wide by 18" deep. Height is 32½".

M 509 ON M 593   *CREDENZA WITH CHINA TOP*   *1953*
Left: China top measures 50" wide, 14" deep, and 39" high. Credenza is fitted with full length top drawer and adjustable shelves inside of cabinets. Top measures 54" by 18". Height is 34". Silver tray in top drawer. Overall height of credenza and china top is 73".

M 198 on M 193   Credenza with Glass-top Hutch   *1948–50*
Fitted with full length bottom drawer and adjustable shelves inside of both cabinets. Buffet top measures 54" by 18", height 31". Plate glass hutch measures 52" wide, 14" deep, and 38" high. Overall height of case 72". Top has six adjustable shelves.

M 995 on M 996   Harmonic China   *1954*
Base measures 36" by 19". Height is 31". China top measures 33" by 15". Height is 31". Overall height is 62".

Harmonic Buffet with
Tambour Door
M 997   *1954*
Fitted with tambour door at cabinet side. Top measures 48" wide and 19" deep. Height is 31".

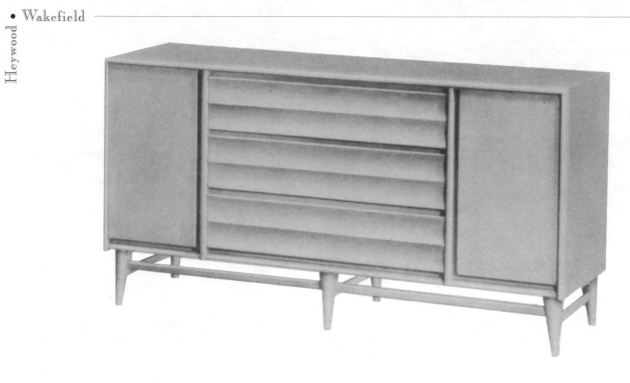

M 998   HARMONIC LARGE BUFFET   1954
Top: Fitted with three drawers, an adjustable shelf in each cabinet section, and a felt-lined silver tray in the top drawer. Top measures 60" by 19". Height is 31".

HARMONIC LARGE BUFFET WITH CHINA TOP
M 909 ON M 998   1954
Left: China top has four adjustable shelves and three drawers. Top is 50" wide by 14" deep. Height of top is 38". Buffet is fitted with three drawers, an adjustable shelf in each cabinet section, and a felt-lined silver tray in the top drawer. Top measures 60" by 19". Height is 31". Full piece has six drawers and two cabinets. Overall height of base and top is 69".

CHINA TOP ON HARMONIC SERVER

M 375 ON M 996   1954

Top Left: The china top has sliding plate-glass doors. It is fitted with two adjustable shelves. Size of top 32½" wide, 14" deep, and 32½" high. Harmonic server is fitted with an adjustable shelf. Top measures 36" by 19". Height is 31". Overall height of base and top 63½".

UTILITY CASE WITH OPEN HUTCH TOP

M 785 ON M 782 W   1953–54

Top Right: Top measures 45" by 12". Height is 25". Top drawer of case opens to a desk top. Base measures 48" by 18". Height is 34". Overall height of base and top is 59". Base has two adjustable shelves in cabinet section.

GLASS TOP HUTCH ON UTILITY CABINET

M 508 ON M 782 W   1952–54

Right: China top is 44" wide, 14" deep, and 26" high. Top drawer of case opens to a desk top. Base measures 48" by 18". Height is 34". Overall height of cabinet and top is 60".

M 1541   *SERVER*   *1956–61*
Top Left: Fitted with full-length drawer. Cabinet has shelf. Top measures 36" by 17". Height is 32".

BUFFET WITH OPEN HUTCH TOP
M 785 ON M 592   *1953–54*
Top Right: Top of buffet measures 48" by 18". Height is 32½". Hutch top measures 45" by 12". Height is 25". Overall height of complete case is 57½".

BUFFET WITH CHINA TOP
M 999 ON M 592   *1954–55*
Left: China top is 46" wide by 14" deep by 26" high. It is fitted with an adjustable shelf. Top of buffet measures 48" by 18". Height is 32½". Fitted with two adjustable shelves in each cabinet compartment. Overall height is 59".

GLASS DOOR HUTCH ON TAMBOUR BUFFET
M1596 ON M1542   *1958–59*

Top Left: Hutch top has glass doors; center section has two adjustable shelves. Top measures 45½" wide, 14¼" deep, 35" high. Buffet is fitted with three drawers and has tambour cabinet with adjustable shelf. Buffet is 50" by 18". Height is 32". Overall height of hutch and buffet is 67".

GLASS DOOR HUTCH ON SERVER
M 1598 ON M 1597   *1962–66*

Top Right: Glass Door Hutch is fitted with two sliding glass doors and an adjustable shelf. It is 36" wide, 13½" deep, and 39" high. Server has a full length drawer with four partitions . The two door storage compartment has an adjustable shelf. Top is 36" by 13½" and it is 30" high.

M 1548 ON M 1541   *CHINA ON SERVER*   *1956–61*

Left: China top has sliding plate glass doors. It is fitted with an adjustable shelf. Top measures 34" wide, 14" deep, 26" high. Server is fitted with full-length drawer. Cabinet has shelf. Top measures 36" by 17". Height 32". Overall height of china and server is 58".

LARGE CROWN GLASS CHINA ON BUFFET
M 1547 ON M 1543   1956–65
Left: China top has three Crown Glass doors. Fitted with two adjustable shelves. Top measures 56" wide, 14¾" deep, 35" high. Credenza is fitted with four drawers and two compartments. Top drawer has silver compartments lined with non-tarnishing cloth. Adjustable shelf in each of the end compartments. Top measures 60" by 18". Height is 32". Overall height of china and buffet is 67".

CHINA ON TAMBOUR CABINET
M 1546 ON M 1592   1957
Bottom Left: China top has sliding plate glass doors. Fitted with adjustable shelf. Top measures 45½" wide, 14" deep, 26" high. Tambour door cabinet has adjustable shelf. Top measures 50" wide by 18" deep. Height is 32".

CROWN GLASS CHINA ON SERVER
M 1545 ON M 1541   1956
Bottom Right: China top has crown glass door panels. It is fitted with two adjustable shelves. Top measures 34" wide, 14" deep, 31" high. Server is fitted with full-length drawer. Cabinet has shelf. Top measures 36" by 17". Height 32". Overall height of china and server is 63".

M 1543   *BUFFET*   *1956–65*

Fitted with four drawers and two compartments. Top drawer has silver compartments lined with non-tarnishing cloth. Adjustable shelf in each of the end compartments. Top measures 60" by 18". Height is 32".

M 1544   *CREDENZA*   *1956–61*

Top left drawer is fitted with tray for silver. Drawer at top right has center partition. Single door compartment at lower left has adjustable shelf. Two door compartment has two tray-drawers. Top measures 60" by 18". Height is 32".

UPHOLSTERED CHAIRS

M 343 C   LADIES' LOUNGE CHAIR   1950
Left: This arm chair has a seat 21" wide by 21" deep. The height of the back is 19". Yardage required: 4¼ yards of 54" material.

M 340 C   ARM CHAIR   1949–52
Bottom Left: The seat of this occasional pull-up chair is 22" wide and 21" deep. The back is 17" high. Yardage required: 2 yards of 54" material.

M 341 C   PULL-UP CHAIR   1949
Bottom Right: The seat is 22" wide and 21" deep. The back is 21" high.

M 342 C MEN'S LOUNGE CHAIR 1949–50
Right: This large arm chair has a reversible seat cushion that measures 21" wide by 22" deep. The back is 24" high. Yardage required: 6 yards of 54" material.

LARGE BARREL WING CHAIR
M 344 C   *1949–57*
Bottom Left: Designed by Edmund Spence. The seat of this deluxe arm chair is 22" wide and 22" deep. The back is 26" high. The width of the back at top is 35". Yardage required: 5½ yards of 54" material.

M 345 C   TUB CHAIR   1950–57
Bottom Right: The circular seat of this arm chair measures 24" wide by 22" deep. The back is 18" high. Yardage required: 4 yards of 54" material.

M 346 C BARREL WING CHAIR 1947–50
The seat of this arm chair measures 24" wide and 21" deep. The back is 21" high. Yardage required: 4¼ yards of 54" material.

M 347 C PULL-UP WING CHAIR 1949–50
This arm chair has a seat that is 22" wide and 18½" deep. The back is 20" high. Yardage required: 2½ yards of 54" material.

M 348 C PULL-UP OCCASIONAL CHAIR 1950
This arm chair seat measures 19" wide and 20" deep. The back is 15½" high. Yardage required: 3 yards of 54" material. Also Shown: M 308 G Step Table.

M 354 C WHEELED TELEVISION CHAIR 1950–52
Fitted with ball-bearing swivel wheels. Circular seat measures 24" wide by 22" deep. Height of back 18", overall height is 30". Yardage required: 4½ yards of 54" material.

LARGE BARREL WING CHAIR
M 384 C   1950–53
Top Left: Seat cushion measures 21"
wide by 21" deep. The height of the
back is 23" and the overall height is
38". Yardage required is 4½ yards of
54" material.

M 85 C   PULL-UP CHAIR   1952
Top Right: The width of the seat of
this "West Coast" only chair is 22½",
the depth is 26", and the height is
32½". Yardage required is 1⅜ yards of
50" material.

M 5608 C   CLUB CHAIR   1952
Right: This "West Coast" only club
chair is 36" wide, 37" deep, and 32"
high. Yardage required is 5½ yards of
50" material. Also Shown: M 3753 G
Step-End Table, "West Coast" only.

M 558 C   *LOUNGE CHAIR*   *1953–54*

Top Left: The width of the seat is 22", the depth of the seat is 20", the height of the back is 20", and the overall height is 34½". Yardage required: 5¾ yards of 54" material.

M 564 C   *SWIVEL TUB CHAIR*   *1951–52*

Top Right: Fitted with ball-bearing Seng swivel mechanism. Width of seat 23", depth of seat 19". Overall height is 31½". Yardage required: 3¼ yards of 54" material.

M 559 C   *HIGH BACK LOUNGE CHAIR*   *1952–57*

Below: The width of the seat is 22", the depth of the seat is 20", the height of the back is 26", and the overall height is 39½". Yardage required: 5½ yards of 54" material.

M 565 C   *HIGH BACK EASY CHAIR*   *1951–52*
Width of seat 23", depth of seat is 22". Overall height is 35".
Yardage required: 5½ yards of 54" material.

M 566 C   *BARREL WING CHAIR*   *1951–52*
Width of seat 21", depth of seat 21". Overall height is 33".
Yardage required: 4 yards of 54" material. Also Shown: M 38 G
Step-End Table.

M 567 C   *LADIES' PULL-UP CHAIR*   *1951–52*
Width of seat 21", depth of seat 20". Overall height is 32".
Yardage required: 4¼ yards of 54" material.

OPEN ARM TUB CHAIR, LADIES' CLUB CHAIR
M 568 C   *1951–58*
The width of the seat is 23", the depth of the seat is 19", and the
overall height is 29½". Also available in the Contract Package.
Yardage required: 3 yards of 54" material.

M 569 C   *PULL-UP CHAIR*   *1951–59*
The width of the seat is 23", the depth of the seat is 19", and the overall height is 32½". This chair was also available in the Contract Package. Yardage required: 2 yards of 54" material.

M 598 C   *LADIES' CLUB CHAIR*   *1953*
The width of the seat is 19", the depth of the seat is 19", and the height of the back is 16". Overall height is 30". Yardage required: 4½ yards of 54" material.

M 797 C   *HIGH BACK BARREL CHAIR*   *1953–54*
Width of seat is 21½", depth of seat is 21", height of back is 22", and overall height is 34". Yardage required: 3¼ yards of 54" material.

M 798 C   *OPEN ARM POSTURE CHAIR*   *1953–54*
Width of seat is 22½", depth of seat is 20", height of back is 20", and overall height is 32". Yardage required: 2½ yards of 54" material.

M 799 C   POSTURE BACK ARM CHAIR   *1953–54*
The width of the seat is 22", the depth of the seat is 20½", the height of the back is 26", and the overall height is 37½". Yardage required: 3½ yards of 54" material.

M 941 C   ARM CHAIR   *1954–55*
Seat: 23" wide by 19" deep. Back height 18". Overall dimensions: 30" wide; 28" deep; 31½" high. Yardage required: 3½ yards of 54" material.

M 945 C   CLUB / LOUNGE CHAIR   *1954–56*
Seat: 23" wide by 19" deep. Back height 18". Overall dimensions: 30" wide; 30" deep; 32½" high. Yardage required: 4 yards of 54" material.

M 946 C   LADIES' CHAIR   *1954–55*
Seat: 21" wide by 20" deep. Back height 18". Overall dimensions: 27" wide; 31" deep; 31½" high. Yardage required: 3 yards of 54" material.

M 947 C   *LOUNGE CHAIR*   *1954–56*
Seat: 22" wide by 20" deep. Back height 21". Overall dimensions: 30" wide; 35" deep; 34" high. Yardage required: 5½ yards of 54" material.

M 948   *ARMLESS PULL-UP CHAIR*   *1954–56*
The back height of this chair is 16" and the seat is 23" wide by 21" deep. The overall dimensions are 23" wide, 25" deep, and 32" high. This chair was also available in the Contract Package. Yardage required: 1½ yards of 54" material.

M 984 C   *WING CHAIR*   *1954–57*
Seat: 24" wide by 20" deep. Back height 20". Overall dimensions: 33" wide; 32" deep; 36" high. Yardage required: 5½ yards of 54" material.

M 1156 C   *WOOD ARMED PULL-UP CHAIR*   *1955–56*
Seat is 22" wide by 18" deep. Back height 17½". Overall dimensions, 27" wide by 26" deep, by 33" high. Yardage required: 2¼ yards of 54" material.

M 1158 C   DANISH OCCASIONAL CHAIR   1955–57
Top Left: Seat: 24" wide by 18" deep. Back height 16". Overall dimensions: 31" wide; 29" deep; 27½" high. Yardage required: 3½ yards of 54" material.

M 1159 C   HIGH BACK BARREL CHAIR   1955–56
Top Right: Seat: 25" wide by 20" deep. Back height 22". Overall dimensions: 32" wide; 31" deep; 33" high. Yardage required: 3 yards of 54" material.

M 1161 C   LADIES' LOUNGE CHAIR   1955–57
Left: Seat: 23" wide by 19" deep. Back height 15". Overall dimensions: 30" wide; 28" deep; 28" high. Yardage required: 4½ yards of 54" material.

M 1163 C — LARGE CLUB CHAIR — 1955–56
Top Left: Fitted with four ball-bearing caster wheels. Seat: 25" wide by 22" deep. Back height 17". Overall dimensions: 36" wide; 36" deep; 31" high. Yardage required: 6¾ yards of 54" material.

M 1794 C — LADIES' CHAIR — 1958
Top Right: Overall dimensions: 31" wide; 32" deep; 27" high. Yardage required: 4 yards of 54" material. Add ¾ of a yard for full self platform under seat cushion. Also Shown: M 1511 Bachelor's Chest.

M 1796 C — PILLOW-BACK ARM CHAIR — 1958
Below: Overall dimensions: 30" wide; 34" deep; 35" high. Yardage required: 5 yards of 54" material. Add ¾ of a yard for full self platform under seat cushion.

OCCASIONAL TABLES

M 902 G   *NEST OF TABLES*   *1954–55*

All tops are same size; 19½" deep by 27" wide. Heights are 24"; 21¾"; and 19½". Also Shown: M 984 C Wing Chair.

M 319 G   *COCKTAIL TABLE*   *1949–54*

The molded and tapered top of this table measures 40" x 22". Height is 16".

275

M 338 G   CORNER TABLE   1950–53
Top: The top measures 32" by 32". Height is 21½". The shelf is 32" by 32".

M 335 G   COCKTAIL TABLE   1950–53
Middle: Size of top 36" by 19". Size of shelf 31¾" by 16¾". Height is 16".

M 312 G   NEST OF TABLES   1949–53
Right: The largest table of this group has a 21" by 15" top. It stands 24"
high. The middle one has a 19" by 13½" top and is 23" high. The
smallest one has a 17" by 12" and stands 22" high.

M 304 G   Two-Tier End Table   1947–49
Right: Two-tier step table has lower shelf. Also Shown: M 360 C Arm Chair.

M 306 G   Round Cocktail Table   1947–55
Bottom Left: The round, revolving top measures 32" in diameter. Height is 16".

M 308 G   Step End Table   1948–53
Bottom Right: This tier-topped table is 22" high. The cushion-height lower shelf measures 30" by 17".

modern

. . . with an air of friendly charm

Heywood-Wakefield's skill with curves brings a new charm to Modern! Finishes are light and designs are "Home-Planned" so you can be sure of a harmonious background as you add pieces to living room, dining room, bedroom. Ask for Heywood-Wakefield Modern at better furniture and department stores.

HEYWOOD-WAKEFIELD
EST. 1826

GARDNER, MASS.

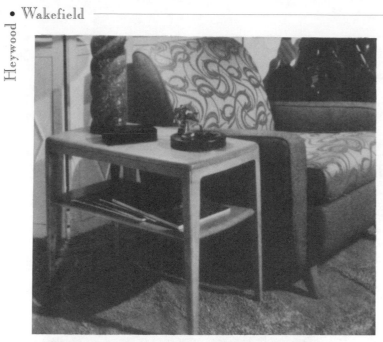

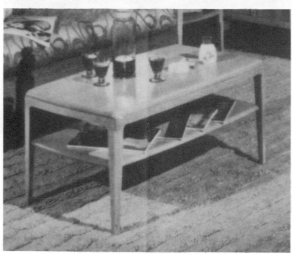

M 317 G   *END TABLE*   1949
Top Left: Top measures 28" by 14". Table is 21" high.
Also Shown: M 350 C Arm Chair.

M 318 G   *LAMP TABLE*   1949
Top Right: Top is 21" square and table stands 21" high.

M 316 G   *COFFEE TABLE*   1949
Middle Left: Fitted with full length shelf. Top measures 36" by 19". It is 16" high.

M 339 G   *CORNER TABLE*   1949
Middle Right: The shaped and molded top is supported by a flush steam-bent rim. The lower shelf is cushion high. Top measures 32" square and is 20" high.

M 3753 G   *STEP-END TABLE*   1952
Left: The top of this California only table measures 14½" by 16½". The middle and bottom shelves are 30" by 15", and the overall height is 22". This table was introduced in 1940 as the C 3753 G and production was continued in California after it was discontinued elsewhere.

M 393 G   CENTER TABLE   *1950–52*
Top: This utility table can be used as a lamp table, picture window unit, or a high corner table. Fitted with 3-legged pedestal base. Top is 30" in diameter. Height is 26".

M 905 G   COCKTAIL TABLE WITH DRAWER   *1954–55*
Right: Fitted with full length drawer. Top measures 40" by 20". Height is 16".

M 938 G   CORNER TABLE   *1954–55*
Below: The top measures 32" by 32". The cushion-high shelf (16" high) is the same size. Height is 24".

M 791 G   End Table   1952–53
Top measures 28" by 16". Height is 21". Also Shown: M 355 C Arm Chair.

M 396 G   *WEDGE-SHAPED TIER TABLE*   *1950–53*
This wedge-shaped table is especially designed to permit curved arrangements with regular seating units. Used between fillers, left and right sectional pieces, and chairs, this table is ideal for curved television arrangements. Size of cushion-height shelf is 22" at back and 12" at front. Length is 30", overall height is 22".

391 G   *END TABLE*   *1950–52*
Top and shelf measure 28" by 16". Height is 22".

280

M 364 G   *LAMP TABLE*   1950–55
Top Left: Size of top is 26" by 24". Height is 26". Size of shelf is 21" by 21".

M 337 G   *LAMP TABLE*   1950–53
Top Right: Top measures 21" by 21". Shelf is 19" by 19". Height is 25".

M 794 G   *STEP END TABLE WITH DRAWER*   1953–55
Right: Fitted with a full length drawer. Cushion-height shelf measures 30" by 18". Overall height is 22".

M 6321 G   *COCKTAIL TABLE*   1952
Below: This cocktail table was available only from the Los Angeles plant. The top measures 48" by 24" and the height is 16".

M 336 G   Step-End Table   1949–50
Top Left: Size of top 28" by 16". Shelf
measures 28" by 16". Height is 21".

Lamp Table with Drawer
M 793 G   1953–55
Top Right: Fitted with a full length
drawer. Top measures 20" by 18".
Height is 25".

M 307 G   Cocktail Table   1949–52
Middle Left: The top of this table is
36" square and the table stands 16"
high. After 1950 this table was available only from the Los Angeles plant.

Square Cocktail Table
M 392 G   1950–55
Bottom Left: This table is also useful as
a low corner table. Size of slightly off-
square top 36" by 36". Height is 16".

M 501 G   *END TABLE*   *1952–53*
Size of top 28" by 16". Height is 21".

M 395   *RECORD CABINET END TABLE*   *1951–52*
Fitted with three compartments for useful storage. Suitable for 12" record albums. Size of top is 28" by 16½". Height is 22".

M 502 G   *LAMP TABLE*   *1952–53*
Top measures 21" by 21". Height is 25".

M 503 G   *MAGAZINE RACK END TABLE*   *1953–57*
Top measures 28" by 15". Height is 22".

M 500 G   COCKTAIL TABLE   *1952–53*
Size of top 40" by 19". Height is 16".

M 795 G   LARGE COCKTAIL TABLE   *1953–55*
This king-size cocktail table has a 50" by 22" top. Height is 16".

M 991 G   COCKTAIL TABLE WITH SHELF   *1954–55*
The top measures 36" by 19". Height is 16".

M 906 G   *WEDGE STEP-END TABLE*   1954–55
Top Left: Length of shelf 30". Width at back 22"; at front 12". Height is 22½".

M 993 G   *LAMP TABLE WITH SHELF*   1954–55
Top Right: The top measures 22" by 20". Height is 25".

M 908 G   *STEP END TABLE*   1954–55
Middle Left: Top measures 16" by 15". Shelf is 30" by 16". Height is 22½".

M 992 G   *END TABLE WITH SHELF*   1954–55
Middle Right: The top measures 28" by 16". Height is 21".

M 1579 G   *SQUARE COCKTAIL TABLE*   1956
Right: Top measures 36" by 36". Height 16".

M 1578 G   ROUND COCKTAIL TABLE   1956
Top measures 38" in diameter. Height 16".

M 1576 G   REVOLVING TOP COCKTAIL TABLE   1956–61
Revolving top measures 32" in diameter. Height 15".

M 1574 G   STEP-END TABLE   1956
Top measures 15" by 18". Shelf is 30" by 18". Height 22".
Also available with plastic top as M 1574 GP.

M 1570 G   CORNER TABLE   1956
Top measures 30" by 30". Cushion-high shelf
is 30" by 30". Overall 32¼" by 32¼". Height
22". Also available with plastic top and shelf as
M 1570 GP.

M 1573 G   *LAMP TABLE*   1956
Top measures 22" by 22". Height 22". Also
available with plastic top as M 1573 GP.

M 1572 G   *END TABLE*   1956
Top measures 28" by 17". Height 22". Also available with
plastic top as M 1572 GP.

M 1571 G   *COCKTAIL TABLE*   1956
Top measures 44" by 20". Height is
14". Also available with plastic top as
M 1571 GP.

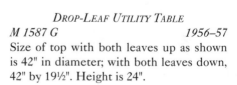

DROP-LEAF UTILITY TABLE
M 1587 G   *1956–57*
Size of top with both leaves up as shown
is 42" in diameter; with both leaves down,
42" by 19½". Height is 24".

M 1581 G   *COCKTAIL TABLE WITH SHELF*   *1956–57*
Top measures 40" by 21". Height 15".

M 1580 G   *COCKTAIL TABLE*   *1956–57*
Top measures 50" by 22". Height 15".

M 1590 G   *CORNER TABLE*   *1956–57*
Top measures 34" by 34". Cushion-high shelf is 29" by 29".

M 1584 G   *STEP-END TABLE*   *1956–57*
Top measures 17" by 16½". Shelf is 30" by 20". Height 22½".

288

M 1583 G   LAMP TABLE   1956–57
Top Right: Fitted with drawer and shelf. Top measures 26" by 24". Height is 24".

LARGE COCKTAIL TABLE WITH DRAWER
M 1585 G   1956–57
Middle: Fitted with drawer. Top measures 54" by 22". Height is 15".

M 1586 G   LAMP TABLE   1956–57
Top Left: Top measures 26" by 24". Height is 26".

M 1507 G   CORNER TABLE   1957–66
Right: Top measures 31" wide by 31" deep. The shelf is 32" square. Shelf height is 15".

M 1502 G   *END TABLE WITH SHELF*   *1957–66*
Top measures 30" long by 20" deep. The shelf is 26½" long
by 16½" deep. Shelf height is 15". Overall height is 21". This
table was also available in the Contract Package.

M 1504 G   *STEP-END TABLE*   *1957–66*
Top measures 20" wide by 15" long. The shelf is 30" long by
20" wide. Shelf height 15".

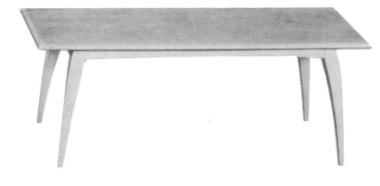

M 1588 G   *LAMP TABLE*   *1958–61*
Top measures 26" by 24". Height 26".

M 1501 G   *COCKTAIL TABLE*   *1957–61*
Top measures 42" long by 20" deep. Height is 15". This table was also
available in the Contract Package.

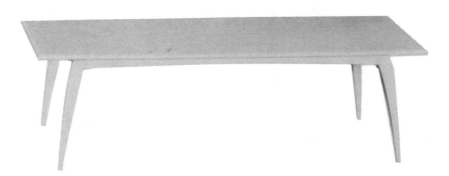

LARGE COCKTAIL TABLE
M 1505 G   *1957–66*
Top measures 52" long by 20" deep.
Height 15".

M 1508 G   ROUND COCKTAIL TABLE   1957–66
Above: Top measures 36" in diameter. Height is 15".

M 1506 G   COCKTAIL / CORNER TABLE   1957
Right: Designed for use as square cocktail or low corner table. Top measures 32" square. Height is 15".

M 1503 G   LAMP TABLE WITH SHELF   1957–63
Below: Top measures 26" wide by 24" deep. The shelf is 22½" wide by 20½" deep. Shelf height is 15", overall height is 21".

ARISTOCRAFT TABLES

Although the Aristocraft "CM" line of tables was designed for use with Aristocraft upholstered pieces, these tables were frequently displayed and sold with other Heywood-Wakefield Modern suites, sectionals, and occasional chairs.

CM 370 G   ARISTOCRAFT CORNER TABLE   1949–53
The cut-back top of this corner table permits full use of the 30" by 30" shelf. The tiered top has the same overall dimensions. Height is 21" overall. Shelf is cushion high.

ARISTOCRAFT COCKTAIL COFFEE TABLE
CM 371 G   1949–53
The molded, shaped top of this table is 36" by 19". Height is 16".

CM 372 G   ARISTOCRAFT END TABLE   1949–53
The molded, shaped top is 28" long and 15" deep. The shelf is full length. Height is 21".

Aristocraft Step End Table
CM 374 G   1950–53
Top Left: The top of this tier table is 22" by 15". Overall height is 22". Large shelf is cushion height.

Aristocraft Lamp Table
CM 373 G   1949–53
Top Right: The molded and shaped top of this table is 20" by 18". Height is 25". Useful as a night stand, too. The shelf is full length.

Aristocraft Corner Table
CM 970 G   1954–55
Right: The cut-back top of this corner table permits full use of the 30" by 30" shelf. The tiered top has the same overall dimensions. Height overall is 23". Shelf is cushion high.

Aristocraft Cocktail Table
CM 971 G   1954–55
Below: The molded, shaped top of this table is 36" by 19". Height is 16".

CM 972 G   *ARISTOCRAFT END TABLE WITH SHELF*   *1954–55*
The molded, shaped top is 28" long and 15" deep. The shelf is
full length.

CM 974 G   *ARISTOCRAFT STEP-END TABLE*   *1954–55*
The top of this tier table is 28" by 15". Overall height is 22". Large
shelf is cushion height.

ARISTOCRAFT LAMP TABLE WITH SHELF
CM 973 G   *1954–55*
The molded and shaped top of this table is 20" by
18". Height is 25". Useful as a night stand, too. The
shelf is full length.

THE ARISTOCRAFT LINE

The Aristocraft line, introduced in 1949, was the creation of W. Joseph Carr, staff designer. Aristocraft was specifically designed to utilize the darker "heart" lumber of the Yellow Birch, which was more plentiful than the "sap" lumber normally used for the production of Modern furniture. The darker "heart" lumber, nearly two-thirds of the tree, was used for Old Colony. The outer portion of the log produced the lighter "sap" lumber. Besides being popular at the factory, Aristocraft was an immediate sales success and Heywood-Wakefield continued to make Aristocraft pieces until the Modern line was discontinued.

CM 367   *ARISTOCRAFT SINGLE FILLER*   *1950–53*
The width of the seat is 22", the depth of the seat is 21", the height of the back is 19", and the overall height is 32". Yardage required in a single fabric all over: 2½ yards of 54" material, or 4 yards of 36" material.

CM 367 LC OR CM 367 RC   *ARISTOCRAFT LEFT OR RIGHT ARM CHAIR*   *1950–54*
Two shown: The width of the seat is 22", the depth of the seat is 21", the height of the back is 19", and the overall height is 32". Yardage required in a single fabric all over: 2½ yards of 54" material or 4 yards of 36" material.

CM 368   *ARISTOCRAFT DOUBLE FILLER*   *1952–53*
Not shown: Same as single filler CM 367 except double wide. The width of the seat is 44", the depth of the seat is 21", the height of the back is 19", and the overall height is 32". Yardage required in a single fabric all over: 4 yards of 54" material or 6 yards of 36" material.

CM 368 LC OR CM 368 RC   *DOUBLE FILLERS WITH LEFT OR RIGHT ARMS*   *1952–53*
Not shown: Same as single filler with arm CM 367 LC or RC except double wide. The width of the seat is 44", the depth of the seat is 21", the height of the back is 19", and the overall height is 32". Yardage required in a single fabric all over: 4 yards of 54" material or 6 yards of 36" material. Also Shown: CM 970 G Corner Table, M 176 Corner Cabinet.

CM 367 C   ARISTOCRAFT ARM CHAIR   1950–53
Top Left: The width of the seat is 22", the depth of the seat is 21", the height of the back is 19", and the overall height is 32". Yardage required: 2½ yards of 54" material.

CM 367 D   ARISTOCRAFT PLATFORM ROCKER   1952–53
Top Right: The width of the seat is 22", the depth of the seat is 21", the height of the back is 25", and the overall height is 37". Yardage required: 2¾ yards of 54" material.

CM 367 R   ARISTOCRAFT HIGH BACK ARM CHAIR   1952–53
Left: The width of the seat is 22", the depth of the seat is 21", the height of the back is 25", and the overall height is 39". Yardage required: 2¾ yards of 54" material.

CM 368-44   *ARISTOCRAFT LOVE SEAT*   *1950–53*
Above: The width of the seat is 44", the depth of the seat is 21", the height of the back is 19", and the overall height is 32". Yardage required: 4 yards of 54" material.

CM 369-66   *ARISTOCRAFT DAVENPORT*   *1950–53*
Below: The width of the seat is 66", the depth of the seat is 21", the height of the back is 19", and the overall height is 32". Yardage required: 6½ yards of 54" material.

CM 388 LC OR CM 388 RC　　　ARISTOCRAFT LEFT OR RIGHT ARM CHAIR　　　*1950–53*
Two shown: The width of the seat is 23", the depth of the seat is 22", the height of the back is 23", and the overall height is 35".
Yardage required: 3 yards of 54" material.

CM 388　　　ARISTOCRAFT SINGLE FILLER　　　*1950–53*
The width of the seat is 23", the depth of the seat is 22", the height of the back is 23", and the overall height is 35". Yardage
required: 3 yards of 54" material. Also shown: M 338 G Corner Table.

CM 388 C　ARISTOCRAFT ARM CHAIR　*1950–53*
The width of the seat is 23", the depth of the seat is 22", the height of the back is 23", and the over-all height is 35". Yardage required: 3 yards of 54" material.

298

ARISTOCRAFT ARM CHAIR LEFT OR RIGHT
CM 727 LC OR CM 727 RC   *1952–53*
Top Left & Right: The width of the seat is 22", the depth
of the seat is 21", the height of the back is 19", and the
overall height is 32". Yardage required: 2½ yards of 54"
material.

CM 727   *ARISTOCRAFT SINGLE FILLER*   *1952–53*
Left: The width of the seat is 22", the depth of the seat is
21", the height of the back is 19", and the overall height
is 32". Yardage required: 2½ yards of 54" material.

ARISTOCRAFT DOUBLE FILLER WITH RIGHT OR LEFT ARM
CM 728 LC OR CM 728 RC   *1952–53*
The width of the seat is 44", the depth of the seat is 21", the height of the back is 19", and the overall height is 32". Yardage required: 5 yards of 54" material.

CM 728   ARISTOCRAFT DOUBLE FILLER   *1952–53*
The width of the seat is 44", the depth of the seat is 21", the height of the back is 19", and the overall height is 32". Yardage required: 4 yards of 54" material.

CM 727 R   ARISTOCRAFT HIGH BACK ARM CHAIR   *1952–53*
The width of the seat is 22", the depth of the seat is 21", the height of the back is 25", and the overall height is 39". Yardage required: 2¾ yards of 54" material.

CM 727 D   ARISTOCRAFT PLATFORM ROCKER   *1952–53*
The width of the seat is 22", the depth of the seat is 21", the height of the back is 25", and the overall height is 37". Yardage required: 2¾ yards of 54" material.

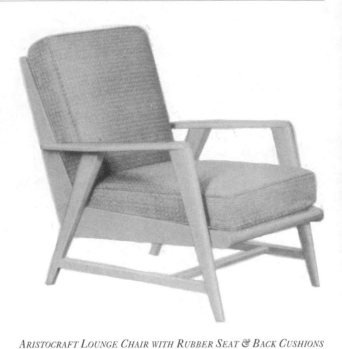

CM 727 C   *ARISTOCRAFT ARM CHAIR*   *1952–53*
The width of the seat is 22", the depth of the seat is 21",
the height of the back is 19", and the overall height is 32".
Yardage required: 2½ yards of 54" material.

ARISTOCRAFT LOUNGE CHAIR WITH RUBBER SEAT & BACK CUSHIONS
CM 724 C   *1953–54*
The width of the seat is 22", the depth of the seat is 21", the
height of the back is 19", and the overall height is 32". Also
available with spring filled cushions as CM 726. Yardage
required: 2½ yards of 54" material.

CM 728-44   *ARISTOCRAFT LOVE SEAT*   *1952–53*
The width of the seat is 44", the depth of the seat is 21", the height of the
back is 19", and the overall height is 32". Yardage required: 4 yards of 54"
material.

CM 927 C   *ARM CHAIR*   *1954–66*
The seat of this chair is 23" wide by 21" deep, and the
back height is 16" . The overall dimensions are 28"
wide, 34" deep, and 31" high. This chair was also
available in the Contract Package. Yardage required:
2½ yards of 54" material.

CM 729-66   ARISTOCRAFT DAVENPORT   *1952–53*

The width of the seat is 66", the depth of the seat is 21", the height of the back is 19", and the overall height is 32". Yardage required: 6½ yards of 54" material.

CM 927   ARISTOCRAFT SINGLE FILLER   *1954–58*

Width of seat is 22", depth of seat is 21". Overall width is 22", overall depth is 34", overall height is 31". Yardage required: 2½ yards of 54" material.

CM 927 LC OR CM 927 RC   ARISTOCRAFT LEFT OR RIGHT ARM CHAIR   *1954–58*

Both shown: Width of seat is 22", depth of seat is 21. Overall width is 25", overall depth is 34", overall height is 31". Yardage required: 2½ yards of 54" material.

CM 928 LC OR RC   ARISTOCRAFT DOUBLE FILLER WITH LEFT OR RIGHT ARM   *1954*

Not shown: Same as CM 927LC or RC except double wide. Width of seat is 44", depth of seat is 21", overall width is 47". Overall depth is 34", overall height is 31". Yardage required: 5 yards of 54" material.

CM 928   ARISTOCRAFT DOUBLE FILLER   *1954*

Not shown: Same as CM 927 single filler except double wide. Width of seat is 44", depth of seat is 21". Overall width is 44", overall depth is 34", overall height is 31". Yardage required: 5 yards of 54" material. Also shown: CM 970 G Corner Table.

ARISTOCRAFT CUSHION VARIATIONS

The Aristocraft CM 927-928-929 series used single cushions. A variation of this series, the CM 931-932 series (not shown), was identical in construction to the CM 927 series but used a single cushion, double wide. For example, the CM 928-44 love seat had four cushions, while the CM 931-44 love seat had only two cushions.

ARISTOCRAFT LOVE SEAT
CM 928-44   1954
Width of seat is 44", depth of seat is 21". Overall width is 50", overall depth is 34", overall height is 31". Yardage required: 5 yards of 54" material.

ARISTOCRAFT DAVENPORT
CM 929-66   1954
Width of seat is 66", depth of seat is 21". Overall width is 72", overall depth is 34", overall height is 31". Yardage required: 7 yards of 54" material.

SECTIONALS, DAVENPORTS, AND LOVE SEATS

M 355   *SINGLE FILLER*   *1950–53*

Three shown: Model number changed to M 955 in 1953. Width of cushion is 23", depth of cushion is 22" . Height of back is 21" and overall height is 32". Yardage required: 3½ yards of 54" material.

M 355 LC OR M355 RC   *LEFT OR RIGHT ARM CHAIR*   *1950–53*

Both shown: Model number changed to M 955 LC or RC in 1953. Width of cushion is 23", depth of cushion is 22". Height of back is 21" and overall height is 32". Yardage required: 4½ yards of 54" material.

M 356 LC OR M 356 RC   *DOUBLE FILLERS WITH LEFT OR RIGHT ARMS*   *1950–53*

Not shown: Model number changed to M 956 LC or RC in 1953. Same as M 355 LC or RC except double wide. Width of seat is 48", depth of seat is 22". Height of back is 21" and overall height is 32". Yardage required: 7 yards of 54" material.

M 356   *DOUBLE FILLER*   *1950–53*

Not shown: Model number changed to M 956 in 1953. Same as M 355 except double wide. Width of seat is 48", depth of seat is 22". Height of back is 21" and overall height is 32". Yardage required: 5½ yards of 54" material. Also Shown: M 392 G Square Cocktail Table.

M 355 C   *ARM CHAIR*   *1950–52*
Model number changed to M 955 C in 1953. Width of seat cushion is 23" and
depth of cushion is 22". Height of back is 21" and overall height is 32". Yardage
required: 5½ yards of 54" material. Also Shown: M 337 G Lamp Table.

M 357   *CURVED SINGLE FILLER*   *1950*
Cushion width at front 22", at back 33", depth of cushion 22". Height of back is 21"
and overall height is 32". Yardage required: 4 yards of 54" material.

M 356–48   *LOVE SEAT*   *1950–53*
Model number changed to M 956–48 in 1953. Width between arms is 48". Depth of seat is 22".
Height of back is 21" and overall height is 32". Yardage required: 8 yards of 54" material.

M 358–68   *DAVENPORT*   *1950–53*
Model number changed to M 958–68 in 1953. Width between arms is 68". Depth of cushions is 22". Height of back is 21" and
overall height is 32". Yardage required: 10½ yards of 54" material.

M 330   *SINGLE FILLER*   *1948–50*
Width of cushion is 23", depth of cushion is 22". Height of back is 21". Overall height is 32". Yardage required: 3½ yards of 54" material.

M 330 LC *OR* **M 330 RC**   *LEFT OR RIGHT ARM CHAIR*   *1948–50*
Width of cushion is 23", depth of cushion is 22". Height of back is 21". Overall height is 32". Yardage required: 4½ yards of 54" material.

M 331   *DOUBLE FILLER*   *1948–50*
Not shown: Same as M 330 Single Filler except double wide. Width of seat is 48", depth of seat is 22". Height of back is 21"; overall height is 32". Yardage required: 5½ yards of 54" material.

M 331 LC *OR* **M 331 RC**   *DOUBLE FILLERS WITH LEFT OR RIGHT ARMS*   *1948–50*
Not shown: Same as M 330 LC or RC Single Filler With Arm except double wide. Width of seat is 48", depth of seat is 22". Height of back is 21", overall height is 32". Yardage required: 7 yards of 54" material. Also Shown: M 339 G Corner Table.

M 330 C   *ARM CHAIR*   *1948–50*
Width of seat cushion is 23", depth of cushion is 22". Height of back is 21". Overall height is 32". Yardage required: 5 yards of 54" material.

M 331–48   LOVE SEAT   *1948–50*
Width between arms is 48". Depth of seat is 22". Height of back is 21"; overall height is 32".
Yardage required: 8 yards of 54" material.

M 332–68   DAVENPORT   *1948–50*
Width between arms is 68". Depth of cushion is 22". Height of back is 21"; overall height is 32". Yardage required: 10½ yards of 54" material.

M 333 OR 353   CURVED SINGLE FILLER   1948–50
Left: This single curved filler was used in both the M 330 and M350 series sectionals. Cushion width at front is 22", at back 33". Depth of cushion is 22". Height of back is 21; overall height is 32". Yardage required: 4 yards of 54" material.

RIGHT AND LEFT ARM CHAIR
M 350 RC OR LC   1948–49
Below: Cushions measure 23" wide and 22" deep. The backs are 21" high.

M 350   SINGLE FILLER   1948–49
Below: Cushion measures 23" wide and 22" deep. The back is 21" high. Also Shown: M 306 G Round Cocktail Table, M 308 G End Table, M339 G Corner Table.

M 352-68   DAVENPORT   1948–49
Above: Between the arms is 68" wide. Cushions are
22" deep and the back is 21" high. Also shown: M
316 G Coffee Table, M 317 G End Table, M 179
Tambour Cabinet.

M 350 C   ARM CHAIR   1948–49
Right: Cushion measures 23" wide and 22" deep.
The back is 21" high. Also shown: M 317 G End
Table.

M 5608 L & R　　　　　　*LEFT AND RIGHT ARM SECTIONAL*　　　　　　*1952*

This sectional was only available from Heywood-Wakefield's Los Angeles plant. The overall length of each piece is 40", the overall depth is 36½", and the overall height is 32½". The depth of the seat is 22½", and the height of the back is 15". Yardage required for each piece is 6¾ yards of 50" material.

M 5628-78　　　　　　*DAVENPORT*　　　　　　*1952*

This davenport was an exclusive "West Coast" design. The overall length is 78". The depth of the seat is 21", the height of the back is 16", and the overall height is 31". Yardage required: 7½ yards of 50" material.

M 5608 LR   *LEG REST*   *1952*

The top of this "West Coast" only leg rest measures 28" square . The height is 17". Yardage required: 2½ yards of 50" material.

M 5608–28   *SINGLE FILLER*   *1952*

This pattern was available only from the Los Angeles plant. The width of the seat is 28", the depth of the seat is 22½", and the height of the back is 15". The overall height is 32½", and the overall depth is 36½". Yardage required: 4 yards of 50" material.

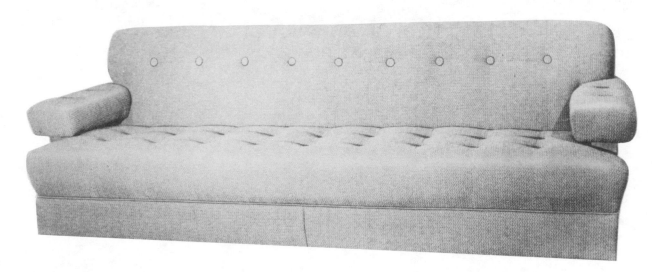

M 5608–100   *DAVENPORT*   *1952*

The overall length of this "West Coast" only davenport is 100", the overall depth is 36½", the overall height is 32½", and the depth of the seat is 22½". The height of the back is 15". Yardage required: 11 yards of 50" material.

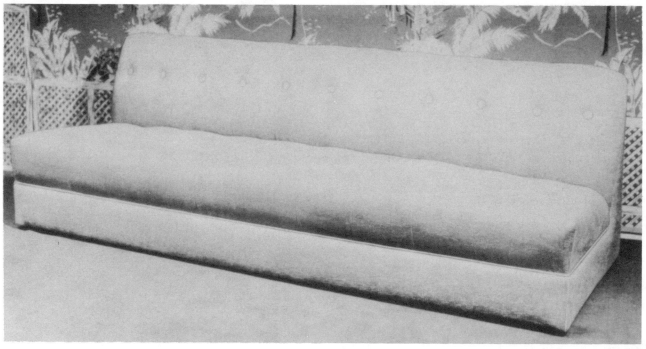

M 5608–95   *ARMLESS DAVENPORT*   *1952*

The overall length of this "West Coast" only davenport is 95", the overall depth is 36½", and the overall height is 32½". The depth of the seat is 22½", and the height of the back is 15". Yardage required: 10 yards of 50" material.

modern furniture

that lives up to its "Nice-to-Live-With" look

M 360 RC or M 360 LC   *RIGHT OR LEFT ARM CHAIR*   *1947–48*
Wood appliqué arms.

M 360   *SINGLE FILLER*   *1947–48*
Sectional filler unit without arms. A curved single filler M 363 was also available. Also shown: M 346 C Wing Chair, M 306 G Round Cocktail Table, and M 311 G Corner Table.

modern

...with an air of friendly charm

Heywood-Wakefield's skill with curves brings a new charm to Modern! Finishes are light and designs are "Home-Planned" so you can be sure of a harmonious background as you add pieces to living room, dining room, bedroom. Ask for Heywood-Wakefield Modern at better furniture and department stores.

HEYWOOD-WAKEFIELD
EST. 1826

GARDNER, MASS.

M 360 C   ARM CHAIR   1947–48
Left: Wood appliqué arms. Also shown: M 304 G Two-Tier End Table.

LEFT OR RIGHT ARM CHAIR
M 560 LC OR M 560 RC   1951–53
Below: Model number changed to M 960 LC or RC in 1953. Width of cushion is 23", depth of cushion is 22". Height of back is 21", overall height is 32". Yardage required: 4½ yards of 54" material.

M 560   SINGLE FILLER   1951–53
Not shown: Model number changed to M 960 in 1953. Same as M 561 Double Filler except half as wide. Width of cushion 23", depth of cushion 22". Height of back 21", overall height is 32". Yardage required: 3½ yards of 54" material.

M 561   DOUBLE FILLER   1951–53
Below: Model number changed to M 961 in 1953. Width of seat 48", depth of seat 22". Height of back 21", overall height is 32". Yardage required: 5½ yards of 54" material.

DOUBLE FILLER WITH RIGHT OR LEFT ARM
M 561 LC OR M 561 RC   1951–53
Not shown: Model number changed to M 961 LC or RC in 1953. Same as M 560 LC or RC except double wide. Width of seat is 48", depth of seat is 22". Height of back is 21", overall height is 32". Yardage required: 7 yards of 54" material. Also shown: M 338 G Corner Table.

M 560 C   ARM CHAIR   *1951–53*
Above: Model number changed to M 960 C in 1953. Width of seat cushion is 23", depth of cushion is 22". Height of back is 21", overall height is 32". Yardage required: 5 yards of 54" material.

M 562–68   DAVENPORT   *1951–53*
Right: Model number changed to M 962–68 in 1953. Width between arms is 68", depth of cushions is 22". Height of back is 21" and overall height is 32". Yardage required: 10½ yards of 54" material.

M 561 48   LOVE SEAT   *1951–53*
Below: Model number changed to M 961–48 in 1953. Width between arms is 48", depth of seat is 22". Height of back is 21" and overall height is 32". Yardage required: 8 yards of 54" material.

M 563   CURVED SINGLE FILLER   *1951–52*

Illustration shows three Curved Fillers. Cushion width at front 22" and at back 33". Depth of cushion 22". Height of back 21". Overall height is 32". Yardage required: 4 yards of 54" material. Also Shown: M 396 G Wedge-Shaped Tier Table (2 shown).

M 595 C   ARM CHAIR   *1952–55*

The width of the seat is 26", the depth of the seat is 22", and the overall height is 30". Yardage required: 4 yards of 54" material.

M 595 RC OR M 595 LC   RIGHT OR LEFT ARM CHAIR   *1952–55*

Right Arm Chair shown: The width of the seat is 26", the depth of the seat is 22", and the overall height is 30". Yardage required: 3½ yards of 54" material.

M 595   SINGLE FILLER   *1952–55*

The width of this seat is 26", the depth of the seat is 22", and the overall height is 30". Yardage required: 3½ yards of 54" material. Also shown: M 392 G Square Cocktail Table, M 338 G Corner Table.

Double Filler with Right or Left Arm
M 596 LC or M 596 RC   *1952–54*
Above: Left Double Filler with Arm shown: The width of the seat is 51", the depth of the seat is 22", and the overall height is 30". Yardage required: 5½ yards of 54" material.

M 596-51   *Love Seat*   *1952–54*
Right: The width of the seat is 51", the depth of the seat is 22", and the overall height is 30". Yardage required: 6¼ yards of 54" material.

M 596   *Double Filler*   *1952–54*
Below: The width of the seat is 51", the depth of the seat is 22", and the overall height is 30". Yardage required: 5 yards of 54" material.

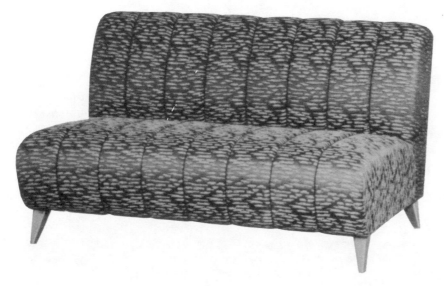

M 597–76   DAVENPORT   *1952–55*
The width of the seat is 76", the depth of the seat is 22", and the overall height is 30". Yardage required: 8 yards of 54" material.

M 755 C   ARM CHAIR   *1954–55*
Seat: 24" wide by 21" deep. Back height 15".
Overall dimensions: 34" wide; 33" deep;
29½" high. Yardage required: 5¾ yards of 54"
material.

M 755   *SINGLE FILLER*   *1954–55*

Seat: 24" wide by 21" deep. Back height 15". Overall dimensions: 24" wide; 33" deep; 29½" high. Yardage required: 3½ yards of 54" material.

M 755 LC or M 755 RC   *LEFT OR RIGHT ARM CHAIR*   *1954–55*

Both shown: Seat: 24" wide by 21" deep. Back height 15". Overall dimensions: 29" wide; 33" deep; 29½" high. Yardage required: 5 yards of 54" material.

M 756   *DOUBLE FILLER*   *1954–55*

Not shown: Same as M 755 except double wide. Seat: 48" wide by 21" deep. Back height 15". Overall dimensions: 48" wide; 33" deep; 29½" high. Yardage required: 5½ yards of 54" material.

M 756 LC or M 756 RC   *DOUBLE FILLER WITH LEFT OR RIGHT ARM*   *1954–55*

Not shown: Same as M 755 LC or RC except double wide. Seat: 48" wide by 21" deep. Back height 15". Overall dimensions: 53" wide; 33" deep; 29½" high. Yardage required: 6½ yards of 54" material. Also shown: M 938 G Corner Table.

M 756–48   *LOVE SEAT*   *1954–55*
Seat: 48" wide by 21" deep. Back height 15". Overall dimensions: 58" wide; 33" deep; 29½" high. Yardage required: 7 yards of 54" material.

M 758–68   *DAVENPORT*   *1954–55*
Seat: 68" wide by 21" deep. Back height 15". Overall dimensions: 78" wide; 33" deep; 29½" high. Yardage required: 10¼ yards of 54" material.

M 965 LC OR M 965 RC   *LEFT OR RIGHT ARM CHAIR*   1953
The width of the cushion is 23", the depth of the cushion is 22", the height of the back is 22", and the overall height is 32". Yardage required: 4½ yards of 54" material.

M 966   *DOUBLE FILLER*   1953
The width of the seat is 48", the depth of the seat is 22", the height of the back is 22", and the overall height is 32". Yardage required: 5½ yards of 54" material.

M 966 LC OR M 966 RC   *DOUBLE FILLER WITH LEFT OR RIGHT ARM*   1953
Not shown: Same as M 965 LC or RC except double wide. The width of the seat is 48", the depth of the seat is 22", the height of the back is 22", and the overall height is 32". Yardage required: 7 yards of 54" material.

M 965   *SINGLE FILLER*   1953
Not shown: Same as M 966 but half as wide. The width of the cushion is 23", the depth of the cushion is 22", the height of the back is 22", and the overall height is 32". Yardage required: 3½ yards of 54" material. Also shown: M 338 G Corner Table.

M 965 C   *ARM CHAIR*   1953
The width of the seat cushion is 23", the depth of the cushion is 22", the height of the back is 22", and the overall height is 32". Yardage required: 5½ yards of material.

M 966–48   LOVE SEAT   *1953*
Top Left: The width between the arms is 48", the depth of the seat is 22", the height of the back is 22", and the overall height is 32". Yardage required: 8 yards of 54" material.

M 968-68   DAVENPORT   *1953*
Middle Left: The width between the arms is 68", the depth of the cushion is 22", the height of the back is 22", and the overall height is 32". Yardage required: 10½ yards of 54" material. Also shown: M 503 G Magazine Rack / End Table.

LEFT OR RIGHT BUMPER END OFFS
M 977 L OR M 977 R   *1954–57*
Below: Seat: 61" wide by 21" deep. Back height is 15". Overall dimensions: 61" wide; 33" deep; 29½" high. Yardage required: 7 yards of 54" material.

M 987   QUARTER ROUND FILLER   *1954–57*
Below: Seat: 28½" at front; 60" at back. Depth of seat is 21". Back height is 15". Overall dimensions: 72" wide; 33" deep; 29½" high. Yardage required: 7¼ yards of 54" material.

LEFT OR RIGHT ASYMMETRICAL CURVED UNITS
M 979 L OR M 979 R   1954–55
Seat: 42" at front; 60" at back. Depth of seat is 21".
Back height is 15". Overall dimensions: 66" wide;
33" on straight side; 38" at curve; 29½" high.
Yardage required: 7 yards of 54" material.

M 986 LC OR *M 986 RC*   DOUBLE FILLER WITH LEFT OR RIGHT ARM   *1954–57*
Seat: 48" wide by 21" deep. Back height is 16". Overall dimensions: 53" wide; 33" deep; 29½" high. Yardage required: 7 yards of 54" material. Also shown: M 908 G Step-End Table.

LEFT OR RIGHT ARM CHAIR
M 975 LC OR *M 975 RC*   *1954–57*
Seat: 24" wide by 21" deep. Back height 16".
Overall dimensions: 29" wide; 33" deep; 29½" high. Yardage required: 4½ yards of 54" material.

M 975   SINGLE FILLER   *1954–57*
Seat: 24" wide by 21" deep. Back height 16".
Overall dimensions: 24" wide; 33" deep; 29½" high. Yardage required: 3½ yards of 54" material.

M 975 C   ARM CHAIR   *1954–57*
Seat: 24" wide by 21" deep. Back height 16".
Overall dimensions: 34" wide; 33" deep; 29½" high. Yardage required: 5½ yards of 54" material.

M 986-48   LOVE SEAT   *1954–57*
Seat: 48" wide by 21" deep. Back height 16".
Overall dimensions: 58" wide; 33" deep; 29½" high. Yardage required: 8 yards of 54" material.

M 986   DOUBLE FILLER   1954–57
Top Left: Seat: 48" wide by 21" deep. Back height 16". Overall dimensions: 48" wide; 33" deep; 29½" high. Yardage required: 5½ yards of 54" material.

M 988–68   DAVENPORT   1954–56
Middle Left: Seat: 68" wide by 21" deep. Back height 16". Overall dimensions: 78" wide; 33" deep; 29½" high. Yardage required: 10½ yards of 54" material.

LEFT OR RIGHT ARM CHAIR
M 935 LC OR M 935 RC   1954–56
Below: Seat: 24" wide by 21" deep. Back height 16". Overall dimensions: 28" wide; 34" deep; 31" high. Yardage required: 5½ yards of 54" material.

M 935   SINGLE FILLER   1954–56
Below: Seat: 24" wide by 21" deep. Back height is 16". Overall dimensions: 24" wide; 34" deep, 31" high. Yardage required: 4 yards of 54" material.

M 936   DOUBLE FILLER   1954–56
Below: Not shown: Same as M 935 except double wide. Seat: 48" wide by 21" deep. Back height 16". Overall dimensions: 48" wide; 34" deep; 31" high. Yardage required: 6½ yards of 54" material.

DOUBLE FILLER WITH LEFT OR RIGHT ARM
M 936 LC OR M 936 RC   1954–56
Below: Not shown: Same as M 935 LC or RC except double wide. Seat: 48" wide by 21" deep. Back height 16". Overall dimensions: 52" wide; 34" deep; 31" high. Material required: 7½ yards of 54" material. Also shown: M 938 G Corner Table.

M 935 C ARM CHAIR 1954–56
Top: Seat: 24" wide by 21" deep. Back height is 16". Overall dimensions: 32" wide; 34" deep; 31" high. Yardage required: 6 yards of 54" material.

M 937–84 DAVENPORT SLEEPER 1954–56
Middle: Illustrations show the M 937–84 set up as a sleeper with the cushions removed and as a conventional davenport. The reversible, foam rubber mattress measures 75" by 30". Seat: 75" wide by 21" deep. Back height is 16". Overall dimensions: 84" wide; 34" deep; 31" high. 12½ yards of 54" material is required.

M 936–48 LOVE SEAT 1954–56
Bottom: Seat: 48" wide by 21" deep. Back height is 16". Overall dimensions: 56" wide; 34" deep; 31" high. Yardage required: 8½ yards of 54" material.

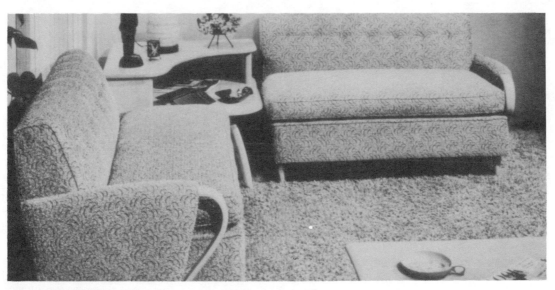

M 981 LC OR M 981 RC   DOUBLE FILLER WITH LEFT OR RIGHT ARM   *1954–55*
Above: Seat: 48" wide by 21" deep. Back height is 15". Overall dimensions: 52" wide; 33" deep; 29½" high. Yardage required: 6½ yards of 54" material. Also shown: M 938 G Corner Table.

M 980   SINGLE FILLER   *1954–55*
Middle Left: Seat: 24" wide by 21" deep. Back height 15". Overall dimensions: 24" wide; 33" deep; 29½" high. Yardage required: 3½ yards of 54" material.

LEFT OR RIGHT ARM CHAIRS
M 980 LC OR M 980 RC   *1954–55*
Middle Left: Seat: 24" wide by 21" deep. Back height is 15". Overall dimensions: 28" wide; 33" deep; 29½" high. Yardage required: 4½ yards of 54" material. Also shown: M 938 G Corner Table.

M 980 C   ARM CHAIR   *1954–55*
Middle Right: Seat: 24" wide by 21" deep. Back height is 15". Overall dimensions: 32" wide; 33" deep; 29½" high. Yardage required: 5½ yards of 54" material.

M 981   DOUBLE FILLER   *1954–55*
Right: Seat: 48" wide by 21" deep. Back height is 15". Overall dimensions: 48" wide; 33" deep; 29½" high. Yardage required: 5½ yards of 54" material.

M 981–48   LOVE SEAT   1954–55
Seat: 48" wide by 21" deep. Back height 15". Overall dimensions: 56" wide; 33" deep; 29½" high. Yardage required: 7 yards of 54" material.

M 982–68   DAVENPORT   1954–55
Seat: 68" wide by 21" deep. Back height 15". Overall dimensions: 76" wide; 33" deep; 29½" high. Yardage required: 10 yards of 54" material.

M 1195   SINGLE FILLER   1955–56
Seat: 26" wide by 22" deep. Back height 17". Overall dimensions: 26" wide; 35" deep; 30" high. Yardage required: 3¼ yards of 54" material.

LEFT OR RIGHT ARM CHAIR
M 1195 LC OR M 1195 RC   1955–56
Right Arm Chair shown: Seat: 26" wide by 22" deep. Back height 17". Overall dimensions: 30" wide; 35" deep; 30" high. Yardage required: 3½ yards of 54" material.

M 1195 C   ARM CHAIR   1955–56
Seat: 26" wide by 22" deep. Back height 17". Overall dimensions: 34" wide; 35" deep; 30" high. Yardage required: 4 yards of 54" material.

LEFT OR RIGHT ARM DOUBLE FILLER
M 1196 LC OR M 1196 RC   *1955–56*
Left Arm Double Filler shown: Seat: 51" wide by 22" deep.
Back height 17". Overall dimensions: 55" wide; 35" deep;
30" high. Yardage required: 5¼ yards of 54" material.

M 1196   *DOUBLE FILLER*   *1955–56*
Seat: 51" wide by 22" deep. Back height 17". Overall
dimensions: 51" wide; 35" deep; 30" high. Yardage
required: 5 yards of 54" material.

M 1196–51   *LOVE SEAT*   *1955–56*
Seat 51" wide by 22" deep. Back height 17". Overall
dimensions: 59" wide; 35" deep; 30" high. Yardage
required: 6 yards of 54" material.

M 1788   *QUARTER ROUND*   *1958*
Designed to be used with either the Gramercy Park or
Monterey Groups. Overall dimensions: 72" wide; 34"
deep; 29" high. Yardage required: 7½ yards of 54" material required. Add two yards for full self platform under
seat cushion.

M 1790 C   GRAMERCY PARK ARM CHAIR   *1958*
Left: Overall dimensions: 36" wide; 34" deep; 29" high. Yardage required: 4½ yards of 54" material. Add ¾ of a yard for full self platform under seat cushion.

M 1197–76   DAVENPORT   *1955–56*
Middle: Seat: 76" wide by 22" deep. Back height 17". Overall dimensions: 84" wide; 35" deep; 30" high. Yardage required: 8 yards of 54" material.

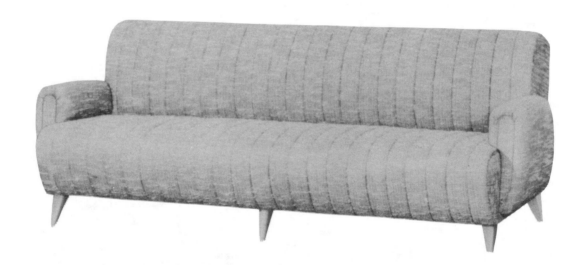

M 1790 LC OR RC   GRAMERCY PARK LEFT OR RIGHT ARM CHAIR   *1958*
Overall dimensions: 30" wide; 34" deep; 29" high. Yardage required: 4 yards of 54" material. Add ¾ of a yard for full self platform under seat cushion.

M 1790   GRAMERCY PARK SINGLE FILLER   *1958*
Overall dimensions: 24" wide; 34" deep; 29" high. Yardage required: 3½ yards of 54" material. Add ¾ yard of a yard for full self platform under seat cushion. Also shown: M 1507 G Corner Table.

GRAMERCY PARK LOVE SEAT

M 1791–60 1958

Right: Overall dimensions: 60" wide; 34" deep; 29" high. Yardage required: 6½ yards of 54" material. Add ¾ yard for full self platform under seat cushion.

RIGHT OR LEFT BUMPER END OFF

M 1789 R OR L 1958

Above: Designed to be used with either the Gramercy Park or Monterey Groups. Overall dimensions: 48" wide; 34" deep; 29" high. Yardage required: 6 yards of 54" material. Add 1¾ yards for full self platform under seat cushion.

M 1792–84 GRAMERCY PARK SOFA 1958

Below: Overall dimensions: 84" wide; 34" deep; 29" high. Yardage required: 10 yards of 54" material. Add 2 yards for full self platform under seat cushion.

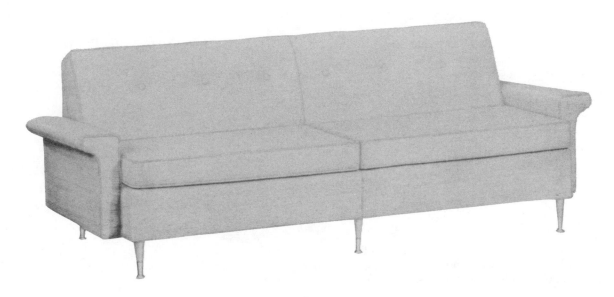

M 1785 C   MONTEREY ARM CHAIR   *1958*

Overall dimensions: 32" wide; 34" deep; 29" high. Yardage required: five yards of 54" material. Add ¾ yard for full self platform under seat cushion.

M 1787–80   MONTEREY SOFA   *1958*

Overall dimensions: 80" wide; 34" deep; 29" high. Yardage required: 9½ yards of 54" material. Add 2 yards for full self platform under seat cushion. Also shown: M 1507 G.

M 1785 & M 1790 SINGLE FILLER   *1958*

Middle Left: Designed to be used with either the Gramercy Park or Monterey Groups. Overall dimensions: 24" wide; 34" deep; 29" high. Yardage required: 3½ yards of 54" material. Add ¾ yard for full self platform under seat cushion.

MONTEREY RIGHT OR LEFT ARM CHAIR
M 1785 RC OR LC   *1958*
Middle Right: Left Arm Chair shown. Overall dimensions are 28" wide, 34" deep, 29" high. Yardage required is 4 yards of 54" material.

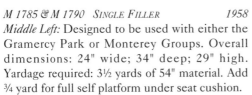

MONTEREY RIGHT OR LEFT ARM SOFA
M 1786 RC OR LC   *1958*
Right: Right Arm Sofa shown. Overall dimensions are 52" wide; 34" deep; and 29" high. Yardage required is 6 yards of 54" material.

M 1786–56　　　　*MONTEREY LOVE SEAT*　　　　*1958*
Overall dimensions: 56" wide; 34" deep; 29" high. Yardage required: 6½ yards of
54" material. Add ¾ yard for full self platform under seat cushion.

GRAMERCY PARK PILLOW BACK SOFA
M 1793–96　　　　　*1958*
Overall dimensions: 96" wide; 34"
deep; 30" high. Yardage required:
13½ yards of 54" material. Add two
yards for full self platform under
seat cushion.

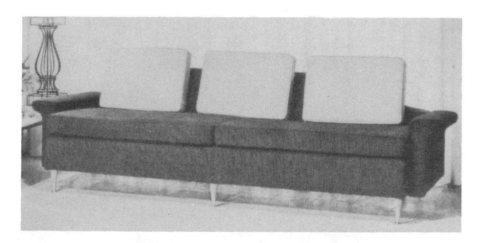

M 1786 & M1791　　　　*DOUBLE FILLER*　　　　*1958*
Designed to be used with either the Gramercy Park or Monterey Groups. Overall dimensions are 52" wide, 34" deep, and 29" high. Yardage required is 5½ yards of 54" material. Also
shown: M 1504 G Step-End Table.

End Notes

— From Country Store to — Modern Furniture

(1) The historical information available, much of which is derived from Heywood-Wakefield's own company histories, seems to offer somewhat conflicting information regarding what machines were invented and designed by Levi Heywood and what machines were invented by Gardner Watkins, his assistant. One can assume that regardless of who invented the machines, Levi Heywood's name likely appeared on patents, which perhaps is the reason why some inventions credited at times to Watkins were also sometimes credited to Heywood.

(2) Again an argument can be made for crediting inventions to both Levi Heywood and Gardner Watkins.

(3) As in the case of Watkins and Heywood, the source of early innovations at Wakefield Rattan is muddy at best. It seems in many instances that Wakefield designed and/or patented machines which were created to put Houston's newly-invented processes to work.

Sources:

A Completed Century, 1826-1926: The Story of the Heywood-Wakefield Company, Heywood-Wakefield Company, Boston, 1926.

"Chronological History of Marshall Burns Lloyd & Lloyd Manufacturing Co.," Lloyd/Flanders Industries, Inc., 1992.

Greenwood, Richard N., *The Five Heywood Brothers (1826-1951): A Brief History of the Heywood-Wakefield Company during 125 Years*, Heywood-Wakefield Company, New York, 1951.

— In the Modern Manner —

Sources:

Greif, Martin, *Depression Modern: The Thirties Style in America*, Universe Books, New York, 1981.

Greenwood, Richard N., *The Five Heywood Brothers (1826-1951): A Brief History of the Heywood-Wakefield Company during 125 Years*, Heywood-Wakefield Company, New York, 1951.

"The Homes of Today and Tomorrow," *Design*, October, 1933, p. 15.

Kennedy, Christopher, Gilbert Rohde: *The Heywood-Wakefield Years*, DESIGNbase, 1993.

"Merchandising Modern for the Masses," *Furniture Record*, March, 1935, p.10.

Pile, John, *Dictionary of 20th Century Design*, Roundtable Press, New York, 1990.

"Steelcraft for 1937," The Murray Ohio Manufacturing Co., Cleveland, 1937.

"What Every Man Should See at the Fair," *Furniture Record and Journal*, June, 1933, p. 25.

"Official Guide Book of the Fair," A Century of Progress, Cuneo Press, Chicago, 1933.

"Again Modern for the Masses," *Furniture Record*, October, 1935.

Note: In compiling the information for this chapter, a variety of other sources were used, including advertisements from trade journals and magazines, company press releases, company catalogs, copies of *Heywood-Wakefield Shop News*, and personal interviews with former employees and their families.

— "Who Serves Our Country Best" —

(1) This 1943 Heywood-Wakefield promotional booklet, apparently geared towards explaining the absence of Heywood-Wakefield furniture to customers and retailers, chronicles the company's transition from peace-time to war-time production. The theme of the booklet: when forced to choose between its own bottom line and the country's well-being, Heywood-Wakefield chose the latter. All subsequent quotes in this chapter, unless otherwise noted, are from this booklet.

(2) This quote was taken from a March 2, 1943, edition of *Heywood-Wakefield Shop News*, where excerpts from Posser's speech were printed.

Sources:

Who Serves Our Country Best, Heywood-Wakefield Company, Gardner Massachusetts, 1943.

Heywood-Wakefield catalogs, including the 1941-42 Modern catalog, and the 1943 and 1944 poster catalogs.

Heywood-Wakefield Shop News: September 1, 1944, March 2, 1945, and April 6, 1945.

— From Boom to Bust —
Sources:

"Changes in Stockholdings Filed With Exchanges, SEC," *The Wall Street Journal*, June 23, 1966, p. 18.

"Chronological History of Marshall Burns Lloyd Manufacturing Co.," Lloyd/Flanders Industries, Inc., 1992.

"Heywood-Wakefield Co. Closes Gardner, Mass., Furniture Plant Today," *The Wall Street Journal*, January 13, 1961, p. 11.

"Heywood-Wakefield Co. Holders to Vote Dec. 14 on Recapitalization Plan," *The Wall Street Journal*, November 23, 1965, p. 10.

"Heywood-Wakefield Co. May Decide Today On Closing Main Plant," *The Wall Street Journal*, January 16, 1961, p. 8.

Heywood-Wakefield Company Annual Report, 1979.

"Heywood-Wakefield's Recapitalization Plan Rejected by Holders," *The Wall Street Journal*, January 31, 1966, p. 18.

"Heywood-Wakefield Set To Refinance Debt; No Preferred Payout Seen," *The Wall Street Journal*, March 29, 1966, p. 27.

Heywood-Wakefield Shop News: March 2, 1945, and September 1, 1944.

"Heywood-Wakefield Will Reopen Gardner Plant as Workers Let 10% Pay Cut Stand," *The Wall Street Journal*, January 19, 1961, p. 8.

Johnson, Ed, "An Era Ends: H-W Closes Shop," *The Gardner News*, June 13, 1979, p. 1.

"Simplex Time Recorder Owner Buys About 40% of Heywood-Wakefield," *The Wall Street Journal*, January 6, 1966.

— It Wasn't All Modern —
Sources:

A Completed Century, 1826 - 1926: The Story of the Heywood-Wakefield Company, Heywood-Wakefield Company, Boston, 1926.

Greenwood, Richard N., *The Five Heywood Brothers (1826-1951): A Brief History of the Heywood-Wakefield Company during 125 Years*, Heywood-Wakefield Company, New York, 1951.

"Chronological History of Marshall Burns Lloyd & Lloyd Manufacturing Co.," Lloyd Flanders Industries, Inc., 1992.

Gebhard, David and Harriette VonBreton, *Kem Weber*, University of Southern California, Santa Barbara, California, 1969.

Loewy, Raymond, *Industrial Design: Raymond Loewy*, Overlook Press, Woodstock, New York, 1979.

Note: In compiling the information for this chapter, a variety of other sources were used, including company press releases, company catalogs, copies of *Heywood-Wakefield Shop News*, and personal interviews with former employees and their families.

— The Crafting of Modern —
Sources:

"Quality Inside and Out," Heywood-Wakefield Co., circa, 1950.

Note: In compiling the information for this chapter a variety of other sources were used, including company press releases, company catalogs, copies of *Heywood-Wakefield Shop News*, and personal interviews with former employees and their families.

— Modern Marks —
Sources:

Heywood-Wakefield Shop News, February 1, 1946.

Note: In compiling the information for this chapter a variety of other sources were used, including company catalogs, copies of *Heywood-Wakefield Shop News*, and personal interviews.

Heywood - Wakefield Modern Value Guide

The market for Heywood-Wakefield has changed dramatically since this book was originally published, and so for this latest edition, I have enlisted the help of Jim Toler of Springdale in Three Oaks, Michigan. Jim is nationally known, specializing in buying and selling Heywood-Wakefield throughout the country. We have arrived at the following guidelines for valuing Heywood-Wakefield Modern.

Prices are national retail prices for mint original condition or professional quality refinish. The Internet has virtually eliminated regional price variations.

Prices are retail prices for Wheat and Champagne finish only; deduct 15% for Platinum or Tampico. Other original finishes are too dark for most collectors and not desirable.

The consensus among Heywood-Wakefield dealers and collectors is that a good quality refinish (one that duplicates the original) is worth as much as the original finish in pristine condition. Heywood-Wakefield was designed to be sleek and modern and is not suited to patina or wear.

Upholstered pieces are desirable because they are completely rare. The configuration of a sectional sofa has a considerable effect on the value — the more pieces or sections, the more value. If there are not enough sections to make a whole sofa, there is limited value. With sectionals, 1+1+1=5.

Style Number	Name	Years of Production	Price Range	Page Number
C2787 C	Upholstered Pull-Up Chair	1936-40	$600.00 – 750.00	61,67,81,84,102
C2794 ACB	Side Chair with Channel Back	1936-40	$450.00 – 550.00	69,93
C2794 A	Side Chair	1937-41	$450.00 – 550.00	54
C2794 C	Arm Chair	1936-41	$500.00 – 600.00	54
C2900	Bed	1936	$250.00 – 325.00	65
C2901	3-Drawer Chest	1936	$600.00 – 750.00	63
C2902	4-Drawer Chest	1936	$600.00 – 750.00	62
C2903	Mirror	1936	$125.00 – 250.00	63,64
C2904	Vanity	1936	$750.00 – 850.00	66
C2905	Mirror	1936	$175.00 – 250.00	66
C2906	Dressing Table	1936	$500.00 – 600.00	64
C2907	Bench	1936	$150.00 – 225.00	64,66
C2908	Night Stand	1936	$250.00 – 325.00	62,65
C2909	Bed	1936	$300.00 – 375.00	62
C2910	Center Cabinet	1936-37	$750.00 – 950.00	54,56,57,63,65
C2911 W	Desk / Chest	1936	$950.00 – 1,100.00	68
C2912	Shelf	1936-37	$200.00 – 300.00	54,56,57,68
C2913	Closed Hutch Cabinet	1936	$300.00 – 400.00	55,65
C2914 L or R	Left or Right Pier Cabinet	1936	$450.00 – 550.00	54,56
C2916 A	Chair	1936	$100.00 – 125.00	55
C2916 G	Extension Table	1936	$400.00 – 500.00	55
C2917	Server	1936	$400.00 – 600.00	54,55,56
C2918 A	Side Chair	1936	$400.00 – 500.00	56
C2918 G	Table with Swing Under Leaves	1936-38	$1,100.00 – 1,200.00	56
C2918 C	Arm Chair	1936	$500.00 – 600.00	56
C2920 C	Arm Chair	1936	$850.00 – 950.00	63,69
C2920–60	Davenport	1936	$1,250.00 – 1,500.00	68
C2921 G	Round Coffee Table	1936-39	$500.00 – 600.00	71,91
C2922 G	Round Corner Table	1936-38	$450.00 – 550.00	68,94
C2923 G	Coffee Table	1936	$350.00 – 450.00	68
C2924 G	Coffee Table	1936	$150.00 – 175.00	72
C2925 G	Console or Game Table	1936-38	$750.00 – 950.00	72,77,97
C2926 G	Chairside Table	1936	$350.00 – 400.00	72
C2927 G	End Table	1936-38	$375.00 – 450.00	71,90,95
C2928	Open Shelf Bookcase	1936-38	$500.00 – 600.00	69
C2929	Compartment Bookcase	1936-38	$800.00 – 950.00	69,70
C2930 W	Kneehole Desk	1936	$950.00 – 1,150.00	67
C2931	5-Drawer Chest	1936	$800.00 – 950.00	64
C2932 G	Extension Table	1936-39	$2,000.00 – 2,500.00	73,99
C3135	Round Mirror	1936	$175.00 – 250.00	60,61
C3150	Zephyr Bed	1936-37	$275.00 – 350.00	58,59
C3151	Zephyr 3-Drawer Dresser	1936-37	$500.00 – 650.00	58
C3152	Zephyr 4-Drawer Chest	1936-37	$550.00 – 700.00	59
C3153 X	Zephyr Oblong Mirror	1936-37	$150.00 – 200.00	58
C3154	Zephyr Vanity	1936-37	$500.00 – 650.00	59
C3155	Mirror	1937-39	$150.00 – 200.00	58,59
C3156	Zephyr Dressing Table	1936	$500.00 – 600.00	58
C3157	Zephyr Bench	1936-37	$200.00 – 250.00	58
C3158	Zephyr Night Stand	1936-37	$200.00 – 275.00	58,59
C3160	Penthouse Bed	1936	$250.00 – 325.00	60
C3161	Penthouse 4-Drawer Chest	1936	$500.00 – 650.00	61
C3162	Penthouse 5-Drawer Chest	1936	$500.00 – 650.00	60
C3163	Oblong Mirror	1936	$200.00 – 275.00	61
C3164	Penthouse Vanity	1936	$850.00 – 1,000.00	61
C3166	Penthouse Dressing Table-Desk	1936	$500.00 – 650.00	60
C3167	Penthouse Bench	1936	$150.00 – 225.00	60,61
C3168	Penthouse Night Stand	1936	$175.00 – 250.00	60
C3170 G	Two-Tier End Table	1936-39	$350.00 – 450.00	70,89,92,112,115
C3171 G	Coffee Table	1936-38	$350.00 – 450.00	70
C3172 C	Arm Chair	1936-37	$850.00 – 1,000.00	70
C3172–63	Davenport	1936-37	$1,200.00 – 1,500.00	70
C3173 C	Arm Chair	1936	$1,000.00 – 1,250.00	71

Heywood

C3173–66	Davenport	1936	$1,750.00 – 2,000.00	71
C3174 C	Arm Chair	1936	$500.00 – 800.00	72
C3174–66	Davenport	1936	$1,000.00 – 1,250.00	72
C3300	Bed	1937-38	$300.00 – 375.00	87
C3301	3-Drawer Dresser	1937-38	$650.00 – 800.00	86
C3302	4-Drawer Chest	1937-38	$700.00 – 850.00	87
C3303	Mirror	1937-38	$175.00 – 250.00	86
C3304	Vanity	1937-38	$650.00 – 800.00	88
C3305	Mirror	1937-38	$175.00 – 225.00	88
C3306	Dressing Table	1937-38	$650.00 – 850.00	88
C3307	Bench	1937-38	$150.00 – 200.00	88
C3308	Night Stand	1937-38	$200.00 – 250.00	87
C3309	Bed	1937-38	$300.00 – 375.00	86
C3310	Chest	1937-39	$480.00 – 600.00	76
C3311 W	Desk Base	1937-39	$650.00 – 800.00	93,116
C3312	Open Shelf Hutch Cabinet	1937-39	$300.00 – 400.00	76,93,116
C3314	Server	1937-38	$500.00 – 700.00	74
C3315	Open Base Buffet	1937-38	$1,250.00 – 1,500.00	74
C3316	Glass Door Cabinet	1937-39	$350.00 – 400.00	73,99
C3317	Airflow Server	1937-39	$850.00 – 1,000.00	73,75,99
C3318	Buffet	1937-39	$1,000.00 – 1,250.00	73,99
C3319 G	Extension Table	1937-39	$400.00 – 500.00	78
C3321 A	Side Chair	1937-39	$75.00 – 100.00	78
C3322 A	Side Chair	1937-39	$100.00 – 125.00	75
C3324 AX	Side Chair	1937-38	$450.00 – 550.00	74,88
C3324 C	Arm Chair	1937-38	$500.00 – 600.00	74
C3325 C	Occasional Chair	1937-40	$700.00 – 800.00	79,83,85,109
C3326 C	Barrel Chair	1937-39	$600.00 – 800.00	89,117
C3327 G	Corner Table	1937-38	$500.00 – 650.00	90,91
C3328 W	Kneehole Desk	1937-39	$900.00 – 1,100.00	95
C3330	Airflow Bed	1937-39	$400.00 – 500.00	82,83
C3331	Airflow 4-Drawer Dresser	1937-39	$900.00 – 1,100.00	83
C3332	Airflow 5-Drawer Chest	1937-39	$1,000.00 – 1,200.00	82
C3333	Airflow Mirror	1937-39	$200.00 – 300.00	83,85
C3334	Airflow Vanity Desk	1937-39	$1,000.00 – 1,200.00	82
C3335	Mirror	1937-39	$175.00 – 200.00	82
C3337	Vanity Bench	1937-38	$200.00 – 250.00	84
C3338	Airflow Night Stand	1937-39	$300.00 – 375.00	82,83,85
C3340	Airflow Vanity	1937-39	$1,200.00 – 1,500.00	84
C3341	Single Filler or Armless Center Section	1937-38	$300.00 – 400.00	90
C3341 RC or LC	Right or Left Arm Chair	1937-38	$400.00 – 500.00	90
C3341 C	Arm Chair	1937-38	$800.00 – 1,000.00	90,91
C3342	Double Filler	1937-38	$300.00 – 400.00	90
C3342–44	Love Seat	1937-38	$1,250.00 – 1,500.00	89
C3343–66	Davenport	1937-38	$2,000.00 – 2,400.00	91
C3345 G	Lamp Table	1938	$350.00 – 450.00	93
C3346 C	Arm Chair	1937-39	$300.00 – 350.00	73
C3346 A	Side Chair	1937-39	$250.00 – 300.00	73
C3347 G	Extension Table	1938-39	$1,800.00 – 2,000.00	74
C3348	Corner Cabinet	1938-39	$900.00 – 1,100.00	76,92
C3348 X	Corner Cabinet	1940-43	$800.00 – 1,000.00	123,135,147,148,171
C3349 G	Gateleg Table	1938-40	$500.00 – 650.00	75,96,137
C3360	Airflow Bed with Cane Panels	1938	$300.00 – 400.00	85
C3361 A	Side Chair	1938-39	$100.00 – 125.00	76
C3361 G	Extension Table	1938-39	$500.00 – 600.00	76,77
C3362	Buffet	1938-39	$750.00 – 900.00	77,101
C3363 A	Side Chair	1938-39	$95.00 – 110.00	77
C3364 G	Cocktail Table	1938	$300.00 – 350.00	92,98
C3365 A	Cane Back Desk Chair	1938	$250.00 – 300.00	95
C3366 W	Desk / Chest Bookcase	1938-39	$1,250.00 – 1,500.00	96
C3367 C	Chair	1938-39	$1,800.00 – 2,200.00	92,114
C3367–66	Davenport	1938-39	$3,500.00 – 4,500.00	92,114
C3368 C	Arm Chair	1938-39	$1,250.00 – 1,750.00	93
C3368 R	Wood Frame Arm Chair	1938	$400.00 – 450.00	94
C3368–63	Davenport	1938	$2,500.00 – 3,000.00	93
C3370	Swedish Modern Bed	1938-39	$350.00 – 425.00	79,80,106,107

C3371–75	Swedish Modern 3-Drawer Dresser	1938-39	$850.00 – 950.00	79,107
C3372	Swedish Modern 4-Drawer Chest	1938-39	$950.00 – 1,100.00	106
C3373	Swedish Modern Mirror	1938-39	$250.00 – 300.00	80,106
C3374	Swedish Modern Vanity	1938 -39	$750.00 – 850.00	80,106
C3376–80	Swedish Modern Vanity, 40" Mirror	1938-39	$850.00 – 950.00	81,105
C3377	Swedish Modern Bench	1938-39	$150.00 – 200.00	80,106
C3378	Swedish Modern Night Stand	1938-39	$225.00 – 275.00	79,80,105,107
C3379	Swedish Modern Vanity Bench	1938-39	$250.00 – 300.00	81,105
C3381 C	Cane Panel Arm Chair	1938-40	$400.00 – 500.00	97,137
C3382 C	Cane Chair with Square Panel	1938-39	$400.00 – 500.00	98
C3383 C	Cane Panel Arm Chair	1938	$400.00 – 500.00	94
C3384 C	Cane Chair with Oval Panel	1938-39	$500.00 – 600.00	98
C3385 C	Open Side Arm Chair	1938-39	$400.00 – 500.00	96
C3386 C	Full Upholstered Arm Chair	1938-39	$850.00 – 1,000.00	96
C3387 C	Arm Chair	1938-40	$1,000.00 – 1,250.00	95,100,136
C3388 C	Upholstered Arm Chair	1938-39	$750.00 – 900.00	97,105
C3389 G	Console Table	1939-42	$750.00 – 850.00	118,120,121,146
C3521 R	Barrel Chair	1939	$500.00 – 600.00	116
C3526 A	Side Chair	1939-40	$375.00 – 450.00	100
C3530 A	Side Chair	1939-42	$150.00 – 225.00	99,172
C3530 C	Arm Chair	1939-42	$175.00 – 250.00	99
C3531 G	End Table	1939	$100.00 – 150.00	100,114
C3532 G	Coffee Table	1939	$200.00 – 250.00	114,115
C3533 G	Lamp Table	1939	$100.00 – 150.00	114
C3534	Bookcase	1939	$250.00 – 450.00	117
C3535 A	Side Chair	1939-43	$300.00 – 400.00	104,116,138,149,150
C3535 C	Arm Chair	1939-43	$350.00 – 450.00	117,138
C3536 A	Side Chair	1939-40	$125.00 – 175.00	101,121
C3537 G	Extension Table	1939	$650.00 – 800.00	101
C3538 G	Side Extension Table	1939	$800.00 – 950.00	100
C3539 W	Crescendo Vanity / Desk	1939-40	$1,500.00 – 1,800.00	104,117
C3540 G	Corner Table	1939-40	$650.00 – 800.00	112,130
C3541	Single Filler	1939-40	$300.00 – 400.00	112,130
C3541 C	Arm Chair	1939-40	$850.00 – 1,000.00	113
C3541 RC or LC	Right or Left Arm Chair	1939-40	$350.00 – 450.00	112,130
C3542	Double Filler	1939-40	$400.00 – 500.00	112,130
C3542–44	Love Seat	1939-40	$1,250.00 – 1,500.00	131
C3543–66	Davenport	1939-40	$1,500.00 – 1,800.00	113
C3544	Pier Cabinet	1939-40	$650.00 – 800.00	136
C3545	Bookcase	1939-40	$500.00 – 550.00	136
C3546 G	End Table	1939-40	$600.00 – 750.00	113
C3547 G	Oval Cocktail Table	1939-40	$800.00 – 900.00	113
C3548 G	Cocktail Table	1939-40	$350.00 – 450.00	112,130
C3549 G	Lamp Table	1939-40	$450.00 – 500.00	113,165,169
C3550	Crescendo Bed	1939-40	$300.00 – 375.00	103
C3551–55	Crescendo Dresser with Mirror	1939-40	$800.00 – 950.00	103
C3552	Crescendo 5-Drawer Chest	1939-40	$1,000.00 – 1,250.00	104
C3553	Hanging Mirror	1939-40	$100.00 – 200.00	104
C3554	Crescendo Vanity	1939-40	$1,000.00 – 1,250.00	102
C3557	Vanity Seat	1939-40	$225.00 – 275.00	102
C3558	Crescendo Night Stand	1939-40	$400.00 – 550.00	103
C3559	Crescendo Blanket Chest	1939	$800.00 – 1,000.00	103
C3560	Skyliner Bed	1939-40	$300.00 – 375.00	108,109
C3561	Skyliner 3-Drawer Dresser	1939-40	$1,000.00 – 1,250.00	109
C3562	Skyliner 4-Drawer Chest	1939-40	$1,000.00 – 1,250.00	108
C3563	Skyliner Mirror	1939-40	$200.00 – 300.00	108,109
C3564	Skyliner Vanity	1939-40	$850.00 – 1,000.00	108
C3567	Skyliner Bench	1939-40	$250.00 – 350.00	108
C3568	Skyliner Night Stand	1939-40	$500.00 – 600.00	108,109
C3570	Bed	1939	$300.00 – 350.00	110,111
C3571	3-Drawer Dresser	1939	$700.00 – 800.00	111
C3572	4-Drawer Chest	1939	$850.00 – 950.00	110
C3573	Mirror	1939	$175.00 – 225.00	110,111
C3574	Vanity	1939	$650.00 – 750.00	110
C3577	Bench	1939	$150.00 – 200.00	110
C3578	Night Stand	1939	$250.00 – 300.00	110,111

C3579 C	Arm Chair	1939	$1,000.00 – 1,250.00	115
C3579–63	Davenport	1939	$2,000.00 – 2,500.00	115
C3582	Corner Bookcase	1940	$650.00 – 750.00	136
C3583	Cabinet Bookcase	1940	$750.00 – 850.00	136
C3584	Chest Base	1940	$800.00 – 900.00	121
C3584 W	Desk / Chest	1940	$800.00 – 900.00	133
C3585	Hutch Top	1940-42	$200.00 – 350.00	121,133,139,143,167
C3586 W	Desk / Chest Bookcase	1940	$1,250.00 – 1,500.00	137
C3588 A	Side Chair	1940	$100.00 – 125.00	123
C3589–66	Davenport	1940	$1,750.00 – 2,250.00	132
C3589 C	Arm Chair	1940	$850.00 – 1,100.00	132
C3594 G	Extension Table	1940	$600.00 – 750.00	120
C3595 A	Side Chair	1940-44	$135.00 – 170.00	144,155
C3595 C	Arm Chair	1940-44	$160.00 – 190.00	144
C3596 C	Arm Chair	1940-44	$200.00 – 225.00	120,126,139
C3596 A	Side Chair	1940-44	$175.00 – 200.00	120,139,153
C3700 A	Side Chair	1941-44	$100.00 – 125.00	147
C3701 A	Side Chair	1940	$150.00 – 175.00	118
C3701 C	Arm Chair	1940	$175.00 – 200.00	118
C3702 A	Side Chair	1940-42	$90.00 – 120.00	143
C3702 C	Arm Chair	1940-42	$100.00 – 125.00	143
C3703 G	Extension Table	1940	$400.00 – 500.00	122
C3704 G	Oval Extension Table	1940-41	$800.00 – 900.00	143,144
C3705	Tea Table	1940-42	$750.00 – 900.00	119
C3706 G	Extension Table	1940-42	$1,000.00 – 1,250.00	118
C3707 G	Extension Table	1940-41	$1,000.00 – 1,250.00	138
C3708	Buffet	1940-42	$900.00 – 1,100.00	118,138
C3709	Buffet	1940-42	$1,250.00 – 1,500.00	120,142,144
C3710	Server	1940-44	$500.00 – 600.00	140
C3711	China Top	1940	$300.00 – 350.00	140
C3711 X	China Top	1941-44	$300.00 – 350.00	140,142
C3712 G	Extension Table	1940	$400.00 – 500.00	123
C3713 G	Extension Table	1940	$700.00 – 850.00	121
C3714 A	Side Chair	1940-42	$100.00 – 125.00	122,145
C3715 A	Side Chair	1940-42	$150.00 – 175.00	119,157
C3716 G	Console Extension Table	1940	$750.00 – 900.00	119
C3717 G	Drawer-Top Cocktail Table	1940-42	$750.00 – 900.00	132,165,166
C3718 G	Hunt Cocktail Table	1940-42	$850.00 – 1,000.00	168
C3719 G	End Table	1940-42	$450.00 – 600.00	131,163
C3720	Cameo Bed	1940-42	$500.00 – 600.00	154
C3721–725	Cameo Dresser with Mirror	1940-42	$400.00 – 500.00	154
C3722	Cameo 4-Drawer Chest	1940-42	$600.00 – 700.00	154
C3723	Hanging Mirror	1940-42	$175.00 – 225.00	155
C3724	Cameo Vanity	1940-42	$300.00 – 500.00	155
C3726	Cameo Vanity Base	1940-42	$500.00 – 600.00	155
C3727	Cameo Vanity Seat	1940-42	$150.00 – 175.00	155
C3728	Cameo Night Stand	1940-42	$150.00 – 200.00	154
C3730	Plaza Bed	1940	$300.00 – 400.00	125
C3731–733	Plaza Dresser with Mirror	1940	$800.00 – 950.00	125
C3732	Plaza 5-Drawer Chest	1940	$900.00 – 1,050.00	126
C3733	Hanging Mirror	1940	$125.00 – 175.00	125
C3734	Vanity	1940	$850.00 – 1,000.00	127
C3735	Hanging Mirror	1940-42	$150.00 – 225.00	126,149,156
C3736	Plaza Vanity Base / Desk	1940	$1,000.00 – 1,150.00	126
C3737	Vanity Pouffe	1940	$160.00 – 200.00	127
C3738	Plaza Night Stand	1940	$300.00 – 350.00	125
C3739	Blanket Bench	1940-42	$800.00 – 1,000.00	124,153
C3740	Challenger Bed	1940	$250.00 – 300.00	128
C3741	Challenger 3-Drawer Dresser	1940	$400.00 – 550.00	128
C3742	Challenger 4-Drawer Chest	1940	$450.00 – 600.00	129
C3743	Hanging Mirror	1940	$175.00 – 225.00	128,129
C3744	Challenger Vanity Base	1940	$250.00 – 375.00	129
C3747	Challenger Vanity Bench	1940	$125.00 – 165.00	129
C3748	Challenger Night Stand	1940	$175.00 – 200.00	128
C3750 G	Kidney-shaped Cocktail Table	1940	$375.00 – 450.00	131,135
C3751 G	Clover Leaf Cocktail Table	1940	$450.00 – 550.00	132

C3752 G	End Table	1940	$325.00 – 425.00	132,134,135
C3753 G	2-Tier End Table	1940-44	$400.00 – 500.00	130,164,169
C3754 G	Lamp Table	1940	$325.00 – 425.00	134
C3755 G	Corner Table	1940-44	$325.00 – 425.00	130,164
C3756 G	Oblong Coffee Table	1940-42	$450.00 – 550.00	134,169
C3757	Table Desk	1940-42	$650.00 – 750.00	173
C3760–72	Davenport	1940	$1,800.00 – 2,000.00	135
C3760 C	Arm Chair	1940	$1,000.00 – 1,200.00	135
C3761–72	Davenport	1940	$1,500.00 – 1,800.00	134
C3761 C	Arm Chair	1940	$750.00 – 850.00	134
C3762 C	Arm Chair	1940	$850.00 – 1,000.00	133
C3763 LR	Leg Rest	1940	$350.00 – 450.00	133
C3764 R	Wing Chair	1940	$650.00 – 750.00	133
C3765 C	Arm Chair	1940-42	$600.00 – 750.00	128,160
C3766	Barrel Chair	1940	$500.00 – 650.00	137
C3767 C	Reading Chair	1940-42	$900.00 – 1,000.00	137,167
C3770	Single Headboard for Twin Beds	1941-42	$500.00 – 650.00	156
C3771 X	Studio End Table	1941-42	$400.00 – 450.00	166
C3777 WX	Bookcase-End Desk	1941-42	$600.00 – 700.00	172
C3790	Rio Bed	1943-44	$400.00 – 500.00	174
C3791	Rio 3-Drawer Dresser	1943-44	$600.00 – 700.00	174
C3791–795	Rio 3-Drawer Dresser with Mirror	1943-44	$650.00 – 750.00	174
C3792	Rio 4-Drawer Chest	1943-44	$800.00 – 900.00	174
C3796	Rio Vanity with Mirror	1943-44	$600.00 – 700.00	175
C3797	Vanity Poutte	1943-44	$200.00 – 250.00	175
C3798	Rio Night Stand	1943-44	$250.00 – 300.00	175
C3900	Catalina Bed	1941-42	$250.00 – 300.00	160
C3901	Catalina Dresser Base	1941-42	$400.00 – 500.00	160
C3901–725	Catalina Dresser with Round Mirror	1941-42	$450.00 – 550.00	158
C3902	Catalina 4-Drawer Chest	1941-42	$450.00 – 550.00	159
C3903	Hanging Mirror	1941-42	$150.00 – 175.00	159,160
C3904	Catalina Vanity Base	1941-42	$450.00 – 550.00	160
C3904–923	Catalina Vanity with Attached Mirror	1941-42	$450.00 – 550.00	160
C3907	Catalina Vanity Bench	1941-42	$175.00 – 200.00	159
C3908	Catalina Night Stand	1941-42	$175.00 – 200.00	160,173
C3910	Miami Bed	1941-42	$400.00 – 500.00	157
C3911–725	Miami Dresser with Attached Mirror	1941-42	$825.00 – 1,000.00	157
C3911	Miami 3-Drawer Dresser	1941-42	$650.00 – 800.00	157
C3912	Miami 4-Drawer Chest	1941-42	$800.00 – 900.00	158
C3913	Hanging Mirror	1941-42	$175.00 – 200.00	157
C3914	Miami Vanity Base	1941-42	$600.00 – 750.00	156
C3915	Hanging Mirror	1941-42	$175.00 – 200.00	157
C3916	Miami Vanity	1941-42	$750.00 – 850.00	158
C3917	Miami Vanity Bench	1941-42	$200.00 – 225.00	158
C3918	Miami Night Stand	1941-42	$250.00 – 275.00	157
C3920	Niagara Bed	1941-42	$400.00 – 500.00	152
C3921–725	Niagara Dresser with Round Mirror	1941-42	$1,000.00 – 1,200.00	152
C3921–923	Niagara Dresser with Mirror	1941-42	$1,000.00 – 1,150.00	152
C3922	Niagara 5-Drawer Chest	1941-42	$1,100.00 – 1,250.00	153,154
C3923	Hanging Mirror	1941-42	$150.00 – 200.00	153
C3924	Niagara Vanity / Desk	1941-42	$900.00 – 1,000.00	151,153
C3926	Niagara Vanity	1941-42	$1,000.00 – 1,200.00	151
C3927	Niagara Vanity Seat	1941-42	$350.00 – 450.00	151
C3928	Niagara Night Stand	1941-42	$350.00 – 450.00	152
C3930	Coronet Bed	1941-42	$400.00 – 500.00	150
C3931–933	Coronet Dresser with Mirror	1941-42	$1,000.00 – 1,250.00	150
C3932	Coronet 5-Drawer Chest	1941-42	$1,200.00 – 1,500.00	149
C3933	Hanging Mirror	1941-42	$150.00 – 200.00	150
C3934	Coronet Vanity Base / Desk	1941-42	$900.00 – 1,000.00	149
C3936	Coronet Vanity	1941-42	$1,250.00 – 1,500.00	151
C3937	Coronet Vanity Pouffe	1941-42	$275.00 – 350.00	151
C3938	Coronet Night Stand	1941-42	$400.00 – 450.00	150
C3940 A	Side Chair	1941-42	$150.00 – 175.00	141
C3940 C	Arm Chair	1941-42	$175.00 – 200.00	141
C3940 G	Extension Table	1941-42	$650.00 – 800.00	146
C3941 G	Extension Table	1941-42	$650.00 – 800.00	141

C3942 G	Oblong Coffee Table	1941-44	$350.00 – 400.00	162,171
C3943 G	End Table	1941-44	$300.00 – 350.00	161,162
C3944 G	Lamp Table	1941-44	$350.00 – 400.00	162
C3945 RC or LC	Right or Left Arm Chair	1941-42	$600.00 – 700.00	161
C3945 C	Arm Chair	1941-42	$850.00 – 950.00	162
C3945	Single Filler	1941-42	$500.00 – 600.00	161
C3946–44	Love Seat	1941-42	$1,500.00 – 1,700.00	163
C3946	Double Filler	1941-42	$650.00 – 800.00	161
C3947–66	Davenport	1941-42	$1,800.00 – 2,000.00	162
C3948 C	Channel Side Arm Chair	1941-42	$750.00 – 800.00	163
C3950 A	Side Chair	1941-43	$100.00 – 125.00	148
C3950 C	Arm Chair	1941-43	$125.00 – 150.00	148
C3950 G	Extension Table	1941-43	$400.00 – 500.00	148
C3951 A	Side Chair	1941-42	$250.00 – 325.00	140
C3952 A	Side Chair	1941-42	$155.00 – 170.00	146
C3953 C	Arm Chair	1941-42	$200.00 – 225.00	142
C3953 A	Side Chair	1941-42	$175.00 – 200.00	142
C3954	Credenza / Buffet	1941-44	$450.00 – 550.00	141
C3955 G	Extension Table	1941-42	$450.00 – 600.00	145,147
C3956 G	Extension Table	1941-44	$650.00 – 800.00	142
C3957 G	Gateleg Table	1941-42	$650.00 – 750.00	140,172
C3958 G	Drop-Leaf Extension Table	1941-42	$600.00 – 750.00	139
C3960 G	Corner Table	1941-42	$550.00 – 650.00	161
C3961 G	Oval Cocktail Table	1941-42	$800.00 – 900.00	164,166
C3962 G	End Table	1941-42	$650.00 – 700.00	165,168,171
C3963 G	Round Cocktail Table	1941-42	$400.00 – 450.00	163
C3964 G	Round Cocktail Table	1941-44	$300.00 – 400.00	161
C3970	Straight Front Bookcase	1941-44	$500.00 – 600.00	172,179
C3971	Corner Bookcase	1941-44	$600.00 – 700.00	179
C3972	Cabinet Base	1940-42	$650.00 – 800.00	143,145
C3973	3-Drawer Bookcase / Chest	1941-42	$600.00 – 700.00	171
C3974	Pier Cabinet	1941-42	$600.00 – 750.00	172
C3975	Cabinet	1941-42	$650.00 – 800.00	139,142,146
C3975 W	Desk / Chest	1941-42	$650.00 – 750.00	167
C3976 W	Desk / Chest Bookcase	1941-42	$1,500.00 – 1,750.00	170
C3977 W	Desk / Chest Bookcase	1941-42	$1,800.00 – 2,000.00	170
C3978 W	Kneehole Desk	1941-44	$1,300.00 – 1,500.00	166
C3980–68	Davenport	1941-44	$2,000.00 – 2,200.00	171
C3980 C	Arm Chair	1941-44	$1,200.00 – 1,500.00	171
C3981 C	Arm Chair	1941-42	$800.00 – 1,000.00	169
C3981–68	Davenport	1941-42	$2,000.00 – 2,200.00	171
C3985	Single Filler	1941-44	$500.00 – 600.00	164
C3985 C	Arm Chair	1941-44	$900.00 – 1,000.00	165
C3985 RC or LC	Right or Left Arm Chair	1941-44	$600.00 – 700.00	164
C3986	Double Filler	1941-43	$800.00 – 900.00	166
C3986–44	Love Seat	1941-43	$1,600.00 – 1,800.00	165
C3987–66	Davenport	1941-44	$1,800.00 – 2,000.00	165
C3989 C	Arm Chair	1941-42	$800.00 – 900.00	168
C3990 LR	Leg Rest	1941-42	$350.00 – 450.00	170
C3991 C	Wood Frame Arm Chair	1941-47	$750.00 – 850.00	173
C3992 C	Upholstered Arm Chair	1941-42	$800.00 – 900.00	173
C3994 C	Channel Back Arm Chair	1941-44	$750.00 – 850.00	179
C3995 C	Open Frame Arm Chair	1941-42	$1,000.00 – 1,200.00	170
C3996 R	Wing Chair	1941-44	$800.00 – 850.00	167
C3997 C	Upholstered Arm Chair	1941-42	$650.00 – 750.00	170,172
C4140	Victory Bed	1943-44	$300.00 – 350.00	176
C4141	Victory Dresser Base	1943-44	$400.00 – 450.00	176
C4141–795	Victory Dresser with Mirror	1943-44	$475.00 – 525.00	176
C4142	Victory 4-Drawer Dresser	1943-44	$600.00 – 700.00	177
C4143	Hanging Mirror	1943-44	$150.00 – 200.00	176
C4144	Victory Vanity Base	1943-44	$400.00 – 500.00	177
C4146	Victory Vanity with Mirror	1943-44	$550.00 – 650.00	177
C4147	Victory Vanity Bench	1943-44	$150.00 – 175.00	177
C4148	Victory Night Stand	1943-44	$250.00 – 300.00	177
C4154 G	Extension Table	1943-44	$950.00 – 1,100.00	178
M 85 C	Pull-Up Chair	1952	$250.00 – 300.00	267

M 110	Bed	1947-48	$350.00 – 400.00	187
M 111	3-Drawer Dresser	1947-48	$650.00 – 750.00	188
M 112	5-Drawer Chest	1947-48	$850.00 – 1,000.00	188
M 114	Mr. & Mrs. Dresser	1947-48	$800.00 – 950.00	187
M 115	Hanging Mirror	1947-48	$125.00 – 175.00	188
M 116	Deluxe Vanity	1947-48	$450.00 – 600.00	187
M 117	Vanity Bench	1947-48	$175.00 – 200.00	187
M 118	Night Stand	1947-48	$300.00 – 400.00	187
M 135	Hanging Mirror	1947	$150.00 – 200.00	187
M 140	Kohinoor Bed	1949-51	$400.00 – 500.00	184
M 141	Kohinoor Dresser	1949-51	$800.00 – 900.00	182
M 141–M145	Kohinoor Dresser with Attached Mirror	1949-51	$900.00 – 1,000.00	182
M 142	Kohinoor Chest	1949-51	$1,000.00 – 1,100.00	183
M 144	Kohinoor Mr. & Mrs. Dresser	1949-51	$1,100.00 – 1,250.00	181
M 145	Hanging Mirror	1950	$75.00 – 150.00	182
M 146	Kohinoor Vanity	1949-51	$800.00 – 1,000.00	181
M 147	Kohinoor Vanity Bench	1949-51	$250.00 – 300.00	183
M 148	Kohinoor Night Stand	1949-51	$350.00 – 450.00	181
M 149 on M 141	Kohinoor Dresser with Deck Top	1949-51	$1,350.00 – 1,550.00	182
M 149	Kohinoor Deck Top	1949-51	$500.00 – 600.00	182
M 151 A	Side Chair	1950	$175.00 – 225.00	243
M 152 A	Side Chair	1947-1950	$125.00 – 175.00	243
M 153 A	Side Chair	1950	$125.00 – 175.00	243
M 154 A	Side Chair	1950-55	$275.00 – 350.00	232,243
M 154 C	Arm Chair	1950-55	$300.00 – 400.00	243
M 155 A	Side Chair	1947-50	$250.00 – 300.00	244
M 155 C	Arm Chair	1947-50	$275.00 – 325.00	244
M 157 A	Side Chair	1947-50	$275.00 – 325.00	244
M 157 C	Arm Chair	1947-50	$300.00 – 350.00	244
M 158 A	Side Chair	1950	$200.00 – 250.00	244
M 158 C	Arm Chair	1950	$300.00 – 350.00	244
M 160 G	Dinette Extension Table	1950	$550.00 – 650.00	233
M 163 G	Junior Dining Extension Table	1947-49	$650.00 – 800.00	232
M 165 G	Large Dining Extension Table	1947-52	$1,250.00 – 1,500.00	233
M 166 G	Drop-Leaf Dining Table	1947-55	$750.00 – 850.00	233
M 167 G	Drop-Leaf Extension Table	1949	$1,000.00 – 1,100.00	233
M 168 G	Oval Dining Table	1950	$750.00 – 850.00	234
M 169 G	Junior Dining Extension Table	1950-55	$650.00 – 800.00	234
M 170	Server Base	1947	$400.00 – 450.00	252
M 173	Credenza	1947	$850.00 – 950.00	252
M 175	Glass Top Hutch	1947-53	$400.00 – 450.00	252
M 175 on M 194	China Top on Server	1950	$1,000.00 – 1,150.00	255
M 175 on M 170	China Top on Server Base	1947	$800.00 – 900.00	252
M 175 on M 190	China	1948-50	$850.00 – 950.00	232,253
M 175 on M 334	Glass Top Hutch on Utility Case	1949	$900.00 – 1,000.00	253
M 176	Corner Cabinet	1948-55	$1,000.00 – 1,250.00	252
M 177	Tambour Front Chest	1947-48	$1,800.00 – 2,000.00	230
M 178	Tambour Front 4-Drawer Chest	1947-48	$1,800.00 – 2,000.00	229
M 179	Tambour Utility Case	1950-54	$950.00 – 1,100.00	229
M 180	Riviera Bed	1947-48	$300.00 – 350.00	186
M 181	Riviera 3-Drawer Dresser	1947-48	$700.00 – 800.00	186
M 182	Riviera 4-Drawer Chest	1947-48	$800.00 – 900.00	186
M 186	Riviera Vanity	1947-48	$600.00 – 750.00	185
M 187	Revolving Pouffe	1947-48	$225.00 – 250.00	185
M 188	Riviera Night Stand	1947-48	$225.00 – 275.00	186
M 189 G	Junior Dining Extension Table	1951-55	$800.00 – 950.00	234
M 190	Server Base	1948-50	$400.00 – 450.00	253
M 192	3-Drawer Buffet	1948-50	$850.00 – 950.00	232,256
M 193	Credenza	1948-50	$900.00 – 1,000.00	257
M 194	Server	1950	$500.00 – 600.00	255
M 195	Junior Buffet	1950	$1,000.00 – 1,200.00	255
M 196 W	Credenza with Desk Drawer	1950	$1,250.00 – 1,500.00	254
M 197 G	Pedestal Drop-Leaf Extension Table	1948-55	$1,250.00 – 1,500.00	235
M 198 on M 193	Credenza with Glass Top Hutch	1948-50	$1,800.00 – 2,200.00	257
M 198 on M 196	Credenza with Glass Top Hutch	1950	$2,000.00 – 2,500.00	255
M 199 G	Console Extension Table	1950-52	$800.00 – 900.00	235

M 304 G	Two-Tier End Table	1947-49	$450.00 – 500.00	277
M 306 G	Round Cocktail Table	1947-55	$400.00 – 500.00	277
M 307 G	Cocktail Table	1949-52	$450.00 – 500.00	282
M 308 G	Step End Table	1948-53	$225.00 – 275.00	277
M 312 G	Nest of Tables	1949-53	$550.00 – 700.00	276
M 313 G	Pivot Top Console Table	1951-52	$800.00 – 850.00	236
M 314 W	Student's Desk	1950-51	$900.00 – 1,100.00	225
M 315 W	Kneehole Desk	1947-49	$1,500.00 – 1,800.00	224
M 316 G	Coffee Table	1949	$400.00 – 450.00	278
M 317 G	End Table	1949	$350.00 – 400.00	278
M 318 G	Lamp Table	1949	$400.00 – 450.00	278
M 319 G	Cocktail Table	1949-54	$400.00 – 550.00	275
M 320 W	Kneehole Desk	1950-65	$1,500.00 – 1,800.00	225
M 321	Straight Bookcase	1947-65	$500.00 – 600.00	227
M 322	Corner Bookcase	1947-61	$650.00 – 800.00	227
M175 on M 324	China Top on Utility Chest	1947-48	$900.00 – 1,000.00	253
M 326	Cabinet Bookcase	1952-61	$650.00 – 800.00	227
M 327 W	Table Desk	1950-54	$750.00 – 950.00	223
M 328 W	Desk Bookcase	1951-54	$1,350.00 – 1,500.00	223
M 330	Single Filler	1948-50	$400.00 – 450.00	308
M 330 C	Arm Chair	1948-50	$1,250.00 – 1,500.00	308
M 330 LC or M 330 RC	Left or Right Arm Chair	1948-50	$600.00 – 750.00	308
M 331–48	Love Seat	1948-50	$1,500.00 – 1,750.00	309
M 331 LC or M 331 RC	Double Fillers with Left or Right Arms	1948-50	$800.00 – 1,000.00	308
M 331	Double Filler	1948-50	$500.00 – 600.00	308
M 332–68	Davenport	1948-50	$1,800.00 – 2,200.00	309
M 333 or 353	Curved Single Filler	1948-50	$500.00 – 650.00	310
M 334	Utility Cabinet	1949	$650.00 – 700.00	253
M 335 G	Cocktail Table	1950-53	$400.00 – 500.00	276
M 336 G	Step End Table	1949-50	$200.00 – 250.00	282
M 337 G	Lamp Table	1950-53	$375.00 – 425.00	281
M 338 G	Corner Table	1950-53	$400.00 – 475.00	276
M 339 G	Corner Table	1949	$500.00 – 650.00	278
M 340 C	Arm Chair	1949-52	$500.00 – 600.00	264
M 341 C	Pull-Up Chair	1949	$450.00 – 500.00	264
M 342 C	Man's Lounge Chair	1949-50	$450.00 – 500.00	265
M 343 C	Ladies' Lounge Chair	1950	$900.00 – 1,000.00	264
M 344 C	Large Barrel Wing Chair	1949-57	$1,500.00 – 1,800.00	265
M 345 C	Tub Chair	1950-57	$600.00 – 850.00	265
M 346 C	Barrel Wing Chair	1947-50	$800.00 – 900.00	266
M 347 C	Pull-Up Wing Chair	1949-50	$450.00 – 550.00	266
M 348 C	Pull-Up Occasional Chair	1950	$450.00 – 550.00	266
M 350 C	Arm Chair	1948-49	$800.00 – 900.00	311
M 350	Single Filler	1948-49	$250.00 – 300.00	310
M 350 RC or LC	Right and Left Arm Chair	1948-49	$300.00 – 400.00	310
M 352–68	Davenport	1948-49	$1,000.00 – 1,250.00	311
M 354 C	Wheeled Television Chair	1950-1952	$400.00 – 500.00	266
M 355	Single Filler	1950-53	$300.00 – 350.00	305
M 355 C	Arm Chair	1950-52	$850.00 – 1,000.00	306
M 355 LC or M 355 RC	Left or Right Arm Chair	1950-53	$450.00 – 550.00	305
M 356	Double Filler	1950-53	$600.00 – 700.00	305
M 356–48	Love Seat	1950-53	$1,500.00 – 1,750.00	307
M 356 LC or M 356 RC	Double Fillers with Left or Right Arms	1950-53	$600.00 – 700.00	305
M 357	Curved Single Filler	1950	$500.00 – 650.00	306
M 358–68	Davenport	1950-53	$1,500.00 – 1,750.00	307
M 360 RC or M 360 LC	Right or Left Arm Chair	1947-48	$550.00 – 650.00	315
M 360 C	Arm Chair	1947-48	$800.00 – 900.00	316
M 360	Single Filler	1947-48	$250.00 – 400.00	315
M 364 G	Lamp Table	1950-55	$400.00 – 450.00	281
CM 367	Aristocraft Single Filler	1950-53	$250.00 – 300.00	295
CM 367 C	Aristocraft Arm Chair	1950-53	$850.00 – 1,000.00	296
CM 367 D	Aristocraft Platform Rocker	1952-53	$1,000.00 – 1,250.00	296
CM 367 LC or CM 367 RC	Aristocraft Left or Right Arm Chair	1950-54	$400.00 – 450.00	295
CM 367 R	Aristocraft High Back Arm Chair	1952-53	$900.00 – 1,050.00	296
CM 368 LC or CM 368 RC	Double Fillers with Left or Right Arms	1950-53	$600.00 – 700.00	295
CM 368–44	Aristocraft Love Seat	1950-53	$900.00 – 1,100.00	297

CM 368	Aristocraft Double Filler	1950-53	$400.00 – 500.00	295
CM 369-66	Aristocraft Davenport	1950-53	$1,250.00 – 1,500.00	297
CM 370 G	Aristocraft Corner Table	1949-53	$300.00 – 350.00	292
CM 371 G	Aristocraft Cocktail Coffee Table	1949-53	$200.00 – 250.00	292
CM 372 G	Aristocraft End Table	1949-53	$275.00 – 325.00	292
CM 373 G	Aristocraft Lamp Table	1949-53	$275.00 – 325.00	293
CM 374 G	Aristocraft Step End Table	1950-53	$225.00 – 275.00	293
M 375 on M 996	China Top on Harmonic Server	1954	$800.00 – 900.00	259
M 384 C	Large Barrel Wing Chair	1950-53	$1,000.00 – 1,200.00	267
CM 388	Aristocraft Single Filler	1950-53	$400.00 – 500.00	298
CM 388 C	Aristocraft Arm Chair	1950-53	$1,000.00 – 1,250.00	298
CM 388 LC or CM 388 RC	Aristocraft Left or Right Arm Chair	1950-53	$550.00 – 650.00	298
M 389 W	Desk / Chest	1952-54	$1,000.00 – 1,250.00	224
M 391 G	End Table	1950-52	$325.00 – 400.00	280
M 392 G	Square Cocktail Table	1950-55	$600.00 – 800.00	282
M 393 G	Center Table	1950-52	$650.00 – 800.00	279
M 394 G	Service Wagon	1951-52	$1,000.00 – 1,250.00	236
M 395	Record Cabinet End Table	1951-52	$900.00 – 1,100.00	283
M 396 G	Wedge-Shaped Tier Table	1950-53	$325.00 – 400.00	280
M 500 G	Cocktail Table	1952-53	$425.00 – 525.00	284
M 501 G	End Table	1952-53	$350.00 – 425.00	283
M 502 G	Lamp Table	1952-53	$350.00 – 425.00	283
M 503 G	Magazine Rack End Table	1953-57	$400.00 – 500.00	283
M 504 under M 505	Room Divider	1953-56	$2,500.00 – 2,800.00	231
M 508 on M 782 W	Glass Top Hutch on Utility Cabinet	1952-54	$1,250.00 – 1,550.00	259
M 509 on M 593	Credenza with China Top	1953	$1,750.00 – 1,900.00	256
M 510	Bed	1948-53	$350.00 – 450.00	189
M 511–515	Encore 3-Drawer Dresser with Mirror	1948-50	$700.00 – 900.00	196
M 512	Encore 4-Drawer Chest	1948-50	$850.00 – 1,000.00	196
M 515	Mirror	1948-50	$75.00 – 150.00	196
M 516	Vanity	1948-49	$650.00 – 750.00	192
M 517	Vanity Bench	1948-49	$150.00 – 175.00	192
M 518	Encore Night Stand	1948-55	$275.00 – 350.00	189
M 520	Shelf Headboard Bed	1952-53	$300.00 – 400.00	197
M 521–525	Encore 4-Drawer Dresser with Mirror	1948-55	$650.00 – 850.00	195
M 521	Encore 4-Drawer Chest	1948-55	$450.00 – 600.00	195
M 522	Encore 5-Drawer Chest	1948-55	$1,000.00 – 1,200.00	197
M 523	Encore Utility Case	1948-54	$650.00 – 800.00	193
M 524	Encore Mr. & Mrs. Dresser	1948-55	$900.00 – 1,100.00	189
M 525	Large Mirror	1948-59	$200.00 – 250.00	189
M 526	Utility Cabinet	1952-53	$650.00 – 850.00	226
M 527 on M 526	China with Open Hutch	1952-53	$900.00 – 1,000.00	254
M 528	Pier Cabinet	1952-54	$650.00 – 800.00	226
M 529–575	Encore Triple Dresser with Mirror	1952-55	$2,000.00 – 2,300.00	194
M 530	Bed	1950-53	$650.00 – 850.00	199
M 532	Encore Double Chest	1954-55	$1,800.00 – 2,200.00	193
M 534	Encore Utility Cabinet	1950-53	$650.00 – 800.00	195
M 536	Encore Vanity	1950-53	$900.00 – 1,100.00	190
M 537	Vanity Bench	1950-53	$350.00 – 450.00	190
M 538	Encore Night Stand	1950-55	$350.00 – 450.00	192
M 539–575 X	Blanket Chest with Mirror	1952-53	$1,250.00 – 1,500.00	189
M 540 6/6	Double Utility Headboard with Swing-Apart Twin Bed Frames	1953-54	$375.00 – 475.00	198
M 540	Utility Headboard	1950-53	$375.00 – 475.00	198
M 546	Kohinoor Desk / Vanity	1949	$2,200.00 – 2,500.00	183
M 549 C	Captains Chair	1953-66	$45.00 – 90.00	206,245
M 551 A	Side Chair	1952-55	$175.00 – 200.00	245
M 552 A	Side Chair	1953-55	$225.00 – 275.00	245
M 552 C	Arm Chair	1953-55	$250.00 – 300.00	245
M 553 A	Side Chair	1950-53	$175.00 – 225.00	246
M 553 C	Arm Chair	1950-53	$200.00 – 250.00	246
M 554 A	Side Chair	1953-55	$175.00 – 225.00	246
M 554 C	Arm Chair	1953-55	$200.00 – 250.00	246
M 555 A	Side Chair	1950-55	$300.00 – 350.00	246
M 555 C	Arm Chair	1950-55	$350.00 – 400.00	246
M 556 A	Side Chair	1952-54	$350.00 – 400.00	247

Heywood

M 556 C	Arm Chair	1952-54	$375.00 – 425.00	247
M 557 A	Side Chair	1952	$250.00 – 300.00	247
M 557 C	Arm Chair	1952	$300.00 – 350.00	247
M 558 C	Lounge Chair	1953-54	$450.00 – 500.00	268
M 559 C	High Back Lounge Chair	1952-57	$500.00 – 600.00	268
M 560 C	Arm Chair	1951-53	$1,000.00 – 1,250.00	317
M 560	Single Filler	1951-53	$400.00 – 450.00	316
M 560 LC or M 560 RC	Left or Right Arm Chair	1951-53	$600.00 – 750.00	316
M 561–48	Love Seat	1951-53	$1,350.00 – 1,550.00	317
M 561 LC or M 561 RC	Double Filler with Right or Left Arm	1951-53	$800.00 – 1,000.00	316
M 561	Double Filler	1951-53	$500.00 – 600.00	316
M 562–68	Davenport	1951-53	$1,600.00 – 2,000.00	317
M 563	Curved Single Filler	1951-52	$450.00 – 500.00	318
M 564 C	Swivel Tub Chair	1951-52	$500.00 – 600.00	268
M 565 C	High Back Easy Chair	1951-52	$750.00 – 850.00	269
M 566 C	Barrel Wing Chair	1951-52	$950.00 – 1,050.00	269
M 567 C	Ladies' Pull-Up Chair	1951-52	$750.00 – 850.00	269
M 568 C	Open Arm Tub Chair, Ladies' Club Chair	1951-58	$850.00 – 950.00	269
M 569 C	Pull-Up Chair	1951-59	$500.00 – 600.00	270
M 570	Trophy Suite Bed	1951-52	$375.00 – 450.00	202
M 571–573	Trophy Suite Dresser with Mirror	1951-52	$850.00 – 950.00	202
M 572	Trophy Suite Chest	1951-52	$900.00 – 1,000.00	202
M 574–575	Trophy Suite Mr. and Mrs. Dresser with Mirror	1951-52	$900.00 – 1,000.00	202
M 576	Trophy Suite Deluxe Vanity	1951-52	$850.00 – 1,000.00	201
M 577	Vanity Bench	1951-52	$250.00 – 300.00	190
M 578	Trophy Suite Night Stand	1951-52	$350.00 – 400.00	201
M 583	Hanging Mirror	1953	$125.00 – 150.00	191
M 586	Encore Deluxe Vanity	1953-54	$1,250.00 – 1,500.00	191
M 587	Vanity Bench	1953	$350.00 – 450.00	191
M 590	Server	1950-55	$550.00 – 650.00	254
M 593	Credenza	1950-55	$900.00 – 1,000.00	256
M 595	Single Filler	1952-55	$300.00 – 400.00	318
M 595 RC or M 595 LC	Right or Left Arm Chair	1952-55	$450.00 – 500.00	318
M 595 C	Arm Chair	1952-55	$900.00 – 1,000.00	318
M 596–51	Love Seat	1952-54	$1,250.00 – 1,500.00	319
M 596	Double Filler	1952-54	$450.00 – 550.00	319
M 596 LC or M 596 RC	Double Filler with Right or Left Arm	1952-54	$700.00 – 900.00	319
M 597–76	Davenport	1952-55	$2,000.00 – 2,200.00	320
M 598 C	Ladies' Club Chair	1953	$500.00 – 600.00	270
CM 708	Night Stand	1956-57	$100.00 – 200.00	208
CM 712	4-Drawer Chest	1956-57	$300.00 – 400.00	208
CM 714	Double Dresser	1956-57	$400.00 – 500.00	209
CM 715	Table / Desk	1956-57	$250.00 – 350.00	209
CM 716	Dresser / Desk	1956-57	$300.00 – 400.00	208
CM 717	Luggage Bench	1956-57	$75.00 – 100.00	209
CM 724 C	Aristocraft Lounge Chair with Rubber Seat and Back Cushions	1953-54	$650.00 – 800.00	302
CM 727	Aristocraft Single Filler	1952-53	$250.00 – 300.00	299
CM 727 C	Aristocraft Arm Chair	1952-53	$850.00 – 1,000.00	302
CM 727 D	Aristocraft Platform Rocker	1952-53	$1,000.00 – 1,250.00	301
CM 727 LC or CM 727 RC	Aristocraft Arm Chair Left or Right	1952-53	$400.00 – 450.00	299
CM 727 R	Aristocraft High Back Arm Chair	1952-53	$900.00 – 1,050.00	301
CM 728–44	Aristocraft Love Seat	1952-53	$900.00 – 1,100.00	302
CM 728 LC or CM 728 RC	Aristocraft Double Filler with Right or Left Arm	1952-53	$600.00 – 700.00	300
CM 728	Aristocraft Double Filler	1952-53	$400.00 – 500.00	301
CM 729–66	Aristocraft Davenport	1952-53	$1,250.00 – 1,500.00	303
M 755 C	Arm Chair	1954-55	$750.00 – 850.00	320
M 755 LC or M 755 RC	Left or Right Arm Chair	1954-55	$350.00 – 450.00	321
M 755	Single Filler	1954-55	$250.00 – 300.00	321
M 756–48	Love Seat	1954-55	$950.00 – 1,100.00	322
M 756 LC or M 756 RC	Double Filler with Left or Right Arm	1954-55	$500.00 – 600.00	321
M 756	Double Filler	1954-55	$300.00 – 400.00	321
M 758–68	Davenport	1954-55	$1,250.00 – 1,500.00	322
M 770	Bed	1952-59	$375.00 – 475.00	203
M 771–525	Sculptura Single Dresser with Mirror	1952-56	$850.00 – 950.00	204
M 772	Sculptura Chest	1952-59	$1,000.00 – 1,100.00	203

M 774–525	Sculptura Mr. & Mrs. Dresser with Mirror	1952-59	$1,000.00 – 1,200.00	205
M 776	Sculptura Vanity	1952-59	$900.00 – 1,100.00	204
M 777	Vanity Bench	1952-59	$350.00 – 400.00	204,211
M 778	Sculptura Night Stand	1952-59	$500.00 – 600.00	203,204
M 779–575	Sculptura Triple Dresser with Mirror	1952-59	$1,800.00 – 2,000.00	203
M 780 4/6	Cabinet Utility Headboard	1952-55	$650.00 – 850.00	194
M 781 on M 771	Sculptura Deck Top on Sculptura Single Dresser	1952-53	$1,250.00 – 1,500.00	205
M 783 W	Student's Desk	1952-61	$900.00 – 1,100.00	225
M 785 on M 782 W	Utility Case with Open Hutch Top	1953-54	$1,250.00 – 1,500.00	259
M 785 on M 592	Buffet with Open Hutch Top	1953-54	$1,250.00 – 1,500.00	260
M 786 G	Pedestal Extension Table	1952-55	$1,250.00 – 1,500.00	237
M 787 G	Game Dining Table	1952-53	$650.00 – 750.00	237
M 788 G	Extension Game Dining Table	1953-54	$750.00 – 850.00	237
M 789 G	Large Dining Extension Table	1953-55	$1,500.00 – 1,800.00	238
M 790 6/6	Double Utility Headboard	1953-54	$1,000.00 – 1,250.00	199
M 790	Utility Headboard	1953-55	$375.00 – 475.00	200
M 791 G	End Table	1952-53	$350.00 – 425.00	280
M 792	Sculptura 5-Drawer Chest	1953-59	$1,200.00 – 1,400.00	205
M 793 G	Lamp Table with Drawer	1953-55	$450.00 – 600.00	282
M 794 G	Step End Table with Drawer	1953-55	$475.00 – 525.00	281
M 795 G	Large Cocktail Table	1953-55	$550.00 – 650.00	284
M 797 C	High Back Barrel Chair	1953-54	$650.00 – 750.00	270
M 798 C	Open Arm Posture Chair	1953-54	$650.00 – 750.00	270
M 799 C	Posture Back Arm Chair	1953-54	$800.00 – 900.00	271
M 902 G	Nest of Tables	1954-55	$1,000.00 – 1,250.00	275
M 905 G	Cocktail Table with Drawer	1954-55	$600.00 – 750.00	279
M 906 G	Wedge Step End Table	1954-55	$325.00 – 375.00	285
M 908 G	Step End Table	1954-55	$300.00 – 350.00	285
M 909 on M 998	Harmonic Large Buffet with China Top	1954	$1,500.00 – 1,750.00	258
M 910	Harmonic Bed	1954	$375.00 – 450.00	210
M 911–573	Harmonic Dresser with Mirror	1954	$850.00 – 950.00	210
M 912	Harmonic 5-Drawer Chest	1954	$1,000.00 – 1,100.00	210
M 914	Harmonic Mr. & Mrs. Dresser	1954	$1,000.00 – 1,100.00	211
M 916	Harmonic Desk Vanity	1954	$950.00 – 1,050.00	211
M 918	Harmonic Night Stand Lamp Table	1954	$350.00 – 450.00	211
M 920	Bed	1954-55	$300.00 – 400.00	200
M 923	Chest Mirror	1954-55	$400.00 – 550.00	197
M 926	Vanity Desk	1954-56	$2,000.00 – 2,500.00	222
CM 927	Aristocraft Single Filler	1954-58	$200.00 – 250.00	303
CM 927 C	Arm Chair	1954-66	$650.00 – 800.00	302
CM 927 LC or CM 927 RC	Aristocraft Left or Right Arm Chair	1954-58	$300.00 – 350.00	303
CM 928	Aristocraft Double Filler	1954	$300.00 – 350.00	303
CM 928–44	Aristocraft Love Seat	1954	$800.00 – 900.00	304
CM 928 LC or RC	Aristocraft Double Filler with Left or Right Arm	1954	$400.00 – 500.00	303
CM 929–66	Aristocraft Davenport	1954	$1,000.00 – 1,250.00	304
M 930	Bed	1954-55	$350.00 – 400.00	200
CM 931	Double Filler	1954-58	$300.00 – 500.00	304
CM 931–44	Love Seat	1954-57	$800.00 – 900.00	304
CM 931–50	Love Seat	1958	$800.00 – 900.00	304
CM 931 LC or CM 931 RC	Double Filler with Right or Left Arm	1954-58	$400.00 – 500.00	304
CM 932–66	Davenport	1954-57	$1,000.00 – 1,250.00	304
M 934	Starter Chest	1954	$800.00 – 950.00	228
M 934 W	Starter Chest with Desk Drawer	1954	$900.00 – 1,050.00	228
M 935	Single Filler	1954-56	$200.00 – 250.00	327
M 935 C	Arm Chair	1954-56	$800.00 – 900.00	328
M 935 LC or M 935 RC	Left or Right Arm Chair	1954-56	$400.00 – 500.00	327
M 936	Double Filler	1954-56	$300.00 – 400.00	327
M 936–48	Love Seat	1954-56	$950.00 – 1,100.00	328
M 936 LC or M 936 RC	Double Filler with Left or Right Arm	1954-56	$500.00 – 600.00	327
M 937–84	Davenport Sleeper	1954-56	$1,250.00 – 1,500.00	328
M 938 G	Corner Table	1954-55	$400.00 – 475.00	279
M 941 C	Arm Chair	1954-55	$750.00 – 800.00	271
M 945 C	Club / Lounge Chair	1954-56	$650.00 – 750.00	271
M 946 C	Ladies' Chair	1954-55	$650.00 – 750.00	271
M 947 C	Lounge Chair	1954-56	$650.00 – 750.00	272
M 948	Armless Pull-Up Chair	1954-56	$200.00 – 250.00	272

M 950 G	Round Extension Table	1954-55	$1,800.00 – 2,000.00	238
M 952 G	Plastic Top Dining Extension Table	1955	$250.00 – 350.00	238
M 953 C	Arm Chair	1954-55	$275.00 – 325.00	248
M 953 A	Side Chair	1954-55	$175.00 – 225.00	248
M 965	Single Filler	1953	$300.00 – 350.00	323
M 965 C	Arm Chair	1953	$850.00 – 1,000.00	323
M 965 LC or M 965 RC	Left or Right Arm Chair	1953	$450.00 – 550.00	323
M 966	Double Filler	1953	$400.00 – 500.00	323
M 966 LC or M 966 RC	Double Filler with Left or Right Arm	1953	$600.00 – 700.00	323
M 966-48	Love Seat	1953	$1,250.00 – 1,500.00	324
M 968-68	Davenport	1953	$1,500.00 – 1,700.00	324
CM 970 G	Aristocraft Corner Table	1954-55	$300.00 – 350.00	293
CM 971 G	Aristocraft Cocktail Table	1954-55	$175.00 – 225.00	293
CM 972 G	Aristocraft End Table with Shelf	1954-55	$225.00 – 275.00	294
CM 973 G	Aristocraft Lamp Table with Shelf	1954-55	$225.00 – 275.00	294
CM 974 G	Aristocraft Step End Table	1954-55	$200.00 – 225.00	294
M 975	Single Filler	1954-57	$200.00 – 300.00	326
M 975 C	Arm Chair	1954-57	$800.00 – 900.00	326
M 975 LC or M 975 RC	Left or Right Arm Chair	1954-57	$400.00 – 500.00	326
M 977 L or M 977 R	Left or Right Bumper End Offs	1954-57	$650.00 – 850.00	324
M 979 L or M 979 R	Left or Right Asymmetrical Curved Units	1954-55	$500.00 – 600.00	325
M 980	Single Filler	1954-55	$100.00 – 200.00	329
M 980 C	Arm Chair	1954-55	$300.00 – 600.00	329
M 980 LC or M 980 RC	Left or Right Arm Chairs	1954-55	$200.00 – 400.00	329
M 981 LC or M 981 RC	Double Filler with Left or Right Arm	1954-55	$200.00 – 400.00	329
M 981-48	Love Seat	1954-55	$380.00 – 720.00	330
M 981	Double Filler	1954-55	$100.00 – 200.00	329
M 982-68	Davenport	1954-55	$600.00 – 1,200.00	330
M 984 C	Wing Chair	1954-57	$650.00 – 750.00	272
M 986	Double Filler	1954-57	$350.00 – 450.00	327
M 986 LC or M 986 RC	Double Filler with Left or Right Arm	1954-57	$500.00 – 600.00	326
M 986-48	Love Seat	1954-57	$950.00 – 1,100.00	326
M 987	Quarter Round Filler	1954-57	$450.00 – 550.00	324
M 988-68	Davenport	1954-56	$1,250.00 – 1,500.00	327
M 989 G	Harmonic Drop-Leaf Extension Table	1954-55	$950.00 – 1,100.00	239
M 991 G	Cocktail Table with Shelf	1954-55	$450.00 – 550.00	284
M 992 G	End Table with Shelf	1954-55	$375.00 – 425.00	285
M 993 G	Lamp Table with Shelf	1954-55	$400.00 – 450.00	285
M 995 on M 996	Harmonic China	1954	$850.00 – 950.00	257
M 997	Harmonic Buffet with Tambour Door	1954	$800.00 – 900.00	257
M 998	Harmonic Large Buffet	1954	$850.00 – 950.00	258
M 999 on M 592	Buffet with China Top	1954-55	$1,250.00 – 1,500.00	260
M 1156 C	Wood Armed Pull-Up Chair	1955-56	$250.00 – 350.00	272
M 1158 C	Danish Occasional Chair	1955-57	$850.00 – 950.00	273
M 1159 C	High Back Barrel Chair	1955-56	$500.00 – 600.00	273
M 1161 C	Ladies' Lounge Chair	1955-57	$400.00 – 450.00	273
M 1195	Single Filler	1955-56	$200.00 – 300.00	330
M 1195 C	Arm Chair	1955-56	$800.00 – 900.00	330
M 1195 LC or M 1195 RC	Left or Right Arm Chair	1955-56	$350.00 – 450.00	330
M 1196	Double Filler	1955-56	$350.00 – 450.00	331
M 1196-51	Love Seat	1955-56	$1,000.00 – 1,250.00	331
M 1196 LC or M 1196 RC	Left or Right Arm Double Filler	1955-56	$500.00 – 700.00	331
M 1197-76	Davenport	1955-56	$1,800.00 – 2,000.00	332
M 1500	Encore Bed	1956-66	$350.00 – 450.00	214
M 1501 G	Cocktail Table	1957-61	$250.00 – 325.00	290
M 1502 G	End Table with Shelf	1957-66	$250.00 – 300.00	290
M 1503 G	Lamp Table with Shelf	1957-63	$300.00 – 350.00	291
M 1504 G	Step End Table	1957-66	$200.00 – 250.00	290
M 1505 G	Large Cocktail Table	1957-66	$300.00 – 350.00	290
M 1506 G	Cocktail / Corner Table	1957	$250.00 – 300.00	291
M 1507 G	Corner Table	1957-66	$300.00 – 350.00	289
M 1508	Encore Night Stand	1956	$250.00 – 300.00	214
M 1508 G	Round Cocktail Table	1957-66	$250.00 – 300.00	291
M 1509	Encore Cane Door Chest	1956-59	$500.00 – 600.00	212
M 1510	Panel Bed	1956	$350.00 – 450.00	214
M 1511	Bachelor's Chest	1958-59	$550.00 – 650.00	213

M 1512	Encore 5-Drawer Chest	1956-61	$900.00 – 1,000.00	215
M 1514–1515	Encore Double Dresser with Mirror	1956-57	$900.00 – 1,000.00	216
M 1514–1525	Double Dresser with Mirror	1956-61	$900.00 – 1,100.00	212
M 1518	Encore Night Stand / Pier Cabinet	1956	$350.00 – 450.00	216
M 1519–1525	Encore Triple Dresser with Attached Mirror	1956	$1,500.00 – 1,700.00	216
M 1520	Utility Headboard Bed	1956-66	$325.00 – 375.00	217
M 1521	Single Dresser	1956	$750.00 – 900.00	213
M 1522	Encore 5-Drawer Chest	1956-66	$950.00 – 1,100.00	217
M 1524–1515	Encore Double Dresser with Mirror	1956-66	$900.00 – 1,000.00	217
M 1528	Encore Night Stand	1956-66	$300.00 – 375.00	214
M 1529–1525	Encore Triple Dresser with Mirror	1956-66	$1,500.00 – 1,700.00	215
M 1530 4/6 with M 1518	Utility Headboard Bed with Night Stands	1956	$400.00 – 500.00	212
M 1531 on M 1521	Encore 3-Drawer Deck on Single Dresser	1956	$800.00 – 950.00	213
M 1533	Hanging Mirror	1958-66	$60.00 – 120.00	206
M 1534–1533	Encore Double Dresser with Mirror	1958-59	$850.00 – 950.00	218
M 1536 on M 1521	Encore Tambour Deck Utility Cabinet on Single Dresser	1956	$950.00 – 1,050.00	218
M 1538	Encore Lamp Table / Night Stand	1958-59	$350.00 – 425.00	213
M 1539–1535	Encore Triple Dresser with Mirror	1958-59	$1,300.00 – 1,500.00	218
M 1540	Cabinet Utility Headboard Bed	1956-57	$750.00 – 950.00	215
M 1541	Server	1956-61	$750.00 – 850.00	260
M 1543	Buffet	1956-65	$1,000.00 – 1,200.00	263
M 1544	Credenza	1956-61	$1,000.00 – 1,200.00	263
M 1545 on M 1541	Crown Glass China on Server	1956	$1,500.00 – 1,800.00	262
M 1546 on M 1592	China on Tambour Cabinet	1957	$1,250.00 – 1,500.00	262
M 1547 on M 1543	Large Crown Glass China on Buffet	1956-65	$2,800.00 – 3,200.00	262
M 1548 on M 1541	China on Server	1956-61	$900.00 – 1,100.00	261
M 1549 G	Drop-Leaf Extension Table	1956-66	$950.00 – 1,100.00	239
M 1550 G	Round Extension Table	1956	$1,800.00 – 2,000.00	239
M 1551 A	Side Chair	1956-66	$150.00 – 175.00	207,248
M 1551 C	Arm Chair	1956-66	$175.00 – 200.00	248
M 1552 A	Side Chair	1956	$175.00 – 200.00	248
M 1552 C	Arm Chair	1956	$200.00 – 250.00	248
M 1553 A	Side Chair	1956-66	$300.00 – 350.00	249
M 1553 C	Arm Chair	1956-66	$325.00 – 375.00	249
M 1554 A	Side Chair	1956-66	$275.00 – 325.00	249
M 1554 C	Arm Chair	1957-58	$300.00 – 400.00	249
M 1555 A	Side Chair	1956 -59	$275.00 – 325.00	249
M 1555 C	Arm Chair	1956-59	$325.00 – 375.00	249
M 1556 G	Two Pedestal Drop-Leaf Extension Table	1956-61	$1,250.00 – 1,400.00	240
M 1557 G	Three-Pedestal Drop-Leaf Extension Table	1956-66	$1,150.00 – 1,400.00	240
M 1558 G	Encore Junior Dining Extension Table	1956-66	$550.00 – 600.00	240
M 1559 G	Large Dining Extension Table	1956-61	$600.00 – 700.00	241
M 1560	Bed with or without Footboard	1958-65	$300.00 – 350.00	206,207,221
M 1561 A	Side Chair	1958-59	$175.00 – 200.00	250
M 1561 C	Arm Chair	1958-59	$200.00 – 225.00	250
M 1562 A	Cane Side Chair	1956	$125.00 – 150.00	250
M 1562 C	Cane Arm Chair	1956	$150.00 – 175.00	250
M 1563 A	Side Chair	1956	$125.00 – 150.00	250
M 1563 C	Arm Chair	1956	$150.00 – 175.00	250
M 1564 A	Side Chair	1956-61	$150.00 – 175.00	251
M 1564 C	Arm Chair	1956-61	$200.00 – 225.00	251
M 1566 G	Drop-Leaf Dining Table	1956	$500.00 – 600.00	241
M 1567 G	Dining Extension Table	1958-59	$450.00 – 550.00	241
M 1568 G	Round Dining Extension Table	1958-59	$1,500.00 – 1,800.00	242
M 1569 G	Junior Dining Extension Table	1956	$500.00 – 600.00	242
M 1570 G	Corner Table	1956	$200.00 – 225.00	286
M 1571 G	Cocktail Table	1956	$250.00 – 300.00	287
M 1572 G	End Table	1956	$375.00 – 450.00	287
M 1573 G	Lamp Table	1956	$375.00 – 450.00	287
M 1574 G	Step End Table	1956	$175.00 – 200.00	286
M 1576 G	Revolving Top Cocktail Table	1956-61	$375.00 – 425.00	286
M 1578 G	Round Cocktail Table	1956	$300.00 – 350.00	286
M 1579 G	Square Cocktail Table	1956	$300.00 – 350.00	285
M 1580 G	Cocktail Table	1956-57	$325.00 – 400.00	288
M 1581 G	Cocktail Table with Shelf	1956-57	$300.00 – 350.00	288

M 1582	Encore 5-Drawer Chest	1958-59	$850.00 – 950.00	219
M 1583 G	Lamp Table	1956-57	$400.00 – 450.00	289
M 1584 G	Step End Table	1956-57	$275.00 – 325.00	288
M 1585 G	Large Cocktail Table with Drawer	1956-57	$425.00 – 475.00	289
M 1586 G	Lamp Table	1956-57	$300.00 – 400.00	289
M 1587 G	Drop-Leaf Utility Table	1956-57	$450.00 – 500.00	287
M 1588 G	Lamp Table	1958-61	$275.00 – 325.00	290
M 1589 G	Large Dining Extension Table	1962-66	$550.00 – 650.00	242
M 1590 G	Corner Table	1956-57	$300.00 – 350.00	288
M 1593	Side Chair	1958-59	$125.00 – 150.00	251
M 1594 C	Arm Chair	1958-59	$175.00 – 200.00	251
M 1594 A	Side Chair	1958-59	$150.00 – 175.00	251
M 1596 on M 1542	Glass Door Hutch on Tambour Buffet	1958-59	$1,200.00 – 1,400.00	261
M 1598 on M 1597	Glass Door Hutch on Server	1962-66	$850.00 – 1,000.00	261
M 1785 C	Monterey Arm Chair	1958	$200.00 – 400.00	334
M 1785 RC or LC	Monterey Right or Left Arm Chair	1958	$200.00 – 400.00	334
M 1785 & M 1790	Single Filler	1958	$75.00 – 150.00	334
M 1786 RC or LC	Monterey Right or Left Arm Sofa	1958	$150.00 – 300.00	334
M 1786–56	Monterey Love Seat	1958	$300.00 – 600.00	335
M 1786 & M1791	Double Filler	1958	$75.00 – 150.00	335
M 1787–80	Monterey Sofa	1958	$500.00 – 1,000.00	334
M 1788	Quarter Round	1958	$200.00 – 400.00	331
M 1789 R or L	Right or Left Bumper End Off	1958	$200.00 – 400.00	333
M 1790	Gramercy Park Single Filler	1958	$75.00 – 150.00	332
M 1790 C	Gramercy Park Arm Chair	1958	$200.00 – 400.00	332
M 1790 LC or RC	Gramercy Park Left or Right Arm Chair	1958	$150.00 – 300.00	332
M 1791–60	Gramercy Park Love Seat	1958	$300.00 – 600.00	333
M 1791	Gramercy Double Filler	1958	$75.00 – 150.00	335
M 1791 LC or RC	Gramercy Left or Right Arm Sofa	1958	$150.00 – 300.00	334
M 1792–84	Gramercy Park Sofa	1958	$500.00 – 1,000.00	333
M 1793–96	Gramercy Park Pillow Back Sofa	1958	$500.00 – 1,000.00	335
M 1794 C	Ladies' Chair	1958	$250.00 – 300.00	274
M 1796 C	Pillow-Back Arm Chair	1958	$250.00 – 300.00	274
CM 1908	Night Table with Plastic Top	1958	$100.00 – 150.00	206
CM 1911	Bachelor's Chest with Plastic Top	1958	$300.00 – 400.00	206
CM 1912	4-Drawer Chest with Plastic Top	1958	$300.00 – 400.00	207
CM 1914–1535	Double Dresser with Plastic Top and Attached Mirror	1958	$400.00 – 500.00	207
CM 1915	Table Desk with Plastic Top	1958	$150.00 – 250.00	206
CM 1916	Desk / Dresser	1958	$200.00 – 300.00	207
CM 1917	Luggage Bench	1958	$75.00 – 100.00	207
M 1920	King-size Headboard	1962-65	$500.00 – 650.00	219
M 1921	Straight Bookcase	1958-59	$250.00 – 325.00	231
M 1922	Corner Bookcase	1958-59	$325.00 – 400.00	231
M 1923	Corner Desk	1958-59	$300.00 – 350.00	230
M 1924	Wall Cabinet	1958-59	$200.00 – 300.00	230
M 1925	Corner Cabinet	1958-59	$250.00 – 350.00	230
CM 1927	Arm Chair	1958	$250.00 – 300.00	207
M 1930	Encore Bookcase Headboard Bed	1958-59	$350.00 – 400.00	219
M 1932	Symphonic 4-Drawer Chest	1958-59	$700.00 – 800.00	220
M 1934–M 1533	Symphonic Double Dresser with Hanging Mirror	1958-59	$750.00 – 850.00	220
M 1938	Symphonic Night Stand	1958-59	$275.00 – 325.00	221
M 1939–1535	Symphonic Triple Dresser with Attached Mirror	1958-59	$900.00 – 1,000.00	221
M 1940	Encore Utility Headboard	1958-61	$600.00 – 750.00	220
M 3753 G	Step End Table	1952	$400.00 – 500.00	278
M 5608–28	Single Filler	1952	$100.00 – 200.00	313
M 5608–95	Armless Davenport	1952	$1,250.00 – 1,500.00	314
M 5608–100	Davenport	1952	$1,250.00 – 1,400.00	313
M 5608 C	Club Chair	1952	$300.00 – 350.00	267
M 5608 L & R	Left and Right Arm Sectional	1952	$500.00 – 600.00	312,313
M 5608 LR	Leg Rest	1952	$500.00 – 600.00	313
M 5628–78	Davenport	1952	$2,200.00 – 2,500.00	312
M 6107 C	Arm Chair	1952	$250.00 – 300.00	247
M 6107 A	Side Chair	1952	$225.00 – 275.00	247
M 6321 G	Cocktail Table	1952	$325.00 – 350.00	281